INTERNATIONAL
BUSINESS

INTERNATIONAL
BUSINESS

Selected, Edited, and with Introductions and Summaries by

Christopher J. Robertson
Northeastern University

Mc Graw Hill **Contemporary Learning Series**

To my wife, Valerie, para siempre

Photo Acknowledgement
Corbis/Royalty Free

Cover Acknowledgement
Maggie Lytle

Compositor: Hurix Systems

Manufactured in the United States of America

First Edition

1234567890DOCDOC0987

MHID: 0-07-339750-4
ISBN: 978-0-07-339750-4
ISSN: 1930-7039

Printed on Recycled Paper

CONTENTS IN BRIEF

CONTENTS

UNIT 2   OPERATING IN A GLOBAL ECONOMY   90

PREFACE

Only as high as I reach can I grow
Only as far as I seek can I go
Only as deep as I look can I see
Only as much as I dream can I be
—Karen Ravn (1903–1970)

All travel has its advantages. If the passenger visits better countries, he may learn to
improve his own. And if fortune carries him to worse, he may learn to enjoy it.
—Samuel Johnson (1709–1784)

In order to fully understand a topic, one must recognize the controversies and the various angles surrounding the subject. **Roundtable Viewpoints** is designed to address a number of different issues within a specific discipline. The issues are supported by readings that provide articulate argumentation, debate, and various points of view. Upon completion of an issue, students are ready to take a specific point of view based on the analysis of perspectives in the material they've just read.

Each **Roundtable Viewpoints** issue question is relevant to the discipline issues today, compels the student, and guides them through the readings. The issue questions are pertinent to the area of study as it is currently handled in classrooms today.

The reading selections within each issue are intriguing and lively, while academically challenging and even rigorous to a student. The 5 selections per issue are current, culled from a variety of sources, and relate to the most popular issues within each discipline. In addition, each reading takes a recognizable position or perspective on the issue. The controversy and differing views among the readings are readily apparent to the student and invite discussion.

International business is complex. Issues such as outsourcing and globalization tend to trigger an array of reactions from people around the world. Most topics in the realm of international business can be analyzed from a number of different angles as well; there isn't just a pro and con side to each issue. In this book, *Roundtables Viewpoints: International Business*, a total of 45 articles that relate to eight different issues have been selected. Each article examines either a unique aspect of the corresponding issue or takes a stand for or against the underlying principles of the issue. As a reader of this book, you should try to see as many sides of an issue as possible with an open mind, then develop your own worldview after assessing the many diverse perspectives. Also, it is worth noting that some of the issues presented in this book have overlapping themes, and most issues are very interrelated. This interconnectedness is by design as it reflects one of the major challenges of decision making in the real world. Every day, managers must assess numerous situations and evaluate multiple alternatives and the ramifications of each possible decision.

The idea of having a roundtable discussion of issues is an extension of an earlier format where taking one side of an issue in a debate was the tradition. In the corporate boardroom, where international business topics are examined with great rigor, there are generally multiple solutions to a problem based on extremely different opinions. It is an important intellectual exercise to try and suspend any preconceived notions you may have about an issue before reading the various perspectives on each issue. Developing an ability to incorporate a range of opinions and paradigms should facilitate a stronger, deeper, understanding of each issue. Also, when attempting to envision potential solutions to a situation, trying to determine the implications for the many stakeholders involved, both domestically and abroad, is a worthwhile exercise.

Structure of this book This book is organized in three units: "Ethical Issues in International Business," "Operating in a Global Economy," and "Managing in a Foreign Environment." Each unit contains three issues, and each issue has five corresponding articles that represent a major theme related to the particular issue. Within each issue, an *introduction* sets the stage for the selected articles. An *issue summary* ties the debate together after reading the articles. After the issue summary, three more sections are provided to encourage deeper thinking and analysis: *highlights, critical thinking,* and *additional readings and resources* (including Web resources). *Challenge questions* are also provided throughout the book. These end-of-chapter materials can be used as mechanisms for developing more detailed solutions or as platforms for creating additional questions. Finally, the book concludes with a brief biographical sketch of each contributing author. The selected authors represent a broad array of professions, including economists, reporters, professors, corporate executives, consultants, and one ambassador.

A word to the instructor An *Instructor's Manual* complete with a brief synopsis of the issue, follow-up activities, collaborative learning exercises, and testing material (multiple-choice and essay questions complete with answers and suggested answers) is available through the publisher for classroom use. A correspondence service for **Roundtable Viewpoints** adopters can be found at http://www.mhcls.com/roundtable/.

Acknowledgments I would like to thank my wife, Valerie, and my children, Avery, Cálem, and Ian, for their patience, love, and understanding throughout the process of writing this book. Thanks to my parents and my brother, for encouraging me to see the world with passion and an open mind. Also, thanks to Jill Peter, my editor at McGraw-Hill Contemporary Learning Series, for her encouragement, patience, and professionalism. And finally thanks to Northeastern University, the Universidad de Lima, and Professor Daniel J. McCarthy for unconditional support.

GUIDED TOUR

UNIT OPENER

Designed to outline related issues and capture student interest, each unit opener provides general information for the upcoming issues. The unit openers conclude with a list of issue questions covered in each unit.

ISSUE INTRODUCTIONS

Designed to introduce the issue to the reader, the issue introduction states an issue question, provides history, current events, a list of the upcoming article selections for the issue, and relevant information about the issue to help facilitate discussion.

ISSUE SUMMARIES

Issue summaries appear at the end of each issue text. The summary brings the readings together, offers concluding observations, and suggests new directions for the student to take to further explore the issue.

HOW ARE IMPLEMENTATION AND ENFORCEMENT MONITORED?

To ensure the effective implementation of the Convention and of the revised Recommendation, Parties adopted a monitoring process based on the OECD peer-review principles.

The monitoring process is divided in two main phases.

Phase 1 evaluates whether the legal texts through which State Parties implement the Convention meet the standard set by the Convention.

Phase 2 studies the structures put in place to enforce the laws and rules implementing the Convention and the Revised Recommendation and to assess their application in practice. This includes reviewing national investigations and prosecutions and conducting "on site" interviews with government and regulatory authorities and other persons concerned with application of the Convention.

The OECD Working Group on Bribery in International Business Transactions (the "Working Group") is in charge of monitoring the implementation of the Convention and the related instruments.

The Phase 1 reviews, which began in April 1999 when the Convention was ratified, are almost completed, with 33 countries having been examined by the Working Group. These reviews have found that overall, national standards are in line with the Convention; where necessary, remedial measures were recommended. Several Parties have taken action to implement these recommendations. Others are in the process of amending their legislation.

What responsibility should multinational firms hold for the actions of their contract manufacturers overseas?

CHALLENGE QUESTIONS

Each issue contains challenge questions, in the form of marginal notes, designed to stimulate critical thinking and discussion. The challenge questions are thought-provoking and relevant to the issue and its selections.

ISSUE HIGHLIGHTS

- The reduction of trade barriers has for many years been encouraged by world leaders as a mechanism for stimulating more international trade.
- The EU has expanded dramatically since its creation and now includes 25 member nations and a number of applicant nations.
- The EU faces a difficult challenge as many potential immigrants from former colonies attempt to enter EU member nations and obtain citizenship.
- At the Summit of the Americas meeting, the Free Trade Area of the Americas (FTAA) is continually discussed. The FTAA is a proposed freetrade zone that would cover over 90 percent of the Western hemisphere.
- The World Trade Association has a number of responsibilities, including monitoring and arbitrating over trade disputes among member nations.
- Regional trade agreements, such as ASEAN, MERCOSUR and CAFTA, have also garnered interest and respect in recent years.

ISSUE HIGHLIGHTS

Highlights appear at the end of each issue and help to identify important information and details about the issue. The main points covered in the readings are recapped in the issue highlights.

CRITICAL THINKING

1. Language is a complex yet important part of culture. Yet languages tend to vary within countries, across borders, and in dialects. It is important for managers to recognize both the official and unofficial languages of a target nation. Expatriates preparing for foreign assignments should also make a reasonable attempt to learn the local language even if their native tongue happens to be the lingua franca in the assigned country. This will enhance credibility and respect, while opening up more windows into the local culture.
2. A number of researchers have examined how the importance of the context of a situation varies across cultures. In many Asian nations, for example, people place a significantly higher emphasis on the context of a situation than their Western counterparts. Western societies tend to emphasize the content of a situation more so than the context; as a result, communication in Western societies tends to be more explicit and precise.
3. Many cultures today are the result of the integration of various cultures over time. A number of factors influence the dominant set of cultural values at a specified point in time. Immigration patterns, colonial history, form of government, local indigenous groups, and prevalent subcultures all play a major role in the shaping of a nation's culture.

CRITICAL THINKING

Found at the end of each issue, this essential feature provides key strategies for using critical thinking skills in discussing the issues and forming an educated and well-thought-out opinion.

ADDITIONAL READING RESOURCES

D. Barboza and M. Barbero, "Wal-Mart is said to be acquiring a chain in China," *The New York Times*, October 17, 2006, Section A, Page 1–2.
A. DeRosa, "Sealed Air alters global strategies; Canada site to close," *Plastics News*, July 31 2006, Page 1–2.
J. Main, "How to go Global and Why," *Fortune*, August 28, 1989, pp. 70–76.
Michael E. Porter, *The Competitive Advantage of Nations*, New York: Free Press, 1990.
H. K. Steensma, L. Marino & K.M. Weaver, "Attitudes toward cooperative strategies: A cross-cultural analysis of entrepreneurs," *Journal of International Business Studies*, 4th Quarter, 2000, pp. 591–609.
www.playmobil.com, The Web site for Playmobil toys.
www.compete.com, The Council on Competitiveness, a nonprofit group that focuses on enhancing competitiveness domestically and abroad.
www.bestbuy.com, The Web site for Best Buy.

ADDITIONAL READING RESOURCES

This feature encourages further research relevant to each issue. Many perspectives frame each issue, and these resources provide additional material related to the topic being discussed.

INTRODUCTION

International business is no longer a topic that is exclusively discussed in the corporate boardrooms of massive multinational organizations. The combination of astounding advances in technology with rapidly falling trade barriers has made *going international* a feasible and profitable proposition for even the smallest of firms. Yet engaging in trade with people and firms from nations with different laws, values, and traditions is still an extremely complex endeavor. Many of the issues that managers face when going abroad, such as how to handle certain ethical dilemmas, have a number of different sides to them, and managerial opinions vary with regard to how to best develop a sustainable long-term policy to deal with potential problems. In this book, a number of articles that explore salient international business topics from different perspectives are presented and examined. The result is a virtual international business roundtable discussion that has been designed to facilitate a more in-depth understanding of the selected topics and underlying issues.

The articles that have been chosen for this book are grouped into three distinct categories: "Ethical Issues in International Business," "Operating in a Global Economy," and "Managing in a Foreign Environment." Each category, or unit, contains either three issues, and each issue has five articles that address the corresponding issue from a different angle. Indeed, many of the issues overlap conceptually, and the relationship among the various topics is deeply connected by design. A possible solution that may be plausible for one issue may be completely inappropriate for a different issue due to the potentially less-than-optimal outcomes. Therefore it is important to consider, when assessing potential courses of action related to an issue, how your views and opinions may directly or indirectly affect other issues if a particular policy is implemented. When assessing different scenarios, you should try to envision solutions or strategies that will satisfy a broad range of constituents for a sustainable period of time. Your overall objective should be to develop a more open-minded, comprehensive, worldview with respect to international business.

In this introduction, an overview of each of the three parts of this book is presented. A brief examination of the theoretical and practical implications related to each issue is provided along with an analysis of the interrelationships among the issues. A review of current applicable theories is provided to foster a deeper understanding of why certain international business phenomena exist. Each theory is also applied to common international business management practices. In addition, an initial assessment of practical implications for managers is explored from a multidisciplinary perspective. Finally, each section of this introduction concludes with a brief synopsis of the main theme of each article.

ETHICAL ISSUES IN INTERNATIONAL BUSINESS

Cultural beliefs about what is right or wrong tend to vary greatly based on a number of factors such as religious beliefs, traditions, rituals, and form of government. Further, the historical values that form the moral base of a society are also shaped over time by outside influences, such as immigration patterns and foreign investors. One of the major dilemmas that managers face when working abroad is attempting to discern what is deemed morally appropriate behavior in a particular foreign environment. The development of a viable policy that incorporates a broad spectrum of potential conflicts is a key ingredient to success overseas. Although many firms have implemented formal codes of ethics, the relevance of such instruments in certain foreign markets is oftentimes marginal at best. Firms must also strike a balance between home and host country laws when developing policies geared toward managing ethical behavior. Oftentimes it can be advantageous for a firm to set the moral bar higher than the local prevailing standards when abroad in order to minimize potential conflicts that could lead to significant damage to a firm's reputation and image. Many multinational firms today uphold standards abroad that are well above what is required by local law. Although these standards may still be below what the home country requires, the local government and workers tend to appreciate the positive direction that has been set.

Two theoretical concepts that provide insight into the international business ethics debate are moral absolutism and ethical relativism. Moral absolutism is a term that refers to the concept of a universal moral standard that is applied worldwide. Thus if bribery is viewed as unacceptable behavior in Sweden, a Swedish moral absolutist would argue that a global policy that prohibits employees from paying bribes should be implemented for his firm. At the opposite end of the continuum is the idea of ethical relativism. An ethical relativist believes that it is morally appropriate to shift or adapt standards to the local cultural norms. Therefore a Swedish ethical relativist would argue that it is perfectly acceptable for her firm to pay bribes in a country where bribery is a common practice and culturally acceptable. The dilemma here is that a practical reality falls somewhere between moral absolutism and ethical relativism. For this reason, it is common to find multinational firms that have country-specific policies and code of ethics that are based on local laws, customs, and rituals. Nevertheless, on some issues, such as child labor and environmentalism, firms may elect to uphold universal standards that are well above the local norms. While this strategy certainly helps develop goodwill in the local market, it also helps quell potentially damaging negative publicity back home.

From a practical perspective, multinational firms wrestle with a wide range of ethical issues on a daily basis. Managers must continually make decisions related to issues such as outsourcing, bribery, safe work conditions, environmental degradation, insider trading, software piracy, and various forms of discrimination. While taking into consideration laws, both at home and abroad, is a key element in the ethical decision-making process, firms must develop internal policies that are effective mechanisms in the quest to curb unethical behavior. Corporate leaders must also be aware of how their global image and reputation is affected in major consumer markets. Massive multinational companies, such as Wal-Mart and Nike, have experienced sharp sales declines in recent years shortly after negative publicity was released surrounding their operations abroad. Cutting corners on business ethics and corporate social responsibility can cost companies dearly in the long run; therefore, moral decisions should be taken seriously. The bottom line is that each organization must develop a cogent and viable code of ethics that serves as a moral compass for their management teams worldwide. And specific rules, regulations, and policies that guide the behavior of employees should stem from this moral code. A code of ethics that has no policy implications is essentially just a symbolic emblem that in practice is virtually useless.

Three specific issues related to international business ethics are analyzed in this part of the book. The first issue is captured in the question, "What Are the Benefits and Costs of

International Outsourcing?" This issue was a major theme in the 2004 presidential debates in the United States between President George W. Bush and Senator John F. Kerry. Yet this issue is more complex than what can be captured in a few quick sound bites. The ideas of maintaining global competitiveness and protecting local jobs are multifaceted and have many implications for corporate strategy development as well as society. Five articles that reflect a broad range of perspectives on the issue of outsourcing have been selected. In the first article, the author assesses the pros and cons of outsourcing and attempts to calculate the employment implications for the U.S. economy. The second article is essentially a window into the European perspective on outsourcing with an emphasis on call centers that have surfaced in Barcelona. In the third article, the authors utilize a number of statistics and benchmarks to assess long-term implications of outsourcing for various stakeholders. The fourth article is an assessment of a number of claims about outsourcing that may have been criticized as unfounded. The author, Daniel W. Drezner, contends that, in the long run, outsourcing is a profitable and worthwhile policy for a national government to embrace because the benefits outweigh any potential costs. The final article in this issue examines the state of legal outsourcing to India, a country that has a competitive advantage in this industry due to educational and legal similarities with both the United States and the United Kingdom.

The second ethical issue that is debated is captured in the question "What Are the Standards and Practices Surrounding Sweatshops?" Although most people clearly conclude that sweatshops are morally reprehensible, it is difficult to find agreement on what exactly constitutes a sweatshop. Indeed, poor and unsafe work conditions, low wages, underage workers, and abusive management are all characteristics of a sweatshop, yet where to draw the line is the dilemma that most multinational firms face when operating facilities abroad. Five articles have been selected that address the concept of sweatshops, each from a different perspective. The first article describes how the Cambodian government has implemented a new law that forces factory managers to uphold higher work standards and foster more transparency. The second article examines one of Nike's contract manufacturers in China and reports on some of the policies that Nike has enforced to facilitate higher workplace standards. The third article takes a look at a new company, No Sweat Apparel, that is using its sweatshop-free manufacturing approach to create a positive public perception that will hopefully translate into a competitive advantage. The fourth article in this issue explores the intersection between sweatshops and globalization. The author, Radley Balko, argues that sweatshops may be a necessary step on the road to economic development. Although Balko takes a controversial position on this issue, he does articulate an interesting perspective related to the steps that must be taken to foster the economic transition of a nation toward prosperity. The fifth article assesses the recent challenges that Coca-Cola has faced with respect to the firm's moral reputation.

The third question surrounding ethical issues in international business is, "What Are the Best Approaches to Minimizing Global Corruption?" Indeed, corruption is a major factor to consider when firms contemplate trade with firms from new potential markets abroad. Corruption levels tend to vary significantly by country, and different forms of corruption are more or less rampant in certain countries, depending on cultural beliefs and local perceptions of morally acceptable behavior. Take software piracy, for example. In the United States, the software piracy rate tends to hover around 25 percent, while in China it is closer to 90 percent (see Business Software Alliance, http://www.bsa.org). This moral gap with respect to intellectual property can be partly attributed to different cultural beliefs and legal systems. Five articles have been selected related to international anti-corruption agreements and how a firm can best prevent unethical behavior, both within and beyond the firm. The first article summarizes and critiques a number of recent country-level anti-corruption agreements. David Zussman describes how the OECD and United Nations have made significant strides lately in their collective attempts to create a more level moral playing field in the global economy. In the next article, an interview with an expert, Owen Pell, on the U.S. Foreign Corrupt Practices Act is presented. Although this law, passed in 1977, has traditionally been used sparingly to prosecute U.S. managers from paying bribes to foreign government officials, the momentum for convictions has increased recently due to the Sarbanes Oxley Act in 2001. Attorney Pell provides keen insight into the law and outlines a number of strategies for firms that are trying to develop policies to prevent potential violations. The third article in this issue examines how corporate codes of ethics can help establish stronger standards of behavior for firms that are operating abroad, regardless of the size of the company. The fourth article, by Alex Brummer, looks into the state of corruption in Nigeria and one woman's fight to help change the global perception of Nigeria as a haven for corrupt activities. The final article in this issue is an OECD brief that summarizes the state of the OECD anti-bribery pact, while also providing valuable information on the implementation and enforcement status of the pact.

OPERATING IN A GLOBAL ECONOMY

The second part of this book focuses on issues related to managing and operating a business in a truly international setting. People tend to have different perceptions of globalization, and firms must take the public perception of multinational organizations into account when making decisions about various potential target markets. The interface between business and government is also a key factor in the international business arena, especially when considering the implications of free-trade agreements and tariff structures. Although many nations from around the world have now entered into some form of trade agreement, there is still strong resistance to free trade in many parts of the world. Indeed, the advances in global transportation and communications systems have been undeniably helpful as well in the acceleration of global trade patterns. Many small firms, and firms from developing countries, can now quickly and effectively enter foreign markets thanks to modern logistics and supply systems. Many firms that 20 years ago had virtually no interest in international trade because of the high taxes and complicated logistical challenges are now fully engaged in export operations.

A major side effect of globalization has been the gradual shift in cultural values around the world. Each year, more and more people are exposed to Western values through television, the Internet, tourism, and multinational firms. People tend to have different responses to this exposure to foreign cultures over time. In some societies, the local people embrace the influx of Westernization. This is referred to as cultural convergence since the local cultures tend to accept Western values and shift away from local traditions. Other cultures have a negative reaction to Westernization and, as a result, the local people gravitate back to their traditional values. This is referred to as cultural divergence. A third possibility is the true blending of cultures, or crossvergence, where a new hybrid culture is created based on traditional values and newly adopted Western values. Many scholars argue that Hong Kong is an excellent example of a society that has integrated the values of two traditional cultures, British and Chinese. It is also possible that a country can experience a combination of these cultural shifts depending on the variation in values within the country. As global trade continues to accelerate and reach remote sections of the world, these patterns of cultural transformation will likely evolve over time.

From a practical perspective, the idea of globalization is extremely important to managers. Many markets that were untapped a decade ago now contain many mature, educated consumers. Moreover, as multinational firms look to certain destinations abroad as potential contract manufacturing sites, the local beliefs and attitudes toward globalization must be incorporated into the decision-making process. A nation that embraces an anti-globalization sentiment is far more likely to elect public officials that will implement policies that may be costly for foreign firms operating in local markets. Local policies, such as higher import taxes, also tend to impact the international position of a government on important issues such as free-trade agreements. From a shipping and logistics perspective, globalization has had a profound impact on large and small firms worldwide. The level and scope of services that international courier firms offer today has made it more efficient and profitable for firms to sell their goods abroad.

In this part of the book three issues related to operating in a global economy are examined in detail. The first issue surrounds the question, "How Does Globalization Affect the World?" Although globalization is not a new concept, it has received a significant amount of attention in recent years due to the rapid annual growth of international trade since the early 1980s. Many scholars attribute this rapid growth to key factors such as falling trade barriers and advances in international communication and shipping. Indeed, other important ingredients to globalization also include television, the Internet, and modern transportation systems. Globalization has become a controversial topic with many supporters and critics. Those in favor of globalization argue that free and far-reaching trade has created numerous jobs and accelerated economic development; opponents contend that the gap between rich and poor has grown as a result of unfair practices by multinational firms. Five articles have been selected for this roundtable discussion of globalization. In the first article, the author identifies and dismantles a number of myths about globalization. In the second article, a number of pitfalls related to globalization are examined and assessed. The third and fourth articles provide summaries of statistical analyses of the economic impact that globalization has had on the U.S. and world economies. In the fifth and final article, the author looks at globalization from the British perspective with an eye toward global supply chain efficiency.

The second issue is grounded in the question, "How Do Free-Trade Agreements Affect Multinational Firms?" The movement toward free trade has been undeniably strong in the past two decades. While the European Union and NAFTA have received considerable attention by scholars, practitioners, and the popular press, the number and scope of similar agreements around the world is impressive. The Central American Free Trade Agreement (CAFTA) negotiated in 2005 was another step toward the hemispheric reduction of tariffs in the Americas. And although the Free Trade Agreement of the Americas has stalled, a number of nations, such as Chile and Peru, have had significant success with negotiating bilateral accords with trade partners. Other major agreements and organizations, such as the World Trade Organization (WTO) and the Asia Pacific Economic Community, have been working diligently to facilitate the freer movement of goods across borders worldwide. Yet to what extent does free trade affect the decision making of managers in multinational firms? In this roundtable discussion, five articles have been selected to foster a more in-depth ability to answer such a question. The first article wrestles with the issue of immigration in Europe. Although the Muslim uprising in France in the fall of 2005 received worldwide attention, this issue is quite complex and has a number of implications for firms operating in Europe. In the second article, the author examines the potential outcomes of the CAFTA agreement, and he attempts to project the potential winners and losers based on the terms of the agreement. The third article related to free trade looks into possible explanations as to why the Free Trade of the Americas has become unpopular in a few nations and how the supporting nations can press forward toward a more amenable deal. The next article, by Chile's Ambassador of India Jorge Heine, assesses the recently approved free trade accord between China and Chile. Heine also provides a unique perspective from a government insider with respect to Chile's incredible success with using free-trade agreements as a mechanism for economic development. The fifth article explores the protests at the 2005 WTO meetings in Hong Kong. David Armstrong analyzes a number of specific family-owned firms to determine how WTO policies will impact their profitability.

The third issue related to operating in the global economy is captured in the question, "What Are Some Key Strategies for Taking Advantage of Modern Technologies Related to Global Logistics?" As more and more firms go international, opportunities for the transport of products, documents, and supplies will continue to increase substantially. Many global logistics firms have taken advantage of new technologies to offer a wider range of services worldwide. Advances such as refrigerated cargo jets, modern packaging systems, and the ability to process export and import customs documents in-house have triggered a wealth of new service approaches. Moreover, a number of major multinational delivery firms have signed partnering deals with local networks, which has created a broader net of global geographic service. With increased pressure to meet bottom-line objectives, managers have recognized the importance of having a streamlined process of getting their goods from the warehouse to consumers. As a result, many firms have elected to manage their delivery networks in-house to keep costs at a minimum. Five articles have been selected that capture a variety of different international logistics issues. The first article examines the decision by FedEx to stick to its core competencies, while other rival firms have elected to dramatically expand product and service offerings. The second article, by Ian Putzger, takes an in-depth look at how one logistics company has introduced an uninterrupted international cool chain of service for pharmaceutical products such as vaccines. This new technology should create numerous opportunities for the high-speed worldwide export of medicine in the future. In the third article, Roy Kheng critiques the state of logistics in China and identifies a number of major challenges that delivery firms will face in the Chinese market in years to come. The fourth article, by R.G. Edmonson, describes a new technology that has been introduced that enables shippers to track the exact location of containers at any given point in time. In the fifth article, an assessment of the status of the Panama and Suez canals is provided.

Peter Leach evaluates the recent improvements that have been made to the canals, changes in tariff structures, and strategic shipping routes between Asia and the rest of the world.

MANAGING IN A FOREIGN ENVIRONMENT

Perhaps one of the most important factors involved with doing business abroad is developing an ability to adapt to the local culture. For an expatriate to have a successful tour of duty overseas, he or she must be able to function effectively in a foreign environment that may have a dramatically different culture. Managers bring a broad range of skills, backgrounds, and cultural experiences to the table with them, and each individual may react quite differently in certain foreign markets based on prior experience abroad. Moreover, the level and scope of training for the current assignment is a key factor in determining the potential for successful completion of a tour of duty. This part of the book deals with the human side of going international. Although many managers receive training before beginning an assignment in a foreign land, there are still many nuances and complexities that tend to be culturally specific and may create significant challenges for an expatriate. Depending on a manager's emotional and cultural maturity level, and familiarity with the newly assigned country, his or her ability to adapt quickly to the local culture may be hampered by a range of issues. Many organizations now understand the significant costs involved with sending a manager to a foreign assignment, and the early return home of an expatriate, commonly referred to as expatriate failure, can be excessively burdensome for a firm. Indeed, selecting the right individual for an assignment, and providing a reasonable level of training, can help prevent expatriate failure while maximizing performance.

From a human resource management perspective, when the executives of a firm decide to fill a position in one of the company's foreign facilities, a number of possible options exist. For example, let's assume that a shoe company from Boston must assign a plant manager to the firm's new factory in Brazil. One option is to send a manager from the corporate headquarters in Boston to Brazil. This is commonly referred to as an ethnocentric staffing approach since it involves the selection of a home country manager. The advantages of ethnocentric staffing include a common language between the manager and headquarters and a mutual understanding of the company's business philosophy. Disadvantages of this approach include potential language and cultural conflicts abroad and a rudimentary understanding of laws, customs, and business practices in the host country. A second approach would be to hire a Brazilian, or host country, manager to run the operations in Brazil. This approach, referred to as polycentric staffing, has advantages that include the manager's knowledge of the local language, labor laws, workforce trends, and culture. One major disadvantage might be the existence of significantly different managerial and leadership ideologies between the local manager and the headquarters back in Boston. Another approach, referred to as geocentric staffing, would be the firm appointing a manager to the position in Brazil from a third country, such as Portugal or Argentina. In this situation, the best person for the job is selected regardless of nationality, and a major advantage is that the job search can be truly global and comprehensive in nature. One drawback of the geocentric technique is that there is still a potential for a culture clash between the manager and either the local Brazilian workers or the top management team back in Boston. Regardless of which approach is adopted, the top management team must be aware of the cultural risks and ramifications related to each decision.

There are an endless number of practical implications related to managing in a foreign environment. From a motivation and employee commitment perspective, there is evidence that supports the fact that content and well-adjusted employees are more likely to perform at a higher level, more likely to be highly dedicated, and less likely to leave the firm for other employment. Sending a manager on a foreign assignment should be looked upon as an investment in the firm's future. Providing assistance related to finding a home, spousal adjustment, and language training can help with the fluid transition of a manger into the expatriate assignment. Many expatriates become frustrated when they near the completion of their foreign assignment; therefore, it is essential for their organizations to assist with the repatriation process. Help with finding a new job assignment back home, as well as assistance related to personal matters such as help with finding a home or assistance in the transition of children into school can be invaluable. Nevertheless, many expatriates leave their firms after completing a foreign assignment because of either better opportunities elsewhere or a negative experience overall. If the manager's time abroad, and return home, is managed properly, the chances of losing a future star performer to another firm can be minimized.

Three issues have been selected to facilitate a discussion of human and strategic factors involved with going international. The first issue deals with the struggles that managers face when living in a foreign nation and is summarized in the question, "What Are the Major Challenges that Face Expatriates While Living Abroad?" There is no doubt that preparing for an overseas experience significantly increases the chances of successful assignment completion; yet training programs vary considerably, and each expatriate brings his or her own personality and past experience along for the journey. What may be a major challenge to one expatriate may be an immaterial or insignificant event to another. Moreover, the cultural distance, or gap between the home and host culture, also plays a major role in the ability of an expatriate to adapt to local laws, customs, work habits, and cultures. Certainly it is much easier for a U.S. manager to adapt to an assignment in London as opposed to in Lima due to the smaller cultural distance between the U.S. and British cultures. Five articles have been identified that highlight different expatriate challenges while abroad. Clearly there are many additional situations that may trigger unwarranted stress while away from home, but the four articles reviewed in this part of the book focus on pragmatic issues that tend to affect most expatriated workers. The first article, by Gail Reinhart, examines the overseas experience from an employee compensation and benefits perspective. Reinhart emphasizes the importance of issues such as the role that corporate culture plays in the expatriate adjustment process. The second article takes an in-depth look at the long-term financial implications of living abroad. Managers who intend to spend a significant period of time overseas must carefully manage their assets and pay particularly keen attention to applicable tax laws, both at home and in the host country. The third article related to this issue summarizes and explores a number of salient issues related to the return home of an expatriated manager. Many managers experience a form of reverse culture shock or develop a negative attitude toward their firms due to a poor repatriation process. Jan Nelson describes some of the components and benefits of formal repatriation programs. The fourth article related to expatriation looks at the growing trend of managers leaving their firms while working abroad for lucrative positions with local businesses. The recent departure of a number of foreign managers for positions with major Chinese firms is examined in detail. The fifth expatriate article looks at how British expatriates maintain their loyalty to their homeland while working abroad in the United States.

The second issue related to managing in a foreign environment is debated across five articles and is captured in the question, "Why Is It So Important to Understand Cultural Differences When Working Abroad?" There is no doubt that culture is a major factor in international business. Culture is a complex concept that has many layers, and expert opinions on how to cope with cultural differences can vary extensively. The idea of subcultures must also be considered since most nations have multiple cultures within their own borders, thanks to both the perseverance of traditional indigenous cultures and recent patterns of migration worldwide. For example, some nations have multiple official languages that formally acknowledge the subcultures that exist within the nation. French and Flemish are the official languages of Belgium. In Bolivia, Spanish and Aymara are the official languages. Switzerland has four official languages, and India has sixteen. Again, each language is symbolic of a significant subculture that must be carefully considered when doing business in that particular nation. In the first article selected for this topic, the author describes the challenges that an intermediary faces when asked to help facilitate trade between major U.S. and South Korean firms. In the second article, Robert Matthews reports the results of an experiment where cultural context is measured and compared between Eastern and Western counterparts. The next article takes a look at some of the interesting cultural adaptations that Disney made to its Hong Kong theme park, such as offering popular local food and requiring workers to know more than one dialect of Chinese. The fourth article follows a young female expatriate through some of her travails as an expatriate in Milan, Italy, and a number of challenges for young expatriates are identified. In the final article, Rick Vecchio dives into the Peruvian culture and assesses issues such as cultural literacy and racism from a pragmatic perspective.

The final issue related to managing in a foreign environment deals with strategic competitiveness and falls beneath the question, "What Are Some Key Approaches Related to Competing in Foreign Markets?". Although managers must cope with cultural and other challenges while living abroad, decisions related to how to best compete in a foreign environment are essential ingredients to success. Managers must continuously assess the competitive environment in various target markets and adapt strategic plans where necessary. The first article selected for this topic reviews the evolution of the German firm Geobra Brandstatter and how the recent success of the Playmobil toy series came about as a result of adapting to environmental changes. In the second article, K.C. Swanson highlights the competitive strategy of Best Buy related to the firm's entrance into the Chinese market. The third article contains an interview with Jeff Smisek, president of Continental Airlines, that focuses on Continental's decision to extend service to Ireland from the United States. Jeff Schmid, in the fourth article, describes the transformation that has taken place at Rockwell and how the firm has developed unique relationships abroad to gain a competitive advantage. The fifth and final article explores the demand side of business in India and describes how many fashion retailers have entered the India market due to a growing customer base.

Although only nine issues have been selected for this edition of Roundtables, these issues serve well as a foundation for an integrative debate related to international business. As mentioned earlier, many of these issues are interrelated, and it behooves the reader to try to envision how a decision related to one issue affects the outcome of a firm or manager when faced with another issue. A number of other factors exist when managing international operations, and the link between these factors and the issues selected in this book must be evaluated as well. Certainly the particular strategy of the firm, and the direct and indirect competition for each product within a potential target market, must be factored into the decision-making process. For example, a firm that competes with a low-cost strategy in one country may face more or less competition within that strategic group in another country. Consumer preferences, and perceptions of products from certain nations, also tend to vary considerably from country to country and should be considered when formulating a long-term strategic plan. Moreover, managerial styles and motivational tools may need to be altered to create a more efficient and effective operation in an overseas market.

One of the major objectives of this book is to think critically about international business activities and operations. When stimulated properly, analytical skills should facilitate an ability to develop realistic alternative solutions related to potential international business situations and dilemmas. Hopefully the articles, questions, and exercises set forth in the coming sections of the book will help achieve this objective and create a more thorough understanding of the complexities involved with doing business abroad. Although many situations in the world of international business tend to be extraordinarily unique due to cultural, legal, and economic differences, it is important to cultivate an ability to evaluate scenarios based on decisions that other firms have made surrounding similar situations in the past. In the end, each manager will have to step forward and take action based on a combination of experience, analytical competence, and advice from fellow colleagues.

U N I T 1

Ethical Issues in International Business

One of the more complex issues that managers face in international business is the variation in ethical environments from country to country. Managers must often decide whether to follow a relativist approach, where adapting moral standards to the local standard is seen as acceptable, or to take an absolutist approach, where one moral standard is applied globally. Potential ethical dilemmas in international business are plentiful and include such issues as outsourcing, child labor, sweatshops, bribery, insider trading, and environmental degradation. In this section, a number of articles related to outsourcing, sweatshops, and fighting corruption have been selected. Each author takes a unique look at a salient topic that has become increasingly important to multinational managers.

Issue 1: What Are the Benefits and Costs of International Outsourcing?

Issue 2: What Are the Standards and Practices Surrounding Sweatshops?

Issue 3: What Are the Best Approaches to Minimizing Global Corruption?

ISSUE 1

What Are the Benefits and Costs of International Outsourcing?

The general idea of outsourcing has been around for decades, if not centuries. Prudent managers seeking a more refined focus on their core competencies have consistently looked outside the factory walls for lower-cost alternatives to bolster efficiency and productivity. Indeed, U.S. firms have been manufacturing in far-away places such as southeast Asia and Latin America since the advent of the Industrial Revolution. Many European firms have also embraced the idea of shifting some jobs to lower-wage nations, both within Europe and elsewhere.

Why has attention to this issue been so heightened in recent years? One reason is that outsourcing was one of the hot topics that took center stage during the 2004 U.S. presidential election between President George W. Bush and Senator John F. Kerry. Another reason is that the level and degree to which outsourcing has been employed since the late 1990s has increased significantly. Moreover, while manufacturing outsourcing has been around for decades, the recent surge in service outsourcing, partly due to advances in technology, has led to increased concern.

Outsourcing has been defined as an activity that occurs when "a firm subcontracts a business function to an outside supplier" (Drezner, 2004). International outsourcing, or "offshore outsourcing," is therefore the subcontracting of a business function from a domestic facility to a foreign location. Outsourcing is a complicated issue, and analysts draw from a number of related topics such as protectionism, competitiveness, free-trade agreements, and job creation to bolster their positions. When discussing jobs lost due to outsourcing, it is essential to simultaneously discuss jobs gained during the same period. Thus it is the net job count that is important, rather than just one direction of the job flow.

There have been countless studies of offshore outsourcing in the past decade. One estimate by Forrester Research predicts that close to 40 percent of Fortune 1,000 firms have engaged in some form of outsourcing and that more than 3 million whitecollar jobs will leave the United States by 2015. Over 2 million financial-sector jobs have been forecasted, by Deloitte Research, to leave the United States by 2009, and the IT (information technology) sector has already experienced a 10 percent overseas shift in jobs. The legal world has been affected by outsourcing as well. According to Forrester, nearly 80,000 legal jobs are likely to move from the United States to India by the year 2015.

While these predictions and job migration patterns are grim, the overseas shift in jobs is only part of a two-way process that undoubtedly includes significant job *insourcing* and job creation. The size and scope of outsourcing must be put into perspective as well. For example, total employment in the United States is over 130 million, and job creation by 2010 is expected to exceed 20 million. It is also important to assess the proportion of international outsourcing relative to domestic activity. For example, in the U.S. IT sector, close to US$120 billion was spent in 2003, and less than 2 percent of that work was performed offshore (Weidenbaum, 2005). With that data in mind, the percentage of outsourced jobs, depending on which estimate you employ, tends to hover between 1 and 5 percent of total jobs, and that is without adjusting for created jobs. On the insourcing side, it is also noteworthy that over 60 percent of the annual revenues for U.S. IT companies is generated from overseas work performed. From a cost savings and efficiency perspective, many firms are expected to prosper based on the careful use of outsourcing as a mechanism for ratcheting up the bottom line. In the United States, legal research annual savings are expected to surpass US$2 billion annually, and these savings could play a role in curbing health insurance premium inflation.

A range of views regarding offshore outsourcing will be explored in the five articles selected for this chapter. First, in his article "Outsourcing: Pros and Cons," Murray Weidenbaum describes the complexity of outsourcing while assessing the limits and dangers related to this activity. Weidenbaum also takes a pragmatic look at employment implications and the net effect of outsourcing on the United States. Next, in their article "Cafes, Beaches, and Call Centers," Andy Reinhardt and Carlta Vitzthum explore the recent surge of call centers in Southern Europe, particularly in and around Barcelona, Spain. In this article, a number of excellent examples of U.S. firms that now look to Southern Europe as a strategic call center location are provided.

The third article, "Outsourcing: A Policy Agenda" by Sarah Anderson and John Cavanagh, presents a number of strong arguments against the policy of offshore outsourcing. Anderson and Cavanagh support their claims with recent examples and data from industry. The fourth article, by Daniel W. Drezner, offers an opinion in support of outsourcing in "The Outsourcing Bogeyman." Drezner erases numerous doubts cast by anti-outsourcing groups, and he asserts that outsourcing is a profitable and necessary strategy that has an overall positive effect on the U.S. economy. The fifth and final article, by Sufia Tippu, explores the state of legal services outsourcing. In particular, Sharma focuses on the relationship between the United States and India and why India has a competitive advantage in attracting legal work from nations such as the United States and the United Kingdom.

ISSUE ARTICLES

Murray Weidenbaum, "Outsourcing: Pros and Cons," *Business Horizons* (July/August 2005).

Andy Reinhardt and Carlta Vitzthum, "Cafes, Beaches, and Call Centers: Barcelona Has Become the New European Hot Spot for Outsourcing," *Business Week* (September 5, 2005).

Sarah Anderson and John Ca vanagh, "Outsourcing: A Policy Agenda," *Foreign Policy in Focus* (April 2004).

Daniel W. Drezner, "The Outsourcing Bogeyman," *Foreign Affairs* (May/ June 2004).

Sufia Tippu, "Net Value: Legal Services Outsourcing Next Big Trend?" *The Edge Malaysia,* http://www.theedgedaily.com (posted on February 20, 2006).

Outsourcing: Pros and Cons

Murray Weidenbaum

Overseas outsourcing of jobs is far more complicated than is generally understood. Pressures to outsource range from better-serving overseas markets to increasing the competitiveness of American business. Outsourcing—domestic and international—responds to management's desire to focus the firm's in-house activities on its core competence. A negative side to outsourcing results from companies doing so simply because "everybody is doing it." They may be surprised by accompanying factors such as unexpected costs and complications, as well. Governmental policymakers need to realize that foreign companies outsource more business services to the United States than American firms send overseas.

1. THE COMPLEXITIES OF OUTSOURCING

Overseas outsourcing of jobs has quickly become a controversial national issue. Some see outsourcing as a way of maintaining or increasing a company's competitiveness. Many others view outsourcing in a far more negative light, focusing on jobs lost.

Clearly, outsourcing is not a subject that can be effectively dealt with on a bumper sticker or via 30-second sound bites. Let us start with a little background before we ponder on any firm conclusions. Outsourcing involves far more complicated advantages and disadvantages than debaters on either side of the argument are willing to admit.

2. WHY DO COMPANIES OUTSOURCE?

Many service companies started creating jobs overseas to gain access to foreign markets. They had to audit, consult, and repair where customers were located, rather than telling those same overseas customers that they had to come here. Moreover, many foreign markets have been growing quickly, while some domestic areas have become relatively saturated, or at least mature.

The age of economic isolationism has long since passed. Approximately 60% of the revenue of American information technology (IT) companies originates overseas. That is not unique; in various industries, ranging from banking

From *Business Horizons,* vol. 48, issue 4, July/August 2005, pp. 311–315. Copyright © 2005 by Elsevier Science Ltd. Reprinted by permission.

to consumer products to job placement services, leading firms report that their overseas revenues exceed their domestic sales.

Simultaneously, some domestic businesses hired specialized workers overseas to respond to U.S. limits on immigration. When American employers could not get those workers to come here, the need to send the work to them became real. While doing so, the companies learned how to use modern technology to shift the location of work economically. They thus became accustomed to taking advantage of lower costs, both domestic and foreign.

Telecommuting from employees' homes also helped pave the way for some enterprises to extend the process to new suppliers, at home and abroad. Moreover, the shift of some telemarketing and customer service jobs overseas followed an earlier pattern within the United States, when such work was outsourced from urban to rural areas where labor costs were lower.

Most fundamentally, many companies are focusing their efforts on their core competence. It is the rare enterprise that produces an entire product by itself, or even half of the end value. Most businesses subcontract out most of their activities to other companies, mainly domestic. Viewed from that perspective, overseas sourcing is a minor part of the trend to decentralize business operations. Nevertheless, many American corporations came to appreciate how frequently the higher productivity of U.S. workers offset the wage differentials and other costs of operating overseas. Thus, they quickly encountered practical limits to offshore outsourcing. To put the matter bluntly, no company can outsource the management, responsibility, or accountability of its activities.

On the other hand, outsourcing can help a company operate in an increasingly competitive global marketplace. Many U.S. companies learned the benefits of drawing on workers stationed in other countries. Outsourcing can enable a business to provide constant coverage, especially for consumers who need round-the-clock support. It is frequently impractical for a firm to adopt a unilateral policy against outsourcing work, especially when its foreign and domestic competitors are doing so. There is also a growing division of labor. For example, system designers in the United States working closely with retailers may conceive an inventory management software that helps use electronic product tags more effectively, but once the system has been mapped out, the actual software code could be written by programmers in India.

All sorts of adjustments are being made. In 2003, Delta Airlines outsourced 1000 jobs to India, but the US$25 million in savings allowed the company to add 1200 reservation and sales positions within the United States. Large software companies, Microsoft and Oracle, have simultaneously increased outsourcing and their domestic payrolls.

It is important to gain some perspective by seeing the relative importance of domestically and internationally produced services. Much of the current controversy focuses on IT. In 2003, approximately US$120 billion was spent on IT in the United States. While approximately 1.4% was moved offshore, the 98.6% of the work that stayed here was not deemed newsworthy.

In total, about 400,000 U.S. positions in IT have gone overseas. Meanwhile, total U.S. employment rose from 129 million in 1993 to 138 million in 2003, mainly in the service sector. It turns out that, on balance, the international movement of services is quite positive to the American economy.

This is so because American corporations are not the only companies that engage in offshoring. In 2003, for example, the United States imported (i.e., offshored) US$86.7 billion in private business services, which included a lot of relatively low-skilled call center and data entry work done in lower-cost developing countries. However, in the same year, we exported (i.e., companies in other nations offshored to us) US$133.5 billion of private business services. That "insourcing" generated a substantial array of relatively high-skilled jobs in engineering, management consulting, banking, and legal services. On average, "insourced" jobs pay 16% above the national average. A net balance of US$46.8 billion flowed to the United States: a 63% increase over 1994, a decade earlier. Such good news rarely surfaces in the often emotional debate over the issue of offshoring.

3. THE LIMITS TO AND DANGERS OF OUTSOURCING

A word of warning, however, is necessary in the face of current business enthusiasm for overseas workers. Companies who outsource just because "everybody is doing it" may be surprised by unexpected costs and complications. About one-half of the outsourcing arrangements entered into end up being terminated, for a variety of reasons. Some new overseas vendors encounter financial difficulties, or are acquired by other firms with different procedures and priorities.

Businesses that arbitrarily set a fixed percentage of work to be outsourced will likely regret it. Newcomers to overseas contracting may find themselves dealing with unreliable suppliers who put their work aside when they gain a more important client, or their overseas vendor may suffer rapid turnover of skilled employees who find jobs with more desirable firms. Typical Indian operations in business processing (including call centers and offices handling payroll, accounting, and human resources functions) often lose 15–20% of their work forces each year. While software programming skills are plentiful, managerial experience is in very short supply.

Other costly complications may arise. Local highways and transportation networks may be inadequate. Some overseas companies wind up transporting their employees to and from work. Also, electricity may not be as assuredly available as in the United States, where blackouts are very infrequent.

Some American companies are paying much more in real estate fees for their offshoring activities than they would in the United States. This negative differential occurs for two reasons: one is the cost of upgrading poor infrastructure overseas; the second is the fact that inexpensive overseas labor pools are usually found in very large cities, while facilities such as call centers back home are located in lower-cost suburban and rural areas.

Some U.S. companies limit their outsourcing to routine engineering and maintenance tasks because they worry that their core technology might be stolen by vendors in Asia that do not respect intellectual property rights. U.S. firms may also encounter a variety of unanticipated difficulties, such as dealing with arcane legal systems and meeting the requirements of different tax and regulatory agencies. Furthermore, they may more frequently encounter corrupt officials in the public sector.

Additionally, overseas managers often do not understand the American business environment: our customers, lingo, traditions, and high-quality control and expectations for prompt delivery of goods and performance of services. In 2003, Dell moved its call center for corporate business support from India back to the United States after clients complained about non-native English speakers with hard-to-follow accents, giving vague answers to technical questions.

We can recall that many U.S. manufacturing firms stubbed their toes in their initial encounters with new vendors in Asia. They did not plan on geopolitical risks, as in Indonesia, where chaos followed the ousting of the longtime national leader. The recent defeat of the Indian prime minister who promoted economic reforms may also lead to another period of policy uncertainty.

4. WHAT HAPPENS TO THE COMPANY'S EMPLOYEES?

The effect of outsourcing on U.S. employment is far more complicated than it first appears. The visible part, or the tip of the iceberg, is widely known and recognizable: some U.S. employees lose their jobs or get shifted to less desirable positions. Although the iceberg may have had a very large tip in recent years, serious analysis of the issue must encompass the entirety of the iceberg.

The total employment effect of outsourcing is much larger than what appears at first glance. Far more U.S. employees keep their jobs because outsourcing helps companies stay competitive, resulting in many getting new or better jobs due to enhanced financial strength of the firm. For example, as companies upgrade their software systems, there may be less domestic demand for basic programmers, but increased need for higher-paid systems integrators.

Corporate IT departments are changing their mix of in-house skills, and now place more emphasis on managerial experience, business process knowledge, and understanding the domestic customers. All of these capabilities can rarely be provided effectively from an overseas location.

Outsourcing and the savings it generates are the beginning, not the end, of the adjustment process. Cost reductions from outsourcing can open up new market opportunities for U.S. companies, and thus generate additional jobs here at home. Companies also can afford to buy new equipment and expand training programs under this scenario. Hence, higher domestic labor costs can be offset by higher worker productivity.

Over time, there is a positive feedback effect from outsourcing. As poor countries overseas develop their economies, new markets are created for U.S.-made products and services. China has already become a major importer of industrial and consumer goods, as well as of agricultural products and raw materials. In time, India is likely to do the same.

Moreover, economic trends rarely move in a straight line for long periods of time. Salaries of IT personnel in India are reported to be rising at 15–20% a year. A more basic factor reducing the gap with U.S. compensation is the fact that demand for trained IT personnel in India is beginning to exceed the supply. In addition, a lot of hidden costs arise, such as the need for U.S.-based managers to visit the overseas sites from time to time to assure that the work being performed meets the standards of the American firm.

Some historical perspective is also useful. In the early 19th century, the United States was a poor developing country. European capital helped finance our canals, railroads, steel mills, and other factories. American workers began to produce goods that competed with European production. Because markets were relatively open, Europeans as well as Americans benefited in the process. Economic growth and job creation occurred on both sides of the Atlantic. Currently, service providers overseas require American-made computers, telecommunications equipment, and software. They also obtain legal, financial, and marketing services from United States sources. Employees are increasingly becoming customers of American products, as well.

5. WHAT IS THE NET EFFECT ON THE UNITED STATES?

On reflection, most service jobs cannot be outsourced. Personal contact is vital in virtually all business activities. It takes domestic companies to tailor new products and services to the needs of local customers. Most of the people we work with regularly remain close by; we normally do not take long trips to see our doctor or dentist or lawyer or accountant. Much less do we go to New Delhi or Manila for those purposes.

One of the great strengths of the American economy is that we have a very open labor market—a characteristic that is basic to this nation's economic vitality. Approximately 1 million workers are laid off or quit each week, and an equal number are hired in their place. It is much harder to lay off workers in Europe or Japan; however, there is another side to the coin. Employers there are very reluctant to take on new workers. In striking contrast, American companies are much more likely to add personnel, and do so.

Over the years, far more new jobs have been created in the United States than have been outsourced; moreover, many foreign companies have been setting up operations in the United States, and have hired American workers as staff. Our more realistic labor policies do work, while their labor policy "straightjackets" do not. By its nature, a strong and flexible labor market has plenty of movement: out of some jobs, and into others. The bottom line is clear: the United States creates far more new jobs (net of layoffs) than Europe and Japan combined. We have the highest proportion (66%) of the population employed of all industrialized countries.

The record also shows that groundbreaking technology, rather than international competition, is the major cause of layoffs and new hires. Technological progress is the heart of the dynamic American job-creating economy. Our positive technology environment also encourages foreign manufacturers, such as pharmaceutical companies, to set up laboratories here.

How can outsourcing foster economic development?

Adding a factual note to the emotional debate regarding the loss of manufacturing jobs, despite lower wages in some overseas regions, foreign firms have chosen to produce automobiles made by high-wage American workers. Examples include Honda in Ohio, Mercedes Benz in Alabama, BMW in South Carolina, and Toyota in California. Moreover, while direct manufacturing employment has been declining, total U.S. production of manufactured goods has risen by about 40% over the past decade. This is a tribute to rapidly advancing productivity, and the combination of trends is an international phenomenon. In recent years, China, Japan, and Brazil each lost more manufacturing jobs than did the United States.

A portion of the reported decline in manufacturing employment is a statistical quirk, as is a part of the rise in service employment. That offsetting change results when a manufacturing company contracts out some of its overhead activities; after all, converting a business function from an overhead burden center in an industrial corporation to a profit center in a service firm is a prod to achieving greater efficiency and helps keep American businesses more competitive. As for the corporate profits that may result from outsourcing, we tend to forget that the typical shareholder is a pension fund or mutual fund representing ordinary Americans.

6. WHAT SHOULD WE DO?

Do those who advocate laws against American business outsourcing really believe that foreign governments would not retaliate? It is likely that these same people have never given thought to the fact that, in a global marketplace, companies all over the world are outsourcing. The United States is both the world's largest exporter, as well as the world's largest importer. In other words, we have the largest stake in maintaining open markets, both at home and abroad.

As in many other forms of regulation, proposed government restraints on outsourcing would have all sorts of unanticipated adverse consequences. Recently, the University of Maryland requested an exemption from a proposed prohibition on outsourcing by agencies and departments of the federal government. It turns out that the university maintains a network of training centers at many

U.S. overseas installations. The alternative to increasing the skills of Americans stationed overseas via "outsourcing" would be to hire foreigners with the needed skills.

Hysterics aside, the Information Technology Association reports that setting up "do-not-call" lists has already eliminated more call center jobs than all of the outsourcing to India. Conversely, not every job created overseas equates to an American job being lost; for example, in the past, U.S. airlines traditionally did not pursue small billing discrepancies with travel agencies because it was not worth the cost incurred. Now, using cheaper Indian workers, the airlines can afford to correct small billing errors. For the airlines, it is a welcome savings, while the practice has also created new jobs in India. Notably, there is no loss of jobs in the United States as a result.

Ironically, experts on offshoring report that all of the publicity, both unfavorable and favorable, has been generating more awareness on the part of U.S. companies of the potential benefits of overseas outsourcing. Nevertheless, the national debate on offshoring requires a constructive response, especially in a presidential election year. Many of the people who lose their jobs are truly hurting. If old-style protectionism is not a good answer, what should we do?

The positive approach is to enhance the productivity and competitiveness of American workers. IBM recently announced the creation of a new US$25 million retraining program for employees concerned about losing their jobs to outsourcing.

More fundamentally, the fact that the U.S. has the highest high school dropout rate of all industrialized nations is nothing that can be blamed on foreigners. Nor can we be proud of the fact that, at the other end of the skill spectrum, the United States has fallen from third to 17th among nations in terms of the share of 18- to 24-year-olds who earn degrees in science and engineering. Also, let us not overlook all the regulatory and tax barriers to innovation and to more efficient domestic production of goods and services that have been erected by the U.S. government.

An agenda of economic reforms is long overdue in order to make the United States a more attractive place to hire and keep productive employees. Such a debate on outsourcing would lead to real sustainable benefits for American workers.

ARTICLE 1.2

Cafes, Beaches, and Call Centers

Andy Reinhardt and Carlta Vitzthum

The 2002 hit French movie *L'Auberge Espagnole* captured the zeitgeist of contemporary Barcelona. In the film, a group of college students from all over Europe share an apartment (and occasionally each others' beds) as they bond over beer and music. But it's all a bit of a fantasy. In the real Barcelona, those kids would more likely board commuter trains every morning bound for office parks in the suburbs. There, they'd plop down in front of PC screens, strap on headsets, and spend the day fielding inquiries from callers around the Continent.

After a slow start, Europe is finally jumping on the outsourcing bandwagon. Consultancy TPI of Woodlands, Tex., figures that European companies awarded $41 billion in outsourcing contracts in 2004, nearly twice the level of two years earlier. One of the hottest nearby destinations for the work is Spain, where thousands of young Europeans flock every year in search of sun and sangria—and jobs. Some 50,000 people from virtually every European country work in more than 2,000 Spanish call centers and so-called shared service centers, which handle functions such as tech support, accounting, and personnel administration. London-based researcher Datamonitor PLC says the industry will add 30,000 jobs over the next two years.

Spain's appeal is easy to fathom. Wages for service-center workers are about 30% lower than in northern Europe, and social charges add just 35% to the cost per employee, vs. up to 50% in France and Germany. But that's not the only reason multinationals such as Avis, Hewlett-Packard and Citigroup have set up shop in Spain. In a business where employee turnover is the most persistent problem, quality of life makes a crucial difference in attracting and retaining talent. "Instead of sitting in ten inches of snow in Poland, wouldn't you rather be sitting in ten inches of warm sand in Barcelona?" asks Stephen A. Koutros, a partner at TPI.

To be sure, Spain is not the only country parlaying good weather and exciting nightlife into booming call-center business. Despite higher costs, the southern French university towns of Toulouse and Montpellier host service centers for companies such as Dell Inc. and Freescale Semiconductor Inc. of Austin, Tex. Italy's largest call-center operator, Gruppo COS, has operations in Palermo, Naples, and Tunisia. At the same time, Eastern Europe is drumming up business with wages that are a fraction of those in the west. And India remains, by far, the world leader in outsourcing.

Still, Spain offers potent advantages, especially for European companies looking to "nearshore" work close to home. Because it's part of the European Union, people from anywhere in the EU can work there without visas or permits. Spanish facilities can handle sensitive banking and medical transactions that aren't allowed to be sent outside the EU. Those factors, plus a good education system, top-notch telecom infrastructure, and excellent transportation, earned Spain the top ranking among European countries in consultancy A.T. Kearney Inc.'s 2004 Offshore Location Attractiveness Index.

Such qualities prompted Dallas-based Affiliated Computer Services Inc. to hang a shingle in Barcelona three years ago. The $5-billion-a-year company specializes in tech support and back-office outsourcing and has about 1,000 employees in Europe, half of them in the Catalan capital. Most of its Barcelona staffers, who hail from 38 countries and speak 14 languages, provide service to General Motors Europe. On one floor of ACS' nondescript glass office building, a team of 300 handles finance functions such as accounts receivable, tax payments, and a remarkable $50 billion a year in accounts payable. Brian Stones, head of ACS' European business, reckons the company has cut GM's accounting costs by 80%. GM won't confirm the figure, but the Barcelona center "has led to a significant improvement in administrative cost efficiency for GM in Europe," says corporate communications manager Marc Kempe.

Is offshore outsourcing strictly a phenomenon in the United States? If not, which other nations have engaged in outsourcing, and why?

BOLD RECRUITING

Across the hall, another 150 ACS staffers administer GM's European human resources. They do everything from managing Internet self-service programs to fielding calls from GM's 77,000 workers and 35,000 retirees around Europe with questions about benefits or paychecks. Grouped in teams according to their language, the ACS employees, whose average age is 27, speak to callers in their native tongues. That's crucial for a successful call-center operation, says Gianluca Tramacere, an outsourcing analyst with researcher Gartner near London. "As soon as callers pick out an accent, they get resentful."

Barcelona may draw lots of young European job seekers, but ACS still recruits aggressively to find the right talent. Consider Ria Rosechakowski, a 25-year-old German who runs a team developing online training tools for GM. She posted her resumé on the Internet a year ago, and an hour later an ACS manager called her for an interview. Five days later she moved to Barcelona and started work. ACS is also adept at unearthing special skills. Armin Hofer, a 34-year-old German with a degree in tax law, moved to Barcelona five years ago with his Spanish wife and went to work in the tax-compliance group serving GM in Germany. "Where else could I find a job that uses my specific skills and language?" he says. To keep workers loyal, ACS puts on beach parties and sponsors sports leagues for its staff.

What are some cultural challenges related to managing the ACS workforce?

For all its allure, Spain must contend with rising wages, which have climbed 36% at the national level since 1998. That's what dampened growth in the Irish service-center industry. "Calling places like Barcelona 'hot spots' has positive connotations, but it also suggests hype and increasing salaries," says Rene Buck, principal of Buck Consultants International, a Dutch firm that advises clients on outsourcing and site selection. Buck tries to steer clients to less-discovered places. These days many of those are in Eastern Europe.

For now, Spain's outsourcing trend shows no sign of letting up. French information-technology services company Teamlog, for instance, is expanding a 120-person European help center for Hewlett-Packard outside Barcelona. Bayer, Nestle, and Sara Lee handle accounting and legal functions there. Eric Lemeilleur, who runs Teamlog's operation in Barcelona, concedes with a laugh that "most employees here know L'Auberge Espagnole by heart." All that beer and free love are paying off for Spain's economy.

Outsourcing: A Policy Agenda

Sarah Anderson and John Cavanagh

D on't worry; they'll get better jobs in the service sector." During the last three decades of the 20th century, this was the mantra of most government and business leaders when corporations transferred auto or apparel jobs to Mexico or China. That line doesn't work anymore, since U.S. companies have started shifting a wide range of service jobs as well—from high-skill computer programming to entry-level call center jobs—to India and other lower-wage nations. This breaching of the final frontier of American jobs has caused understandable anxiety and has become a hot-button issue in the presidential election campaign.

The trend toward foreign "outsourcing" of service jobs is an extension of a longstanding practice of cutting costs by subcontracting parts of business operations to nonunion shops within the United States. The practice has gone global, in part because of technological changes. Massive amounts of information can now be transmitted across the world at low cost, making geographic distances less important. International financial institutions and trade agreements have also facilitated the trend by promoting investment liberalization and privatization of public services, creating new opportunities for U.S. corporations in overseas markets.

Forrester Research estimates that about 40 percent of Fortune 1,000 firms have already outsourced some work and that at least another 3 million service jobs will leave the United States by 2015, led by information technology work. A study by the University of California, Berkeley estimates that 14 million U.S. jobs (11 percent of the total work force) are vulnerable to being outsourced.

Although the number of jobs lost so far is small relative to the total work force, these layoffs have a huge impact on the affected communities, and the potential for white-collar jobs to be offshored is deeply unsettling for many American workers. In addition to job cuts, service workers must now also contend with the enhanced power of highly mobile, increasingly unregulated global corporations to bargain down U.S. wages and working conditions by threatening to move jobs elsewhere.

According to McKinsey and Company, a consulting firm that helps businesses develop offshore operations, U.S. companies make up about 70 percent of the global outsourcing market. Their top destination in the developing world

From *Foreign Policy In Focus Brief,* Volume 9, No. 2, April 2004, pp. 1–3. Copyright © 2004 by Foreign Policy In Focus. Reprinted with permission.

is currently India, where domestic subcontractors perform a range of services for the U.S. market. At the low-skill end, Indian workers earn $1 or less per hour to handle customer service calls for firms like Earthlink and Travelocity. Among the higher-skill workers are Indian computer programmers, who earn about one-tenth the pay of their U.S. counterparts to write code for multinational corporations like Citigroup. Given a lack of other economic opportunities, Indian workers are often eager to secure new jobs catering to the U.S. market. However, there is also a nagging fear that these jobs may evaporate as soon as companies can find lower costs elsewhere.

China, of course, looms on the horizon. It is already the second-biggest developing-country draw for service work, offering rock-bottom wages and an official ban on basic union rights. Though it lacks India's English-speaking advantage, this may not be the case forever, as Beijing is heavily promoting English-language education. Mexico's experience in competing with China over manufacturing jobs could foreshadow events to come. Although employment in Mexico's border export zone more than doubled after the implementation of the North American Free Trade Agreement (NAFTA) in 1994, the country has in recent years lost several hundred thousand of these jobs, partly in economic flight to lower-wage China. India has even lost some foreign manufacturing jobs to China.

Public pressure has galvanized U.S. state and federal legislators to introduce a flurry of bills to curb outsourcing, primarily by requiring that government contract work not be performed overseas. However, there is stiff resistance from the corporate lobby, such as the new Coalition for Economic Growth and American Jobs, which represents some 200 trade groups, including the U.S. Chamber of Commerce and the Information Technology Association of America. These and other pro-outsourcing groups argue that the practice is good for U.S. workers, because it lowers the cost of services for U.S. consumers and enhances the overall competitiveness of U.S. companies. Another common claim is that recent job losses are due to productivity gains, not outsourcing. However, because workers are facing a "jobless" recovery and see few personal benefits from enhanced productivity, these arguments convince very few.

One reflection of public opinion is that concerns about U.S. trade policy have spread up the income ladder. Lower- and middle-class workers have been consistently skeptical of U.S. trade policies, but a February 2004 University of Maryland poll showed that even among Americans earning over $100,000 a year, support for actively promoting more "free trade" has dropped from 57 percent in 1999 to 28 percent in 2004.

PROBLEMS WITH CURRENT U.S. POLICY

As they vie for votes in layoff-ridden swing states, both presidential candidates are offering solutions to the prevailing American angst about trade and outsourcing. Railing against "Benedict Arnold" companies, Sen. John Kerry has vowed to eliminate government incentives for outsourcing. For example, he would place conditions on most government contracts to require that the work be performed in the United States. He would also eliminate a tax break that currently allows U.S. businesses to defer tax payments on income earned abroad, and he proposes to use the resulting revenue to lower the overall corporate tax rate from 35 to 33.25 percent. Similarly, Kerry would offer incentives to encourage transnational corporations to repatriate earnings and would then channel these revenues into an employer tax credit for new hires. Regarding trade, Kerry has vowed to include stronger labor and environmental protections in future trade pacts and to review all existing agreements.

The Bush administration has delivered mixed messages regarding outsourcing. Two prominent officials have publicly endorsed the practice—Treasury Secretary John Snow and Gregory Mankiw, chairman of the Council of Economic Advisers. Both have argued that foreign outsourcing of service jobs is good for the American economy, because it helps companies become more efficient. Meanwhile, President Bush has sought to distance himself from such statements and instead to focus public attention on his administration's new "21st Century" jobs plan. Bush argues that the real driving forces behind outsourcing are "frivolous" lawsuits, excessive regulation, and high taxes. He also claims that NAFTA and other trade agreements have been good for U.S. workers, and he promises that by breaking down even more trade barriers his policies will boost export-related jobs. "The best product on any shelf anywhere in the world says, 'Made in the USA,'" Bush told an audience of women entrepreneurs in Cleveland.

But the Bush administration's jobs plan ignores the historical record and thus misdiagnoses the problem. Government figures show that U.S. employment for American multinational corporations grew only 25 percent between 1982 and 2001, while employment at their overseas affiliates increased 47 percent. (These figures likely underestimate foreign expansion, because they do not include information on employment through subcontractors, data the U.S. government does not require businesses to report). This period of rapid overseas expansion has coincided with increased trade and investment liberalization and a declining corporate tax burden. U.S. employers are leaders in outsourcing, even though their share of the national tax bill is considerably lower than the average for employers in other industrial nations.

Bush's claim that companies are fleeing "Big Government" is also dubious. McKinsey and Company claims that U.S. corporations have led the outsourcing trend not to escape burdensome regulations, but because the relatively unregulated U.S. labor market facilitates sending jobs abroad. McKinsey, a pro-outsourcing consulting firm, points out that compared to most European counterparts, the United States has "liberal employment and labor laws that allow companies greater flexibility in reassigning tasks and eliminating jobs."

Kerry's early jobs plan is encouraging, but it addresses only one side of the issue. His proposal to end taxpayer subsidies for outsourcing, whether through government contracting or tax breaks, is long overdue. Citizens should not have to pay higher taxes to subsidize the evaporation of their jobs. To ensure effectiveness, any reforms must be carefully crafted to prevent potential loopholes. More effort will also be needed to address the threat posed by existing international agreements to domestic legislation that requires public contract work to be performed in the United States. For example, under World Trade Organization rules, the Government Procurement Agreement bans governments from favoring domestic firms in procurement contracts. Although only 25 countries have signed the agreement thus far, plans are under way to expand its scope and incorporate similar rules in other trade pacts.

Kerry's primary focus on domestic measures will have only a modest impact on the jobs issue, because these policies cannot make up for the extreme gap in labor costs, which is the primary driving force behind outsourcing. McKinsey estimates that global pay gaps result in a net cost savings for outsourcers of at least 45–55 percent (after accounting for higher infrastructure and other costs). If this is true, figures in a 2003 University of California, Berkeley study suggest that companies could save around $300 billion a year if they outsourced all of the estimated 14 million U.S. service jobs considered feasible to transfer overseas.

Kerry's promises to change U.S. trade policy are also a step in the right direction. If there were effective international mechanisms to strengthen labor rights enforcement, developing-country workers would have a better chance of obtaining fair wages. Research commissioned by the AFL-CIO indicates that labor rights violations in China artificially depress wages by 47–86 percent and that if the country were to respect basic internationally recognized labor rights, wages would likely increase 90 to 95 percent. However, the goal of strengthening labor rights protections should be pursued as part of a broader strategy to uplift conditions generally in poorer countries. Without overall economic improvements, developing-country governments will continue to face strong pressure to attract foreign investment by offering lax labor rights enforcement, thereby undermining efforts to maintain high standards in the richer countries.

TOWARD A NEW FOREIGN POLICY

The overall goal of U.S. policy on outsourcing should be to attack the factors that make workers—in the U.S. as well as around the world—vulnerable to exploitation by increasingly mobile and unregulated global corporations. The approach needs to recognize that raising standards overseas is vital to retaining stable and substantial jobs at home. This requires a multifaceted response encompassing changes in domestic tax, procurement and labor laws as well as in multilateral trade, finance and aid policies.

On the domestic side, a first step should be to reform tax and procurement policies at all levels of government to ensure that they support good jobs in the United States. Additional subsidies that enhance the incentives for corporations to shift jobs overseas should also be eliminated. These include risk insurance and loan guarantees provided by the Overseas Private Investment Corporation

What factors does a firm need to consider prior to outsourcing?

as well as technical assistance and other supports offered by the U.S. Trade and Development Agency. Moreover, the U.S. government should ensure that U.S. authorities, as well as their counterparts around the world, have the right to use tax and procurement policies as instruments to support social goals without being undermined by international trade agreements.

The domestic policy response should also involve labor law reforms that reduce current obstacles to union organizing and that beef up rules related to laying off workers. Most European countries require that corporations guarantee higher severance pay based on years of service, which substantially raises the cost of moving jobs. Many European countries also oblige companies that are planning to close an operation to consult with unions and sometimes to negotiate over the decision. By contrast, under U.S. law, unions may only bargain over the effects of a closure. Thus, although European countries also experience outsourcing-related job loss, the practice is not as advanced as in the United States.

However, domestic measures, while significant, do not address the biggest incentive for outsourcing—extreme wage gaps. Tackling this problem will require a long-term commitment to supporting sustainable economic activity in poor countries and should focus on the factors that make workers around the world vulnerable to exploitation by global companies.

One of these factors is lax enforcement of internationally recognized labor rights, which artificially depresses wages. U.S. policymakers must learn from the failure of NAFTA's weak labor rights mechanism and should develop a better model. The Hemispheric Social Alliance has proposed involving the International Labor Organization in monitoring compliance and investigating complaints related to rights violations. If necessary, assistance would be provided to help countries achieve compliance. Only if this approach was unsuccessful would sanctions be applied, and if the perpetrator was a specific company, the punishments would be targeted at the company rather than at the host government.

Any labor rights initiative, however, should be integrated within a broader strategy toward poorer nations. Other factors that make workers vulnerable are high unemployment and poverty. Although national governments are not without responsibility for these problems, international financial institutions and trade agreements have played an exacerbating role. For example, the World Bank, the International Monetary Fund and the World Trade Organization all threaten the livelihoods of tens of millions of farmers by pressuring poor-country governments to eliminate tariffs and agricultural subsidies. Likewise, privatization supported by these international financial institutions has often resulted in mass layoffs and weakened social services. These multilateral agencies should instead join governments in promoting "global green deal" policies that stimulate stable and substantial employment while protecting the environment.

Regarding trade, Washington should withdraw its support for rules—such as in Chapter 11 of NAFTA—that grant excessive protection to U.S. investors

What are some of the risks involved with outsourcing?

against public interest laws and other host government actions that diminish profits. Such trade rules undermine democracy and encourage U.S. firms to shift jobs overseas.

To enhance this new and broader strategy toward poorer nations, the U.S. government should advocate for stronger international mechanisms to transfer resources from richer to poorer countries. Where appropriate, this would include debt reduction or cancellation. Washington could also promote the adoption of international taxes on both foreign exchange transactions and arms sales to generate revenues for development purposes. The U.S. must also revamp its development aid policies to emphasize anti-poverty measures, healthy communities and a clean environment rather than handouts to U.S. corporations like Halliburton and Bechtel.

In short, a comprehensive response to corporate outsourcing requires a sea change in the outlook of both the U.S. public and its politicians toward America's role in the world. Just as Americans are less secure when much of the world is plagued by extreme poverty, inequality and instability, worker exploitation overseas translates into exploited workers and less secure jobs at home. The electoral debate over outsourcing offers an opportunity to create a new policy approach that combines solidarity with self-interest in a whole-scale effort to benefit the entire world.

SOURCES FOR MORE INFORMATION

Organizations

Economic Policy Institute
1660 L St. N.W., Suite 1200
Washington, DC 20036
Voice: (202) 775-8810
Fax: (202) 775-0819
Email: epi@epinet.org
Web site: http://www.epinet.org/

WashTech
2900 Eastlake Avenue East, Suite 200
Seattle, WA 98102
Voice: (206) 726-8580
Fax: (206) 323-6966
Email: contact@washtech.org
Web site: http://www.washtech.org/

Publications

Ashok Deo Bardhan and Cynthia A. Kroll, "The New Wave of Outsourcing," Fisher Center for Real Estate and Urban Economics, University of California, Berkeley, available at: <http:// www.haas.berkeley.edu/ news/Research_Report_Fall_2003.pdf>.

Hemispheric Social Alliance, "Alternatives for the Americas," available at
<http://www.art-us.org/docs/alternatives%20dec%202002.pdf>.

McKinsey Global Institute, "Offshoring: Is It a Win-Win Game?"
available at: <http://www.mckinsey.com/knowledge/mgi/offshore/>.

North American Alliance for Fair Employment, "Outsource This?
American Workers, the Jobs Deficit and the Fair Globalization Solutions," available at: <http://www. fairjobs.org/docs/OutsourceThis!.pdf>.

Web sites

Communications Workers of America
http://www.cwa-union.org/outsourcing/
India Resource Center
http://www.corpwatchindia.org/

ARTICLE 1.4

The Outsourcing Bogeyman

Daniel W. Drezner

THE TRUTH IS OFFSHORE

When a presidential election year coincides with an uncertain economy, campaigning politicians invariably invoke an international economic issue as a dire threat to the well-being of Americans. Speechwriters denounce the chosen scapegoat, the media provides blanket coverage of the alleged threat, and legislators scurry to introduce supposed remedies.

The cause of this year's commotion is offshore outsourcing—the alleged migration of American jobs overseas. The depth of alarm was strikingly illustrated by the firestorm of reaction to recent testimony by N. Gregory Mankiw, the head of President George W. Bush's Council of Economic Advisers. No economist really disputed Mankiw's observation that "outsourcing is just a new way of doing international trade," which makes it "a good thing." But in the political arena, Mankiw's comments sparked a furor on both sides of the aisle. Democratic presidential candidate John Kerry accused the Bush administration of wanting "to export more of our jobs overseas," and Senate Minority Leader Tom Daschle quipped, "If this is the administration's position, I think they owe an apology to every worker in America." Speaker of the House Dennis Hastert, meanwhile, warned that "outsourcing can be a problem for American workers and the American economy."

Critics charge that the information revolution (especially the Internet) has accelerated the decimation of U.S. manufacturing and facilitated the outsourcing of service-sector jobs once considered safe, from backroom call centers to high-level software programming. (This concern feeds into the suspicion that U.S. corporations are exploiting globalization to fatten profits at the expense of workers.) They are right that offshore outsourcing deserves attention and that some measures to assist affected workers are called for. But if their exaggerated alarmism succeeds in provoking protectionist responses from lawmakers, it will do far more harm than good, to the U.S. economy and to American workers.

Should Americans be concerned about the economic effects of outsourcing? Not particularly. Most of the numbers thrown around are vague, over-hyped estimates. What hard data exist suggest that gross job losses due to offshore outsourcing have been minimal when compared to the size of the entire U.S. economy. The outsourcing phenomenon has shown that globalization can affect white-collar professions, heretofore immune to foreign competition, in the same way that it has affected manufacturing jobs for years. But Mankiw's statements on outsourcing are absolutely correct; the law of comparative advantage does not stop working just because 401(k) plans are involved. The creation of new jobs overseas will eventually lead to more jobs and higher incomes in the United States. Because the economy—and especially job growth—is sluggish at the moment, commentators are attempting to draw a connection between offshore outsourcing and high unemployment. But believing that offshore outsourcing causes unemployment is the economic equivalent of believing that the sun revolves around the earth: intuitively compelling but clearly wrong.

Should Americans be concerned about the political backlash to outsourcing? Absolutely. Anecdotes of workers affected by outsourcing are politically powerful, and demands for government protection always increase during economic slowdowns. The short-term political appeal of protectionism is undeniable. Scapegoating foreigners for domestic business cycles is smart politics, and protecting domestic markets gives leaders the appearance of taking direct, decisive action on the economy.

Protectionism would not solve the U.S. economy's employment problems, although it would succeed in providing massive subsidies to well-organized interest groups. In open markets, greater competition spurs the reallocation of labor and capital to more profitable sectors of the economy. The benefits of such free trade—to both consumers and producers—are significant. Cushioning this process for displaced workers makes sense. Resorting to protectionism to halt the process, however, is a recipe for decline. An open economy leads to concentrated costs (and diffuse benefits) in the short term and significant benefits in the long term. Protectionism generates pain in both the short term and the long term.

THE SKY IS FALLING

Outsourcing occurs when a firm subcontracts a business function to an outside supplier. This practice has been common within the U.S. economy for some time. (Witness the rise of large call centers in the rural Midwest.) The reduction of communication costs and the standardization of software packages have now made it possible to outsource business functions such as customer service, telemarketing, and document management. Other affected professions include medical transcription, tax preparation, and financial services.

The numbers that are bandied about on offshore outsourcing sound ominous. The McKinsey Global Institute estimates that the volume of offshore outsourcing will increase by 30 to 40 percent a year for the next five years. Forrester Research estimates that 3.3 million white-collar jobs will move overseas by 2015. According to projections, the hardest hit sectors will be financial services and information technology (IT). In one May 2003 survey of chief information officers, 68 percent of IT executives said that their offshore contracts would grow in the subsequent year. The Gartner research firm has estimated that by the end of this year, 1 out of every 10 IT jobs will be outsourced overseas. Deloitte Research predicts the outsourcing of 2 million financial-sector jobs by 2009.

At first glance, current macroeconomic indicators seem to support the suspicion that outsourcing is destroying jobs in the United States. The past two years have witnessed moderate growth and astonishing productivity gains, but overall job growth has been anemic. The total number of manufacturing jobs has declined for 43 consecutive months. Surely, many observers insist, this must be because the jobs created by the U.S. recovery are going to other countries. Morgan Stanley analyst Stephen Roach, for example, has pointed out that "this is the first business cycle since the advent of the Internet—the enabler of a new real-time connectivity to low-cost offshore labor pools." He adds, "I don't think it's a coincidence that this jobless recovery has occurred in such an environment." Those who agree draw on anecdotal evidence to support this assertion. CNN's Lou Dobbs routinely harangues U.S. companies engaged in offshore outsourcing in his "Exporting America" series.

Many IT executives have themselves contributed to this perception. When IBM announced plans to outsource 3,000 jobs overseas this year, one of its executives said, "[Globalization] means shifting a lot of jobs, opening a lot of locations in places we had never dreamt of before, going where there's low-cost labor, low-cost competition, shifting jobs offshore." Nandan Nilekani, the chief executive of the India-based Infosys Technologies, said at this year's World Economic Forum, "Everything you can send down a wire is up for grabs." In January testimony before Congress, Hewlett-Packard chief Carly Fiorina warned that "there is no job that is America's God-given right anymore."

That last statement chills the blood of most Americans. Few support the cause of free trade for its own sake, out of pure principle. The logic underlying an open economy is that if the economy sheds jobs in uncompetitive sectors, employment in competitive sectors will grow. If hi-tech industries are no longer competitive, where will new jobs be created?

INSIDE THE NUMBERS

Before answering that question, Americans need to separate fact from fiction. The predictions of job losses in the millions are driving the current outsourcing hysteria. But it is crucial to note that these predictions are of gross, not net, losses. During the 1990s, offshore outsourcing was not uncommon. (American Express, for one, set up back-office operations in India more than a decade ago.) But no one much cared because the number of jobs leaving U.S. shores was far lower than the number of jobs created in the U.S. economy.

Similarly, most current predictions are not as ominous as they first sound once the numbers are unpacked. Most jobs will remain unaffected altogether: close to 90 percent of jobs in the United States require geographic proximity. Such jobs include everything from retail and restaurants to marketing and personal care—services that have to be produced and consumed locally, so outsourcing them overseas is not an option. There is also no evidence that jobs in the high-value-added sector are migrating overseas. One thing that has made offshore outsourcing possible is the standardization of such business tasks as data entry, accounting, and IT support. The parts of production that are more complex, inter-active, or innovative—including, but not limited to, marketing, research, and development—are much more difficult to shift abroad. As an International Data Corporation analysis on trends in IT services concluded, "the activities that will migrate offshore are predominantly those that can be viewed as requiring low skill since process and repeatability are key underpinnings of the work. Innova-tion and deep business expertise will continue to be delivered predominantly onshore." Not coincidentally, these are also the tasks that generate high wages and large profits and drive the U.S. economy.

As for the jobs that can be sent offshore, even if the most dire-sounding forecasts come true, the impact on the economy will be negligible. The For-rester prediction of 3.3 million lost jobs, for example, is spread across 15 years. That would mean 220,000 jobs displaced per year by offshore outsourcing—a number that sounds impressive until one considers that total employment in the United States is roughly 130 million, and that about 22 million new jobs are expected to be added between now and 2010. Annually, outsourcing would affect less than .2 percent of employed Americans.

There is also reason to believe that the unemployment caused by outsourc-ing will be lower than expected. Gartner assumed that more than 60 percent of financial-sector employees directly affected by outsourcing would be let go by their employers. But Boston University Professor Nitin Joglekar has examined the effect of outsourcing on large financial firms and found that less than 20 percent of workers affected by outsourcing lose their jobs; the rest are repositioned within the firm. Even if the most negative projections prove to be correct, then, gross job loss would be relatively small.

Moreover, it is debatable whether actual levels of outsourcing will ever match current predictions. Despite claims that the pace of onshore and offshore outsourcing would quicken over time, there was no increase in 2003. In fact, TPI Inc., an outsourcing advisory firm, even reports that the total value of busi-ness process outsourcing deals in the United States fell by 32 percent in 2003.

There is no denying that the number of manufacturing jobs has fallen dra-matically in recent years, but this has very little do with outsourcing and almost everything to do with technological innovation. As with agriculture a century ago, productivity gains have outstripped demand, so fewer and fewer workers are needed for manufacturing. If outsourcing were in fact the chief cause of manufacturing losses, one would expect corresponding increases in manufac-turing employment in developing countries. An Alliance Capital Management study of global manufacturing trends from 1995 to 2002, however, shows that

In the United States, what impact has offshore outsourcing had on domestic jobs?

this was not the case: the United States saw an 11 percent decrease in manufacturing employment over the course of those seven years; meanwhile, China saw a 15 percent decrease and Brazil a 20 percent decrease. Globally, the figure for manufacturing jobs lost was identical to the U.S. figure—11 percent. The fact that global manufacturing output increased by 30 percent in that same period confirms that technology, not trade, is the primary cause for the decrease in factory jobs. A recent analysis of employment data from U.S. multinational corporations by the U.S. Department of Commerce reached the same conclusion.

What about the service sector? Again, the data contradict the popular belief that U.S. jobs are being lost to foreign countries without anything to replace them. In the case of many low-level technology jobs, the phenomenon has been somewhat exaggerated. For example, a Datamonitor study found that global call-center operations are being outsourced at a slower rate than previously thought—only five percent are expected to be located offshore by 2007. Dell and Lehman Brothers recently moved some of their call centers back to the United States from India because of customer complaints. And done properly, the offshore outsourcing of call centers creates new jobs at home. Delta Airlines outsourced 1,000 call-center jobs to India in 2003, but the $25 million in savings allowed the firm to add 1,200 reservation and sales positions in the United States.

Offshore outsourcing is similarly counterbalanced by job creation in the high-end service sector. An Institute for International Economics analysis of Bureau of Labor Statistics employment data revealed that the number of jobs in service sectors where outsourcing is likely actually increased, even though total employment decreased by 1.7 percent. According to the Bureau of Labor Statistics "Occupation Outlook Handbook," the number of IT-related jobs is expected to grow 43 percent by 2010. The case of IBM reinforces this lesson: although critics highlight the offshore outsourcing of 3,000 IT jobs, they fail to mention the company's plans to add 4,500 positions to its U.S. payroll. Large software companies such as Microsoft and Oracle have simultaneously increased outsourcing and domestic payrolls.

How can these figures fit with the widespread perception that IT jobs have left the United States? Too often, comparisons are made to 2000, an unusual year for the technology sector because Y2K fears and the height of the dot-com bubble had pushed employment figures to an artificially high level. When 1999 is used as the starting point, it becomes clear that offshore outsourcing has not caused a collapse in IT hiring. Between 1999 and 2003, the number of jobs in business and financial operations increased by 14 percent. Employment in computer and mathematical positions increased by 6 percent.

It is also worth remembering that many predictions come from management consultants who are eager to push the latest business fad. Many of these consulting firms are themselves reaping commissions from outsourcing contracts. Much of the perceived boom in outsourcing stems from companies' eagerness to latch onto the latest management trends; like Dell and Lehman, many will partially reverse course once the hidden costs of offshore outsourcing become apparent.

If offshore outsourcing is not the cause of sluggish job growth, what is? A study by the Federal Reserve Bank of New York suggests that the economy is undergoing a structural transformation: jobs are disappearing from old sectors (such as manufacturing) and being created in new ones (such as mortgage brokering). In all such transformations, the creation of new jobs lags behind the destruction of old ones. In other words, the recent recession and current recovery are a more extreme version of the downturn and "jobless recovery" of the early 1990s—which eventually produced the longest economic expansion of the post-World War II era. Once the structural adjustments of the current period are complete, job growth is expected to be robust. (And indeed, current indicators are encouraging: there has been a net increase in payroll jobs and in small business employment since 2003 and a spike in IT entrepreneurial activity.)

Offshore outsourcing is undoubtedly taking place, and it will likely increase over the next decade. However, it is not the tsunami that many claim. Its effect on the U.S. economy has been exaggerated, and its effect on the U.S. employment situation has been grossly exaggerated.

THE UPSIDE OF OUTSOURCING

To date, the media's coverage of outsourcing has focused on its perceived costs. This leaves out more than half of the story. The benefits of offshore outsourcing should not be dismissed.

The standard case for free trade holds that countries are best off when they focus on sectors in which they have a comparative advantage—that is, sectors that have the lowest opportunity costs of production. Allowing countries to specialize accordingly increases productivity across all countries. This specialization translates into cheaper goods, and a greater variety of them, for all consumers.

The current trend of outsourcing business processes overseas is comparative advantage at work. The main driver of productivity gains over the past decade has been the spread of information technology across the economy. The commodification of simple business services allows those benefits to spread further, making growth even greater.

The data affirm this benefit. Catherine Mann of the Institute for International Economics conservatively estimates that the globalization of IT production has boosted U.S. GDP by $230 billion over the past seven years; the globalization of IT services should lead to a similar increase. As the price of IT services declines, sectors that have yet to exploit them to their fullest—such as construction and health care—will begin to do so, thus lowering their cost of production and improving the quality of their output. (For example, cheaper IT could one day save lives by reducing the number of "adverse drug events." Mann estimates that adding bar codes to prescription drugs and instituting an electronic medical record system could reduce the annual number of such events by more than 80,000 in the United States alone.)

How does international outsourcing affect domestic consumers?

McKinsey Global Institute has estimated that for every dollar spent on outsourcing to India, the United States reaps between $1.12 and $1.14 in benefits. Thanks to outsourcing, U.S. firms save money and become more profitable, benefiting shareholders and increasing returns on investment. Foreign facilities boost demand for U.S. products, such as computers and telecommunications equipment, necessary for their outsourced function. And U.S. labor can be reallocated to more competitive, better-paying jobs; for example, although 70,000 computer programmers lost their jobs between 1999 and 2003, more than 115,000 computer software engineers found higher-paying jobs during that same period. Outsourcing thus enhances the competitiveness of the U.S. service sector (which accounts for 30 percent of the total value of U.S. exports). Contrary to the belief that the United States is importing massive amounts of services from low-wage countries, in 2002 it ran a $64.8 billion surplus in services.

Outsourcing also has considerable noneconomic benefits. It is clearly in the interest of the United States to reward other countries for reducing their barriers to trade and investment. Some of the countries where U.S. firms have set up outsourcing operations—including India, Poland, and the Philippines—are vital allies in the war on terrorism. Just as the North American Free Trade Agreement (NAFTA) helped Mexico deepen its democratic transition and strengthen its rule of law, the United States gains considerably from the political reorientation spurred by economic growth and interdependence.

Finally, the benefits of "insourcing" should not be overlooked. Just as U.S. firms outsource positions to developing countries, firms in other countries outsource positions to the United States. According to the Bureau of Labor Statistics, the number of outsourced jobs increased from 6.5 million in 1983 to 10 million in 2000. The number of insourced jobs increased even more in the same period, from 2.5 million to 6.5 million.

POLITICAL ECONOMY

When it comes to trade policy, there are two iron laws of politics. The first is that the benefits of trade diffuse across the economy, but the costs of trade are concentrated. Thus, those made worse off by open borders will form the more motivated interest group. The second is that public hostility toward trade increases during economic downturns. When forced to choose between statistical evidence showing that trade is good for the economy and anecdotal evidence of job losses due to import competition, Americans go with the anecdotes.

Offshore outsourcing adds two additional political pressures. The first stems from the fact that technological innovation has converted what were thought to be nontradeable sectors into tradeable ones. Manufacturing workers have long been subject to the rigors of global competition. White-collar service-sector workers are being introduced to these pressures for the first time—and they are not happy about it. As Raghuram Rajan and Luigi Zingales point out in "Saving Capitalism

From the Capitalists," globalization and technological innovation affect professions such as law and medicine that have not changed all that much for centuries. Their political reaction to the threat of foreign competition will be fierce.

The second pressure is that the Internet has greatly facilitated political organization, making it much easier for those who blame outsourcing for their troubles to rally together. In recent years, countless organizations—with names such as Rescue American Jobs, Save U.S. Jobs, and the Coalition for National Sovereignty and Economic Patriotism—have sprouted up. Such groups have disproportionately focused on white-collar tech workers, even though the manufacturing sector has been much harder hit by the recent economic slowdown.

It should come as no surprise, then, that politicians are scrambling to get ahead of the curve. During the Democratic primary in South Carolina—a state hit hard by the loss of textile jobs—billboards asked voters, "Lost your job to free trade or offshore outsourcing yet?" Last Labor Day, President Bush pledged to appoint a manufacturing czar to get to the bottom of the outflow of manufacturing positions. In his stump speech, John Kerry bashes "Benedict Arnold CEOs [who] send American jobs overseas."

Where presidential candidates lead, legislators are sure to follow. Senator Charles Schumer (D-N.Y.) claimed in a January "New York Times" op-ed authored with Paul Craig Roberts that because of increased capital mobility, the law of comparative advantage is now null and void. Senator Tom Daschle (D-S.D.) has observed, "George Bush says the economy is creating jobs. But let me tell you, China is one long commute. And let me tell you, I'm tired of watching jobs shift overseas." Senator Christopher Dodd (D-Conn.) and Representative Nancy Johnson (R-Conn.) are sponsoring the USA Jobs Protection Act to prevent U.S. companies from hiring foreign workers for positions when American workers are available. In February, Senate Democrats announced their intentions to introduce the Jobs for America Act, requiring companies to give public notice three months in advance of any plan to outsource 15 or more jobs. In March, the Senate overwhelmingly approved a measure banning firms from federal contracts if they outsource any of the work overseas. In the past two years, more than 20 state legislatures have introduced bills designed to make various forms of offshore outsourcing illegal.

SPLENDID ISOLATION?

There are clear examples of jobs being sent across U.S. borders because of U.S. trade policy—but not for the reasons that critics of outsourcing believe. Consider the example of candy-cane manufacturers: despite the fact that 90 percent of the world's candy canes are consumed in the United States, manufacturers have sent much of their production south of the border in the past five years. The attraction of moving abroad, however, has little to do with low wages and much to do with protectionism. U.S. quotas on sugar imports have, in recent years, caused the domestic price of sugar to become 350 percent higher than world market prices. As candy makers have relocated production to countries where sugar is cheaper, between 7,500 and 10,000 workers in the Midwest have lost their jobs—victims not of outsourcing but of the kind of protectionism called for by outsourcing's critics.

A similar story can be told of the steel tariffs that the Bush administration foolishly imposed from March 2002 until December 2003 (when a ruling by the World Trade Organization prompted their cancellation). The tariffs were allegedly meant to protect steelworkers. But in the United States, steel users employ roughly 40 times more people than do steel producers. Thus, according to estimates by the Institute for International Economics, between 45,000 and 75,000 jobs were lost because higher steel prices made U.S. steel-using industries less competitive.

These examples illustrate the problem with relying on anecdotes when debating the effects of offshore outsourcing. Anecdotes are incomplete narratives that fail to capture opportunity costs. In the cases of steel and sugar, the opportunity cost of using protectionism to save jobs was the much larger number of jobs lost in sectors rendered less productive by higher input prices. Trade protectionism amounts to an inefficient subsidy for uncompetitive sectors of the economy, which leads to higher prices for consumers and a lower rate of return for investors. It preserves jobs in less competitive sectors while destroying current and future jobs in sectors that have a comparative advantage. Thus, if barriers are erected to prevent offshore outsourcing, the overall effect will not be to create jobs but to destroy them.

So if protectionism is not the answer, what is the correct response? The best piece of advice is also the most difficult for elected officials to follow: do no harm. Politicians never get credit for inaction, even when inaction is the best policy. President George H.W. Bush, for example, was pilloried for refusing to follow Japan's lead by protecting domestic markets—even though his refusal helped pave the way for the 1990s boom by letting market forces allocate resources to industries at the technological frontier. Restraint is anathema to the political class, but it is still the most important response to the furor over offshore outsourcing. As Robert McTeer, president of the Federal Reserve Bank of Dallas, said when asked about policy responses to outsourcing, "If we are lucky, we can get through the year without doing something really, really stupid."

The problem of offshore outsourcing is less one of economics than of psychology—people feel that their jobs are threatened. The best way to help those actually affected, and to calm the nerves of those who fear that they will be, is to expand the criteria under which the Trade Adjustment Assistance (TAA) program applies to displaced workers. Currently, workers cannot apply for TAA unless overall sales or production in their sector declines. In the case of offshore outsourcing, however, productivity increases allow for increased production and sales—making TAA out of reach for those affected by it. It makes sense to rework TAA rules to take into account workers displaced by offshore outsourcing even when their former industries or firms maintain robust levels of production.

Another option would be to help firms purchase targeted insurance policies to offset the transition costs to workers directly affected by offshore outsourcing. Because the perception of possible unemployment is considerably greater than the actual likelihood of losing a job, insurance programs would impose a very small cost on firms while relieving a great deal of employee anxiety. McKinsey Global Institute estimates that such a scheme could be created for as little as four or five cents per dollar saved from offshore outsourcing. IBM recently announced the creation of a two-year, $25 million retraining fund for its employees who fear job losses from outsourcing. Having the private sector handle the problem without extensive government intervention would be an added bonus.

THE BEST DEFENSE

Until robust job growth returns, the debate over outsourcing will not go away—the political temptation to scapegoat foreigners is simply too great.

The refrain of "this time, it's different" is not new in the debate over free trade. In the 1980s, the Japanese variety of capitalism—with its omniscient industrial policy and high nontariff barriers—was supposed to supplant the U.S. system. Fifteen years later, that prediction sounds absurd. During the 1990s, the passage of NAFTA and the Uruguay Round of trade talks were supposed to create a "giant sucking sound" as jobs left the United States. Contrary to such fears, tens of millions of new jobs were created. Once the economy improves, the political hysteria over outsourcing will also disappear.

It is easy to praise economic globalization during boom times; the challenge, however, is to defend it during the lean years of a business cycle. Offshore outsourcing is not the bogeyman that critics say it is. Their arguments, however, must be persistently refuted. Otherwise, the results will be disastrous: less growth, lower incomes—and fewer jobs for American workers.

What are the factors to consider when discussing the impact of outsourcing on job loss, job growth, and job creation?

ARTICLE 1.5

Net Value: Legal Services Outsourcing Next Big Trend?

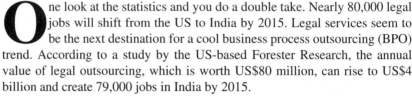

Sufia Tippu

How can outsourcing make a firm more competitive?

One look at the statistics and you do a double take. Nearly 80,000 legal jobs will shift from the US to India by 2015. Legal services seem to be the next destination for a cool business process outsourcing (BPO) trend. According to a study by the US-based Forester Research, the annual value of legal outsourcing, which is worth US$80 million, can rise to US$4 billion and create 79,000 jobs in India by 2015.

"The benefit of the outsourcing companies in the US would translate into a cost saving of about 10% to 12%. The potential of Indian resources to absorb the increasing demand in legal outsourcing is because India enjoys the economic advantage of the wage difference and less perks and overheads," the report says.

The National Association of Software and Service Companies (Nasscom) also projected that legal processing outsourcing (LPO) in India will soon rise to about US$3 billion to US$4 billion. No doubt it is the need for reducing costs, streamlining operations—the same as in outsourcing IT services per se—that seem to be the common drivers for the outsourcing of legal work offshore. Today, legal outsourcing entails supporting the work of corporate legal departments, large law firms and even individual lawyers in activities like drafting contracts, online research, reviewing and reporting documents, litigation support, intellectual property researching and drafting and applying for patents.

Says Jason Brennan, director-legal services, OfficeTiger, which offers legal offshore services in partnership with Hilderbrandt International: "The future of the LPO market is promising. In the US alone, estimated current spending for support services totalled US$19.92 billion in 2004. Assuming a very conservative outsourcing potential of 10%, the resulting opportunity is about US$2 billion. Of this, I believe India can capture a substantial share."

A survey of corporate law departments conducted by the American Corporate Counsel Association suggests that 86% of respondents cited external legal costs as their top concern. This has been the contributing factor in the aggressive search for alternative sources.

But what's exciting about LPO is the fact that till now just a tiny component of the overall BPO industry was coming here but the future is glaringly bright.

"We expect a dramatic and exponential growth, based on the cost pressures currently faced by the US and UK legal markets, and the traction that we are seeing across all of our service lines," says Sanjay Kamlani, co-CEO of legal offshoring outfit Pangea3, which has created a niche market in India for legal offshoring.

Interestingly, a number of US companies, including those part of the Fortune 500, and some of largest law firms in the US, are now outsourcing routine legal work to India.

GE began utilising in-house attorneys located in India as early as 2001, and by 2004, various divisions within GE were each reporting savings in legal costs ranging from US$250,000 to US$700,000 annually. GE, Citigroup, Dupont, Oracle and Cisco are already outsourcing legal services to India. Indigo Lever Shared Services has recently begun outsourcing services in the areas of financial, IT, legal and human resource to Unilever group companies worldwide. Even some state and federal departments in the US have joined the fray though they are under strict non-disclosure agreements.

Apart from these bigger MNCs who have a separate legal unit to handle offshoring, a number of Indian companies—primarily in the BPO segment and a handful from Indian law firms themselves which are setting up new companies to handle overseas legal clients—are coming up fast.

DIFFERENT EMERGING MODELS

Vendors such as Delhi-based Lexadigm Solutions and *lawwave.com* rely exclusively on Indian lawyers to conduct low-level legal work and analysis while others, like Chennai-based OfficeTiger, use a mix of lawyers and trained professionals to handle legal and non-legal tasks such as managing conflicts databases and document management and review. Pangea3 in Mumbai combines US lawyers in New York and Mumbai with Indian lawyers to provide a range of pure play, higher-end lawyer services.

A few vendors specialise. Intellevate, based in Minneapolis, US, has hired Indian lawyers and PhD holders to conduct patent research and other IP work. Another company, ALMT Legal and Atlas Legal Research, does online research, reviewing and reporting documents, drafting, litigation support, and corporate due diligence support at a billing rate of US$80 per hour.

Firms including Ecase Solutions, Evalueserve, Gausa India Ltd, India Legal, Variante Global, Xansa (all based in the National Capital Region of New Delhi and Gurgaon); Mumbai-based Integreon; Indore-based Intercom India; Bangalore-based IPPro, Manthan Services, MindCrest; Chennai-based Oks Span Tech Pvt Ltd, and Thuriam Legal; and Hyderabad-based Quislex, are just a few of the BPOs actively working on LPO projects.

WHY INDIA?

Aside from cost, one of the reasons India has been the main beneficiary of this offshoring drive is the large number of legal professionals available (85,000 at last count)—most of whom are trained in a legal system consistent with US and UK laws. If numbers could win the LPO battle, India's competitors in this space are no match: the Philippines had 44,000 lawyers according to the country's 2003 Law List while Australia's 12 bar associations and law councils comprised only 42,206 members.

Quality of service and speed of delivery are a big draw, too. While LPO is gaining in China and South Korea, the level of Indian attorneys is much higher.

"International attorneys are impressed not only by the labour cost differential, but the speed and quality offered here," says a senior lawyer.

Most LPO outfits like Pangea3, OfficeTiger and Intellevate are staffed 24x7. "By outsourcing to destinations like India, OfficeTiger's clients have seen improvement in operational efficiencies. It allows for 24x7 access to a dedicated staff of legal experts," says Brennan.

Cost-savings is the obvious plus. "It costs a company on average between US$20,000 and US$30,000 to file a patent application in the US. When Pangea3 delivers the same patent application at a price of US$5,000 to US$6,000, a company is suddenly able to file multiple patents within the same budget. Each filed patent generates a whole chain of additional activity including additional legal activity—thus expanding the market," explains Sanjay of Pangea3.

The lower cost allows for more diligent quality control process than is affordable in the US and enables clients to accomplish more within the same or even lower legal budget. "India is a natural fit for this increasing interest in alternative sourcing. India combines a highly-educated and hardworking population, English language capabilities and a stable and continuously improving infrastructure," says Brennan of OfficeTiger.

THE PROBLEMS

On the face of it, the future of LPO in India is bright. But some are not so sure how many of the legal jobs in the US would actually shift to India. For example, while Forrester Research estimates over 12,000 legal jobs were expected to shift from the US by the 2005, Nasscom, India's software services body, estimates less than a few hundred actually moved.

But experts feel that if the quality of legal education is not further improved, it could stymie the flow. The other deterrent could be Foreign Direct Investment norms governing legal services and the existing partnership laws. Nasscom feels India needs to open up its legal services and amend its Partnership Act.

Meanwhile, Khaitan & Co, a leading Kolkata law firm, has already started an LPO by floating a new company Neoworth and has engaged 10 US-enrolled lawyers.

"Although the legal systems in India and the US are different, the analysis part of the work is the same. We are ready to receive high-end jobs," says Rabindra Jhunjhunwala, partner of Khaitan & Co.

Many lawyers are thinking along the same lines. According to them, an Indian lawyer can be as good as his American counterpart in US federal law if properly trained.

What is required of an attorney, either Indian or American, is not that he should be aware of all laws and regulations but that he should be ready to acquire that knowledge.

But Paval Duggal, a Supreme Court advocate and India's foremost authority on cyber and BPO law, believes that high-end legal advisory work may not come to India given the fact there is a huge liability in the US for lawyers. Unlike in India, lawyers can be sued for millions of dollars over dereliction of duty or negligence and most of the law firms pay extremely high insurance costs.

"Patent documentation, legal research, due diligence and other documentation work would be done from here but when it comes to high-end legal advisory work, I doubt whether that could be outsourced to India," Paval added.

Though some consensus exists on the significant potential of legal BPO, the experience of early movers has highlighted a few issues and challenges—some possibly more relevant to this domain. While Indian law firms are not seen as a direct threat to onshore law firms, given the sensitive nature of most legal work, buyer markets have expressed concerns about data security and service quality.

"Some lawyers also have concerns about outsourcing work to professionals whom they have not trained themselves," says a US-based lawyer.

But despite this more cautious line of thought, LPO could well be the next big outsourcing wave from the US and UK.

Why has India become a major destination for legal outsourcing?

ISSUE SUMMARY

As the global trend toward offshore outsourcing continues, there is little doubt that the debate over the advantages and disadvantages of this activity will escalate. Policymakers will need to balance the pressure to embrace free trade with some element of protecting domestic jobs. The challenges for multinational firms will also expand as wages rise in nations such as India and China. Further, as workers from other nations, from regions such as Eastern Europe and Africa, are looked to as offshore employment locations, managers will need to develop additional knowledge related to these developing economies. Many firms have recently taken advantage of an additional benefit of outsourcing, the 24-hour business day.

Proponents of international outsourcing argue that moving jobs abroad is a necessary evil in order to maintain competitive in the global economy. If Nike, for example, was forced to produce all of its athletic shoes in the United States, the costs of production would increase exponentially. This could very well lead to Nike pricing itself out of the market as foreign firms such as Adidas (from Germany) and Asics (from Japan) outsourced production to low-wage nations. The end result could mean significant non-manufacturing job cuts for Nike U.S.A. and perhaps, ultimately, the demise of the firm. Thus, by keeping costs low, Nike can maintain its competitive advantage in the United States and abroad.

On the other hand, to what extent do U.S. firms have a responsibility to employ domestic workers? Opponents of offshore outsourcing emphasize that the rate of jobs flowing away from the United States is increasing, and it appears that this trend will continue for years to come. Moreover, the role of outsourcing and government contracts must be examined with respect to fairness to taxpayers. A number of U.S. citizens could make the claim that they have subsidized foreign firms through tax contributions that led to their own unemployment. Moreover, in certain sectors such as legal services, one potential conflict will be the level of expertise that the foreign affiliate can deliver without having an in-depth understanding of ongoing legal developments within the United States.

Indeed, there are risks that come along with the outsourcing of jobs to some far-away location. First, the local language and customs must be considered. There have been numerous examples of firms that have failed in their overseas efforts due to cultural misunderstandings. And customers, especially in the call center world, tend to be turned off when they encounter the accent of a non-native speaker. Dell actually moved its corporate business support back to the United States from India after experiencing a high volume of complaints. Could this situation occur again in the legal world as many U.S. firms look to outsource legal services to India? Other risks include political instability, rising wages, a lack of quality control, and timeliness of workers.

While the focus of most of the criticism of outsourcing has been on the loss of domestic jobs, a more macro-level analysis from an economic development perspective reveals a positive trend. The developing nations that receive "outsourced" jobs from developed nations tend to experience an injection of above-average wages. In India, for example, close to 80,000 jobs with good salaries are expected to be creaated by 2015 in the legal services sector. This in turn fosters the creation of a class of individuals who have more disposable income that is spent domestically, creating an overall injection of economic growth. As the income levels in these nations continue to climb, the local demand for Western goods will also increase significantly. Ultimately, global economic development should make the world a better place.

ISSUE HIGHLIGHTS

- The concept of outsourcing is not a new phenomenon—firms have been looking offshore for low-cost alternatives for generations.
- Outsourcing, especially in the service sector, has increased rapidly since the late 1990s.
- Many U.S. and European firms have looked to other developed nations, such as Spain and Ireland, as outsourcing alternatives.
- Proponents of outsourcing argue that this activity is necessary to stay competitive in the global economy.
- Opponents of outsourcing contend that sending work to other nations is unjust and harms domestic employment.
- The information technology sector has experienced an extremely rapid increase in the number of jobs that have been outsourced internationally.
- Outsourcing can aid in the economic development of nations through job creation and stable, above-minimum, wages.
- India has become a prime destination for the international outsourcing of legal services from the United States due to similarities in language and legal education.
- Costs savings from legal outsourcing can be massive, with savings of over 75 percent in some services.

CRITICAL THINKING

1. Assessing the net impact of outsourcing on national employment is fairly complicated. It is important to look at both outbound job flows of a nation as well as inbound jobs. When a firm or industry shifts jobs overseas, that firm becomes more competitive, resulting in higher revenues, which in turn could create a number of jobs. The overall growth of an economy and workforce also comes in to play and must be factored into an analysis. With today's global economy, the scope and range of outsourcing activity will likely continue indefinitely.

2. Many firms have embraced the strategy of outsourcing for a variety of reasons. Certainly, procuring lower wages is a major factor. In addition, firms that are global in nature strive to have 24-hour operations, and spanning numerous time zones with their operations and call centers can add to their competitive advantage. Outsourcing can also be looked to as a way of learning about new markets. Many firms that initially looked to China for labor purposes are now keen on selling their products in the Chinese market.

3. Outsourcing can affect the economic development of involved nations. Multinational firms create tens of thousands of jobs each year in developing nations, and these firms typically pay their workers above the prevailing local minimum wage. This injection of cash through job creation assists in economic stability and stimulates internal domestic spending, which can help lead some nations through economic transition. In addition, when local salaries rise, people can begin to look toward imported products as their disposable income increases as well.

4. For a number of reasons, India has become the top destination for legal services outsourcing. Due to the influence on education and legal precedent during the British occupation of India, the Indian legal system is somewhat parallel to that of the United States and United Kingdom. India also has many law schools, and most Indian attorneys have an excellent command of the English language. Moreover, the wage rate in India makes outsourcing to this country a viable option from a cost-savings perspective. Other nations that have entered the global legal outsourcing market, such as the Philippines and Australia, have either fewer attorneys, a weaker command of English, or higher wage rates.

ADDITIONAL READING RESOURCES

Liz Simpson, "Shopping the World for Knowledge," *Training* (July 2002), pages 26–31.

Rammohan Rao, "How to Tap the Opportunities for Outsourcing," *The Financial Times* (August 25, 2004), page 11.

Jonathan Whitaker and M.S. Krishnan, "Outsourcing and Offshoring—Call Center Capabilities—Here Are Some of the Major Issues You Should Look at When Deciding to Outsource Offshore," *Call Center Magazine* (May 1, 2005), page 10.

Priya Srinivasan, "To Be Profitable You Have to Be Offshore," *Business Today* (July 17, 2005), page 102.

Outsource Reporter: http://www.outsourcereporter. com.

FITA (Federation of International Trade Associations): http://www.fita.org.

U.S. Small Business Administration, Office of International Trade: http://www.sba.gov/oit/.

What Are the Standards and Practices Surrounding Sweatshops?

The global scrutiny of sweatshops has been more than comprehensive since a number of major multinational firms have been publicly shamed for manufacturing goods in substandard factories in recent years. With the acceleration of global trade patterns in the 1980s, numerous multinational firms have leveraged their cost advantages by either hiring contract manufacturers or by setting up wholly owned manufacturing facilities overseas. Although many firms have proactively established work conditions that are far superior to the prevailing standards in the local country, others have, albeit unintentionally at times, allowed their standards to slip below an acceptable level. A number of international organizations, such as the International Labor Organization and the Fair Labor Association, have been formed to monitor and assess the work conditions of multinational organizations operating in developing nations.

One person's definition of what constitutes a sweatshop may be quite different from another's. Typically if a firm does not pay wages above the prevailing regional wage rate, does not pay overtime, forbids unionization, and has an unsafe work environment, it approaches the sweatshop threshold. According to Adam Neiman, co-founder of No Sweat Apparel shoes, his product is produced in a sweatshop-free factory because his workers are unionized and "earning at least $90 a month—about 20 percent higher than the minimum wage for the region—with full medical coverage, meal allowances and other benefits." Transparency appears to be a trend lately for firms that are trying to avoid any accusations of making use of sweatshops, and many U.S. firms, such as Nike and Gap, now permit frequent audits of their overseas facilities.

Many developing nations rely on foreign manufacturers to create steady local jobs. In Cambodia, there are 270,000 garment workers, and the vast majority of them produce products for firms such as Disney, Reebok, and Sears. One Nike factory in China generates over $80 million annually from Nike contracts alone. Nike has more than 700 independent contractors in its manufacturing network that spans 50 countries. Wages tend to vary considerably depending on the particular nation. Including overtime, Nike's wages in China hover around $5 a day, well above the market rate for the country. In Cambodia, Vietnam, and other Southeast Asian nations, factory wages tend to range from $2 to $10 a day.

39

International organizations have monitored the benefits and drawbacks related to a complete ban on child labor, which is often a symptom of a sweatshop situation. There have been recent examples of children turning to prostitution and drugs when released from the safety and security of a job with a multinational manufacturer. An example cited by Radley Balko in his article "Sweatshops and Globalization" relays the dire situation that 50,000 children faced when laid off by a German manufacturer in Bangladesh. A number of the children turned to prostitution and crime upon losing their jobs.

In her article about Cambodia's garment industry, Amy Kazmin outlines a new policy approved by the Cambodian government that is designed to elevate national work standards while encouraging more transparency. The program, enacted by the International Labor Organization, encourages cooperation among all players in the contract manufacturing business and increases the number of ongoing factory inspections. Richard Read, in his article titled "At One Nike Contract Plant, No Sweatshop, but Plenty of Sweat," visits a Nike contract manufacturer in China and reports that conditions have improved significantly in recent years. As a result of Nike's questionable practices in the 1990s, the firm has now taken the lead in setting high standards for all of its global manufacturing facilities.

Some firms have been attempting to leverage corporate social responsibility as a competitive advantage. Jenny Strasburg writes about footwear and apparel startup No Sweat Apparel in her article, "Politically Correct Upstart Challenges Nike." Strasburg points out that although No Sweat has not yet established a foothold in the footwear industry, the firm has, through media scrutiny, forced the larger more dominant firms to think twice about their manufacturing standards and work conditions. The fourth article, by Radley Balko, provides an historical perspective on the sweatshop debate. Balko argues that sweatshops may be a stepping stone on the road to prosperity, as was the case in Western Europe and North America. The issues of boycotts and bans, as well as the impact of free trade on sweatshops, are also discussed. The final article related to sweatshops, by David Teather, reviews the situation at Coco-Cola where a number of protesters have accused the firm of unfair labor practices.

ISSUE ARTICLES

Amy Kazmin, "The Rag Trade Patches Up Its Image," *The Financial Times* (September 13, 2005).

Richard Read, "At One Nike Contract Plant, No Sweatshop, but Plenty of Sweat," *The Oregonian* (June 18, 2005).

Jenny Strasburg, "Politically Correct Upstart Challenges Nike," *San Francisco Chronicle* (May 7, 2004).

Radley Balko, "Sweatshops and Globalization," *AWorldConnected.Org* (2004).

David Teather, "Has Coca-Cola Become the New McDonald's?" *The Guardian (London)* (August 18, 2006).

The Rag Trade Patches Up Its Image

Amy Kazmin

In Cambodia, most children have never even heard of Mickey Mouse. But at a factory in Phnom Penh, hundreds of young women have recently been stitching frilly little pajamas with three of Walt Disney's most beloved princesses—Sleeping Beauty, Cinderella, and Belle from Beauty and the Beast—for export to the US.

Disney once banned manufacturers from making its branded clothing in Cambodia after textile factories were accused of hiring underage workers and compelling employees to put in long overtime for little pay.

But Disney's ban has now been lifted due to an International Labour Organisation factory monitoring and improvement programme, which has improved conditions for Cambodia's 270,000 garment workers and is boosting the local clothing industry at a time of intensifying competition.

The initiative is now being recognised in the global rag trade as a model of how western buyers, developing country governments, local factories and organised labour can collaborate to tackle sweatshops and improve the work environment for some of the world economy's most exploited labourers.

Next year, the programme, known as Better Factories Cambodia, will receive its first financial support from big western companies: Gap, Nike, Reebok, Adidas, Levi Strauss, Sears, Wal-Mart, Hennes and Mauritz, the Children's Place Retail Stores and Disney.

"Our hope is that this project ... will allow Cambodia to distinguish itself from the portfolio of emerging countries all competing for this manufacturing business," says Mark Spears, Disney's director of international labour standards. "Part of the difference is not simply price or quality but respect for labour standards and labour rights.

"You are getting government, trade unions, manufacturers and local civil society to literally sit at the same table, at the same time, to address issues in a way that is constructive towards resolution," he says.

As globalisation has made western consumers more aware of the sweatshops in which their clothes are often made, multinational brands have grown increasingly preoccupied with the vexing question of how to ensure decent, fair treatment of workers throughout their supply chain.

How have national governments in developing countries improved work conditions to encourage more foreign firms to use local manufacturers?

Though most garment factories are now subject to dozens of annual inspections by their various western customers, international compliance officers admit the "fragmented" and secretive nature of these efforts means factory managers can falsify records, dupe inspectors or even play buyers off against each other, without substantively changing the way they operate or treat workers.

"Divided, we fall," says a senior executive of one of the companies set to fund the Cambodian initiative. "People are fed up with the existing audit model. When third-party auditors or internal brands go in, it is a complete failure. We've just driven a lot of these issues underground. It is not putting the issues front and centre for everyone to resolve collaboratively."

Cambodia, an impoverished country still haunted by the Khmer Rouge genocide in the 1970s, seems an unlikely place for a national experiment in factory transparency, trade union rights or decent work conditions. But a one-of-a-kind 1999 trade deal between Washington and Phnom Penh laid the crucial groundwork.

Signed in spite of the objections of reluctant local manufacturers, the deal promised greater access to the US textile market if Cambodian factories improved working conditions and respected trade union rights. To export to the US, factories had to submit to surprise inspections by the International Labour Organisation [ILO], which made all its findings public.

With their highly-visible, long-term presence in Phnom Penh and good connections to local labour leaders and community groups, the ILO inspectors proved better able to get a fix on real working conditions than western buyers' own agents on flying, usually pre-announced, visits.

"Workers often just ring us up, and say, 'such and such has happened'," says Ros Harvey, Better Factories' chief technical advisor. "You have local staff that speak the local language and interviews happening away from the workplace—all of these contribute to a much better source of information about what is really happening."

The project's transparency—or "name them and shame them" approach, as one unionist described it—coupled with the promise of more US sales and the threat of strikes, gradually motivated factories to improve.

"Factories have developed good habits, unions have got their act together, the ILO monitoring is credible," says Jason Judd, global campaign director for the American Federation of Labor and Congress of Industrial Organizations. "It's a vindication for anybody who cares about workers rights. You can hold companies accountable, report on the way work is done and grow an industry."

With the end of the global textile quota system last year—and the threat of greater competition from lower-cost China—Phnom Penh decided it would still require all factories to submit to ILO inspections to obtain export licenses. They hoped to save a Dollars 2bn (Pounds 1.1bn) industry that accounts for 80 per cent of national exports, 12 per cent of gross domestic product, and directly or indirectly supported up to 20 per cent of the country's 13m people. Cambodian manufacturers supported the policy, betting that transparency and a reputation for taking labour issues seriously would help them retain or increase orders from image-conscious foreign brands.

So far, the gambit has worked as Cambodia's garment exports to the US, its main market, rose 17 per cent in value terms from January to April this year.

Cambodia is hardly a workers' paradise. Factories still ask staff to do excessive overtime, underpay wages to temporary workers and are lax on safety. Collective labour agreements have been resisted. Chea Vichea, the country's most charismatic trade union leader, was gunned down last year in Phnom Penh, possibly for supporting Cambodia's opposition party.

Yet overall, western buyers say Better Factories' ability to highlight shortcomings gives them a common reference point from which to approach factories.

To deepen the process, the ILO hopes to persuade western buyers to rely only on Better Factories monitoring and to reduce or drop their own audits. Sears Holdings, which owns Sears and K-Mart, has agreed to rely exclusively on ILO inspections, while Disney says they will be the "key basis" for their corporate assessments.

"If you have a national approach or geographically contained approach you can improve the quality and effectiveness of monitoring and also reduce the transaction costs to the factory," Ms Harvey says.

"Just managing 30 different audits by different auditors is a nightmare."

How have independent multinational labor monitoring organizations assisted in the elimination of unfair labor practices?

ARTICLE 2.2

At One Nike Contract Plant, No Sweatshop, But Plenty of Sweat

Richard Read

What constitutes a sweatshop?

More than 4,000 workers who churn out athletic bags in a huge Nike contract factory here breathe ventilated air. They wear earplugs when pounding rivets. They use bathrooms with running water. And they read their rights on wall-mounted bulletins.

Gone are the acrid fumes, the scant protective gear and the foul restrooms evident during past years in plants making Nike products. Workers flocking from poor villages to booming, smog-choked southeast China express eagerness for their jobs here, belying the image of sweatshop exploitation that has plagued the Beaverton-based company for years.

Yet the Golden Prenc factory, which makes about 25,000 bags a day and generates $80 million in annual revenues, is hardly a carefree place. Assembly workers toil long hours at repetitive jobs. Many of them endure separation from families. Their wages are higher than incomes back on the farm, but meager by U.S. standards at an average of $5 a day, including overtime. Workers' modest dreams reveal difficult lives.

"My mother is raising our 3-year-old son back home," says Kuang Wangxin, a 27-year-old floor supervisor. Twice a year, Kuang rides a bus eight hours with his wife, an assembly worker, to see their child. "I hope when he grows up he can start as a manager," Kuang says, "and not go through what I did."

After Nike's recent disclosure of the names and locations of 705 independent contract factories in its network, a plant visit reveals significant improvements since the 1990s. The main issue to surface is one that Nike managers acknowledge as a widespread problem: overtime hours exceeding maximums set by Nike and local laws.

A few hours in one factory is not enough time to thoroughly assess working conditions, and the Golden Prene factory may or may not be representative. Nike still does not release audit scores for individual plants.

A Nike manager hosting the visit substituted Golden Prene for Bonny Sports, another Chinese factory requested from the disclosure list. He said Bonny made products for Bauer Nike Hockey, a subsidiary not yet fully covered by Nike's compliance standards.

At Golden Prene, randomly selected workers voiced few complaints during interviews with and without a Nike manager present. But fundamental issues of fairness linger from the days when activists dragged Nike into the headlines, contrasting factory workers' wages with rising sneaker prices and lavish endorsement contracts.

Nike public-relations officers once bristled at suggestions that their company, dedicated to lofty goals of athletics and achievement, would exploit workers who, in their view, were gaining economic opportunities. But today Caitlin Morris, Nike compliance integration and collaboration director, sticks to a positive message. "The obligation that Nike has is to make good on the concept that foreign investment in these countries does raise standards of living," Morris says. "My aspiration as someone in Nike's corporate-responsibility department is to make a positive contribution to that."

Longtime critics acknowledge progress made by Nike managers, adding that it occurred only due to public pressure. "What they've eliminated is super exploitation, and now they're just down to plain exploitation," says Medea Benjamin, founding director of Global Exchange, a San Francisco human rights organization.

Benjamin says Nike, which reported record profits last year, could afford better wages for its contract workers. She says the company should shun China and other nations that ban unions; Nike managers maintain they can do more to support freedom of association by engaging with China.

Jeff Ballinger, director of Press for Change, a tiny but vocal activist organization in Toronto, says Nike executives should empower workers instead of imposing conveniently crafted initiatives. "They're skating by with some corporate social-responsibility template that's been hammered out by expensive consultants," Ballinger says.

Ballinger and Benjamin grant that consumer outrage has waned. Instead of actively targeting Nike, Global Exchange is pushing U.S. city governments to buy "sweatshop-free" products.

What are some policies that multinational firms have enacted to avert accusations of utilizing sweatshops in foreign contract manufacturing facilities?

CONTRACT PAYROLL INCREASES

Nike's contract work force, meanwhile, has grown to 653,000 in more than 50 countries. One of those workers, Lu Ling, a 26-year-old Golden Prene stitching operator, left her distant rural village eight years ago. She works a standard 60-hour six-day week.

As the eldest child, the middle-school dropout sends money home from her $145 monthly earnings so that her siblings can attend school. Hunched over a sewing machine, she races to exceed hourly production targets so her team can earn more. "Someday," Lu says, "I want to have my own bag factory."

Lu and other workers are so pressed that they don't glance up when visitors come by. They receive health benefits required by Chinese law. They earn enough to buy bicycles—some workers buy motor scooters—but not cars.

The Golden Prene factory, owned by the Guang Der Corp., comprises four hulking manufacturing buildings. The 15-year-old complex is located in the gritty Hua Nan Industrial Zone, one of the many huge new manufacturing districts that sprawl across a mainland Chinese region near Hong Kong.

Factory manager Charles Shang, a former Taiwanese army major who served in a military boot-making plant, says the decision to begin making Nike goods about seven years ago forced changes. Before then, he says, employees worked from 7:30 a.m. until 11 p.m. with two one-hour breaks—every day of the month.

In those days, about 30 percent of the workers failed to return after Chinese New Year holidays. But now, Shang says, annual turnover is under 10 percent.

Nike accounts for between 55 percent and 65 percent of the plant's production. The factory also makes bags for Dakine Hawaii Inc., the Hood River sports-accessory company, and for other brands. Adidas moved out several months ago.

Golden Prene has followed Nike's transition away from oil-based solvents and other hazardous chemicals to water-based materials. Plant managers have grown accustomed to Nike audits, which Shang credits with helping attract customers.

"After they heard we were doing business with Nike," Shang says, "they understood we were qualified."

About 30 Nike employees work in offices inside the Golden Prene plant, with responsibilities ranging from conducting audits to readying Beaverton-designed products for manufacture.

Is it fair for firms like Nike to pay low wages, even though those wages are above the prevailing market rate, given the massive revenues and profits that are realized annually?

GOVERNMENT, FAMILY CONNECTIONS

Golden Prene and other Guangdong-province manufacturers have faced a tightening labor market recently, as workers favor other industrial regions. Instead of raising wages, as some factories have done, the plant works through rural provincial officials, who steer workers its way.

Village and family connections also help. Wan Tianyan, a 21-year-old riveter who projects a macho air, followed his two older sisters to the plant from the family rice paddy. He's saving $97 a month so that he can get married by 25 and give his parents what they want most: a grandson.

"It's not easy here," Wan says.

Does he miss home? Wan shakes his head, but a pained expression flickers across his face.

Politically Correct Upstart Challenges Nike

Jenny Strasburg

Regardless of how sturdy his No Sweat-brand sneakers are, Adam Neiman faces a difficult uphill climb taking on Nike in his latest anti-sweatshop campaign.

Neiman—a roofer by trade who runs his own company in Newton, Mass.—is co-founder and chief executive of No Sweat Apparel. The privately held firm last year sold $150,000 worth of T-shirts, jeans and other clothing made by union workers in developing countries, he said.

Its latest product … has footwear-industry types on their toes. It's a $35 pair of black canvas, rubber-soled sneakers that look like low-rise Converse Chuck Taylors, but lack Converse's trademark star logo.

More remarkable is the one-page flyer that comes in every box.

No Sweat's "labor content disclosure form" offers a new twist in the long-running discussion about fair-labor standards in the globalized footwear industry. The flyer says that unionized workers in Jakarta, Indonesia, made the shoes while earning at least $90 a month—about 20 percent higher than the minimum wage for the region—with full medical coverage, meal allowances and other benefits.

Neiman's contention is that shoe-industry giants can still make good profits even as they do more to promote humane, fair working conditions. Supporting unions and disclosing more information about workers' wages are the best places to start, he said.

"Now you can walk down the street without stepping on the worker who made your shoes," the No Sweat form says. "Sneakers with soul? No sweat." … Neiman, 47, challenged Nike to begin providing a similar form with every pair of shoes it sells.

No stranger to the activist spotlight, Nike said that it already has an effective factory-monitoring and disclosure program.

"As the leading manufacturer and marketer of athletic footwear and apparel, there's more scrutiny applied to what we do" than will ever be applied to a small firm like No Sweat, said Caitlin Morris, Nike's spokeswoman for global issues.

Nike found itself responding to Neiman … after he staged a visit to the company's Beaverton, Ore., headquarters. He asked to speak with Chairman

Can socially responsible firms, such as No Sweat Apparel, compete with success against larger firms such as Nike and Reebok?

and CEO Philip Knight, but Knight wasn't available. Morris said she met with Neiman instead.

Afterward she called No Sweat's business model "interesting and innovative" but said that it's impractical for an $11 billion company that buys products from an ever-shifting base of more than 900 factories in 50-plus countries.

Nike also said in a statement, "While we respect the rights of the protesters to voice their opinions, we believe that our actions to improve the working conditions for the over 600,000 workers who manufacture our products speak just as loudly."

Nike has faced scrutiny for its labor practices since the early 1990s. The attention led eventually to the company's participation in a global factory-monitoring program through the nonprofit Fair Labor Association, an industry-supported labor standards group.

Nike is among more than a dozen companies that help pay for the association to visit hundreds of factories around the world. Some factory surveys are published on its Web site (www.fairlabor.org).

By next year, the association should be able to tell consumers whether Nike meets its minimum standards for factory safety, worker treatment, wages and benefits, said spokeswoman Anne Lally. A comprehensive assessment of the company isn't yet available, she said, because Nike still has one year left in a voluntary, three-year accreditation program.

Lally had just learned of the No Sweat shoes but said they probably will help the association's cause. "It would be great if there's a huge consumer demand because it (would) prove to manufacturers around the world that there is a demand for responsibly-produced shoes."

Neiman said Nike and other companies should take their disclosure steps further by providing more details for shoppers right inside the shoe box.

"We're putting the information right there for consumers to see," he said.

No Sweat is unlikely to become anything more than a tiny player in a giant industry. Its biggest impact may come more from the publicity it attracts than commercial success.

That's not to say that the company doesn't want to move some shoes. Neiman and No Sweat co-founder Jeff Ballinger—who a decade ago wrote a *Harper's* magazine article attacking Nike's labor practices—initially ordered 1,500 pairs of the No Sweat shoes. Internet pre-sales were so strong that they've already ordered another 3,000 pairs, Neiman said. A handful of small retailers supplement online sales (www.nosweatapparel.com), including the activist-operated Global Exchange Fair Trade Stores in San Francisco, Berkeley and Portland, Ore.

"It's a catchy name and a smart marketing ploy," said Kevin Burke, president and CEO of the American Apparel and Footwear Association in Arlington, Va. Neither Nike nor No Sweat belongs to the trade group. Burke said that the industry will watch to see how successful No Sweat is. "If it's true that this company's making the sneaker in the type of conditions in which they say—ethical and humane conditions—I think it's a great idea."

Sweatshops and Globalization

Radley Balko

"In a village in the Mekong delta in Vietnam a woman and her twelve-year old daughter sit all day in the shade from five in the morning until five in the evening making straw beach mats. For their labour they receive $1 a day."

"In China, workers at Wellco Factory making shoes for Nike are paid 16 cents/hour (living wage for a small family is about 87 cents), 11–12 hour shifts, 7 days a week, 77–84 hours per week; workers are fined if they refuse overtime, and they're not paid an extra rate for overtime hours."

Stories like these are common when we hear talk about "sweatshop" plants in the developing world. We hear worse, too—terrible stories about women and children tricked into bondage, of union organizers getting beaten or killed, of terrible working conditions, long hours, and no bathroom breaks.

And yet American companies still operate low-wage factories—"sweatshops"—in developing countries. And there's still a copious source of labor in those countries eager to take the low-paying jobs western factories offer them.

So what's the story on sweatshops? Are they as bad as globalization critics claim they are? Should we boycott companies that operate them? Can they be stopped? Should they be stopped?

THE RACE TO THE BOTTOM

Globalization critics often cite sweatshops as a prime example of the "race to the bottom" phenomenon. A "race to the bottom" is what happens, they say, when world markets are opened to free, unfettered trade. Without transnational labor guidelines and regulations, big corporations will look to place factories and manufacturing plants in countries with the most relaxed environmental and—for our purposes—labor standards.

Developing countries then compete for the patronage of these companies by lowering labor standards—minimum wages and workplace safety requirements, for example. The result: horrendous working conditions like those described above, and no state oversight to make the factories change them.

Critics of free trade say in some countries it's gotten so bad that companies have begun using slave labor, workers compelled to work unpaid by totalitarian governments eager to entertain western businesses.

Some scholars contend that developing countries must pass through a "sweatshop stage" to accelerate economic prosperity. Assess this statement.

In the book *The Race to the Bottom,* author Alan Tonelson describes the process while discussing the 1999 World Trade Organization protests in Seattle:

> Internationally, WTO boosters faced an equally knotty dilemma. Most of the organization's third world members—or at least their governments—opposed including any labor rights and environmental protections in trade agreements. They viewed low wages and lax pollution control laws as major assets they could offer to international investors—prime lures for job-creating factories and the capital they so desperately needed for other development-related purposes. Indeed, they observed, most rich countries ignored the environment and limited workers' power (to put it kindly) early in their economic histories. Why should today's developing countries be held to higher standards?

Tonelson goes on to say that it is workers, then, who must shoulder globalization's burdens, while western companies win cheap labor, western consumers win cheap sneakers and straw hats, and corporate CEOs win eight-figure salaries. And, Tonelson and his supporters argue, it's not just third-world workers. Western workers lose when factories in the U.S. close down, and migrate overseas in search of laborers willing to work for poverty wages.

Critics say sweatshops are a way for corporations to exploit the poverty and desperation of the third world, while allowing them to circumvent the living wages, organization rights, and workplace safety regulations labor activists have fought long and hard for in the west.

WHAT OF SWEATSHOP WORKERS?

When *New York Times* journalists Nicholas Kristof and Sheryl Wudunn went to Asia to live, they were outraged when they first arrived at the sweatshop conditions Asian factory workers worked under. Like most westerners, the thought of 14+ hour shifts six or seven days a week with no overtime pay seemed unconscionable.

After spending some time in the region, however, Kristof and Wudunn slowly came to the conclusion that, while regrettable, sweatshops are an important part of a developing nation's journey to prosperity. The two later documented the role of sweatshops in emerging economies in their book *Thunder from the East.* Kristof and Wudunn relay one anecdote that helped them reach their conclusion in the *New York Times*:

> One of the half-dozen men and women sitting on a bench eating was a sinewy, bare-chested laborer in his late 30's named Mongkol Latlakorn. It was a hot, lazy day, and so we started chatting idly about the food and, eventually, our families. Mongkol mentioned that his daughter, Darin, was 15, and his voice softened as he spoke of her. She was beautiful and smart, and her father's hopes rested on her.
> "Is she in school?" we asked.
> "Oh, no," Mongkol said, his eyes sparkling with amusement. "She's working in a factory in Bangkok. She's making clothing for export to America." He explained that she was paid $2 a day for a nine-hour shift, six days a week.

"It's dangerous work," Mongkol added. "Twice the needles went right through her hands. But the managers bandaged up her hands, and both times she got better again and went back to work."

"How terrible," we murmured sympathetically.

Mongkol looked up, puzzled. "It's good pay," he said. "I hope she can keep that job. There's all this talk about factories closing now, and she said there are rumors that her factory might close. I hope that doesn't happen. I don't know what she would do then."

Globalization's proponents argue that sweatshops, for all their unseemliness, often present developing laborers the best-paid jobs with the best working environment they've ever had; often their other options are begging, prostitution, or primitive agriculture.

Removing the best of a series of bad options, they say, does nothing to better the plight of the world's poor.

BOYCOTTS AND BANS

Anti-sweatshop organizations have achieved an impressive level of organization and influence in the last several years. Campus groups have persuaded university administrators at dozens of colleges around the country to refuse to buy school apparel from companies who use sweatshop labor. The activists demand that corporations pay a "living wage" and agree to international monitoring, or face the loss of collegiate licensing privileges—which amount to some $2.5 billion in annual revenue for the likes of Nike, Reebok and Fruit of the Loom.

So far, evidence has shown that boycotts and public pressure do get results, but perhaps not the kinds of results that are in the best interests of sweatshop workers.

Free traders argue that instead of providing better working conditions or higher wages, which had until then offset the costs of relocating overseas, western companies respond to public pressure by simply closing down their third world plants, or by ceasing to do business with contractors who operate sweatshops.

The result: thousands of people already in a bad situation then find themselves in a worse one.

In 2000, for example, the BBC did an expose on sweatshop factories in Cambodia with ties to both Nike and the Gap. The BBC uncovered unsavory working conditions, and found several examples of children under 15 years of age working 12 or more hour shifts.

After the BBC expose aired, both Nike and the Gap pulled out of Cambodia, costing the country $10 million in contracts, and costing hundreds of Cambodians their jobs.

There are lots more examples like that one.

- In the early 1990s, the United States Congress considered a piece of legislation called the "Child Labor Deterrence Act," which would have taken punitive action against companies benefiting from child labor. The Act never passed, but the public debate it triggered put enormous pressure on a number of multinational corporations. One German garment maker that would have been hit with trade repercussions if the Act had passed laid off 50,000 child workers in Bangladesh. The British charity organization Oxfam later conducted a study which found that thousands of those laid-off children later became prostitutes, turned to crime, or starved to death.

- The United Nations organization UNICEF *reports* that an international boycott of the Nepalese carpet industry in the mid-1990s caused several plants to shut down, and forced thousands of Nepalese girls into prostitution.
- In 1995, a consortium of anti-sweatshop groups threw the spotlight on football (soccer) stitching plants in Pakistan. In particular, the effort targeted enforcing a ban on sweatshop soccer balls by the time the 1998 World Cup began in France. In response, Nike and Reebok shut down their plants in Pakistan and several other companies followed suit. The result: tens of thousands of Pakistanis were again unemployed. According to UPI, mean family income in Pakistan fell by more than 20%.

In his book *Race to the Top*, journalist Tomas Larsson discussed the Pakistani soccer ball case with Keith E. Maskus, an economist at the University of Colorado:

> "The celebrated French ban on soccer balls sewn in Pakistan for the World Cup in 1998 resulted in significant dislocation of children from employment. Those who tracked them found that a large proportion ended up begging and/or in prostitution."

What are some of the potential negative outcomes of firms from industrialized nations banning child labor?

In response, several activist groups have stopped calling for boycotts, and have since started calling for pressure from the governments in whose countries the multinational corporations call home. Still, free traders argue, companies make decisions that are in the best interests of their shareholders and investors, and so if locating overseas isn't offset enough by cheap labor to make the investment worthwhile, companies will merely choose not to invest, costing poor countries thousands of jobs.

ARE SWEATSHOPS A STOP ON THE ROAD TO PROSPERITY?

In his book, Larsson also argues that poor labor standards are usually symptomatic of other problems in a developing country, and that in the long run, they are in fact a *disadvantage* to that country's ability to compete in the international economy. "It is not … countries with the worst human rights records that top the annual rankings of national competitiveness," Larsson writes, "and it is certainly not the countries with the lowest wages and least protection for workers that dominate export markets, or attract the lion's share of foreign direct investment."

Every prosperous country today was once mired in "developing" status. And every prosperous country today once employed child labor in its economic adolescence that would today be considered "sweatshop" working conditions. That includes Britain, France, Sweden, Germany and the United States. Only with the prosperity brought by international trade, globalization's adherents say, can a country then afford to demand better working conditions for its workers.

The economist and syndicated columnist Thomas Sowell writes:

> Half a century ago, public opinion in Britain caused British firms in colonial West Africa to pay higher wages than local economic conditions would have warranted. Net result? Vastly more job applicants than jobs.
>
> Not only did great numbers of frustrated Africans not get jobs. They did not get the work experience that would have allowed them to upgrade their skills and become more valuable and higher-paid workers later on.

Today of course, West Africa is still mired in poverty. Contrast Africa to Hong Kong, or to Taiwan, two countries that embraced an influx of foreign investment, and made a leap to prosperity in just 25 years that took most European countries nearly a century.

Kristof and Wudunn likewise point out that fifty years ago, countries like India resisted allowing foreign investment, while countries like Taiwan and South Korea accepted it—including the poor working conditions that came with it. Today, Taiwan and South Korea boast modern, well-educated, first-world economies. India has become more amenable to investment in the last several years—and its economy has shown promise in response. But for decades, India's refusal to accept foreign "exploitation" wrought wide scale poverty and devastation.

In his book *In Defense of Global Capitalism*, Swedish public policy expert Johan Norberg notes that although India still battles poverty, its improving economy has shrunk its proportion of child laborers from 35% in the 1950s to just 12% in the last few years. Norberg further writes that the burgeoning economies in East and Southeast Asia may enable most of the countries in that region to eliminate child labor altogether by 2010.

Globalists also point out that the modern world economy and its interconnectivity makes it possible for a country to make the transition from an economy where child labor is a necessity to an economy that can afford to ban it in a period of time never before contemplated.

Kristof notes that from the onset of the Industrial Revolution, it took Great Britain 58 years to double its per capita income. In China—where sweatshops are prevalent—per capita income doubles every 10 years. In the sweatshop-dotted southern providence of Dongguan, China wages have increased fivefold in the last few years. "A private housing market has appeared," Kristof writes of Dongguan, "and video arcades and computer schools have opened to cater to workers with rising incomes … a hint of a middle class has appeared."

The anti-sweatshop activists response to these arguments says that because the west has wealth and prosperity, it is the west's responsibility to bring the developing world into modernization without exploiting its laborers. Multi-national corporations can still secure comfortable profit margins without paying miniscule wages, forbidding union organization, and forcing long hours with overtime. As Kevin Danaher of the activist group Global Exchange writes, "Should trade agreements be designed largely to benefit corporations, or should they instead put social and environmental concerns first?"

But free trade advocates say that cheap labor is the one commodity developing nations can offer that first world countries can't. Force corporations to pay artificially high wages in those countries, they say, and there's no incentive for a company to endure the costs of shipping, construction, and risk that come with installing plants overseas. If corporations don't invest, those third world laborers again get forced back into the fields, the alleys, the brothels, and the black market. Better to endure the discomfort of poor working conditions in the short run, so that these countries can begin to build the economies that will enable them to demand better working conditions in the long run.

COMMON GROUND?

In the end, there are at least a few areas in which both free traders and anti-sweatshop crusaders can agree. Most free trade advocates agree, for example, that benefiting from slave labor is no better than theft. Sweatshop workers are often the envy of their communities—they make more money than the farmhands or beggars, for example. But it's important that they're working in factories of their own free will. The key to building prosperity is choice, and if workers don't have the option to quit, or to take a job with a factory across town offering better wages, the "free" in "free trade" is a misnomer, and the benefits of globalization are tainted.

Likewise, free traders and anti-globalization activists usually agree that human rights violations should be documented, and that perpetrators of such violations should be publicized and embarrassed. If in its desire to attract foreign investment a government refuses to police a sweatshop factory where women are being forced into sexual favors, or where union organizers get beaten, it's certainly acceptable—in fact it's imperative—that that government be held accountable in the international community.

The fundamental disagreement in the sweatshop debate seems to be whether or not it's fair for big western companies to benefit from cheap labor in the developing world. Globalists say that menial manufacturing labor is the historical first step in a developing economy's first steps toward prosperity. Sweatshop activists say western corporations can afford to pay artificial "living" wages, and that anything less reeks of exploitation. They further argue that if corporations aren't willing to offer better working conditions on their own, western governments should penalize them, and consumers should refrain from buying their products. Globalists argue that if that happens, corporations would have no incentive to invest in the third world in the first place.

As trade barriers continue to fall, developing countries will continue to choose one track or the other—to embrace foreign investment, or to demand wages not proportional to what their national labor market would naturally allow. Which track delivers prosperity and which track produces continued poverty will lend clues as to who's winning the debate.

FURTHER READING

Global Exchange—An advocacy group that promotes "fair trade" in lieu of "free trade."

Nicholas Kristof—*New York Times* columnist who regularly writes on globalization issues.

Sweatshops.org—Co-op guide to ending America's sweatshops and encouraging "fair trade."

National Labor Committee—is supported by American labor unions to oppose sweatshops in the developing world.

United Students Against Sweatshops—Clearinghouse website for campus anti-sweatshop activists.

www.free-market.net-Free-Market.Net's Globalization Directory—Hosts a litany of articles related to sweatshops and other globalization issues.

David R. Henderson—A Hoover Institution scholar and economist who frequently opposes movements to end sweatshops in the developing world.

Between a Rock and a Hard Place—A Smithsonian Institution history of American sweatshops.

Has Coke Become the New McDonald's?

David Teather

What are the major moral responsibilities of firms such as Coca-Cola when operating in developing countries?

The muffled phone line made the voice in Lagos sound small and distant but there was no mistaking the sense of determination. Ebun-Olu Adegboruwa, a Nigerian lawyer, was explaining how he intended to take on Coca-Cola, the world's largest soft drinks company.

He claims to be acting for some 4,000 people in the port area of Apapa, many of them poor and illiterate, who believe that a local bottling plant has stolen their livelihoods. A lawsuit is planned accusing the company of polluting a lagoon by pumping untreated waste into the water and killing fish. "Like many multinational companies operating in Africa, Coca-Cola is guilty of double standards," he said. "They do what they are unable to do in America and Europe. We feel cheated. People are roaming the streets with no means of making a living."

Welcome to the Coke side of life. The planned legal action is just the latest in a litany of alleged human rights and environmental abuses in developing markets that has made Coca-Cola a cause celebre. When self-described anarchists interrupted the carrier of the Olympic torch on route to Turin ahead of this year's winter games, it was not the athlete's running shoes they objected to, it was the presence of Coca-Cola, which had spent $66m (£35m) to become the main sponsor. Coke is the new Nike.

The latest issue to hobble the company is the renewed allegation that its flagship drink in India contains 27 times the maximum permitted amount of pesticides. A study published by an agency of the UK's Department for Environment, Food and Rural Affairs this week said it detected none of the toxins found by a New Delhi organisation. Nevertheless, a quarter of India's states have imposed partial or total bans so far. Coke's defenders claim the bans are politically driven.

HUNGER STRIKE

Long-simmering claims of ignoring labour abuses in Colombia are still the biggest piece of mud sticking to Coca-Cola, as well as environmental issues in India. A hunger strike was reported last month outside a Coca-Cola plant in

From *The Guardian,* August 18, 2006, pp. 29. Copyright © 2006 by Guardian News & Media Ltd. Reprinted by permission.

Mehdiganj, Uttar Pradesh, which ended when the state government agreed to study charges of pollution and exhaustion of water supplies.

It faces further allegations of union-busting in Pakistan, Guatemala and Nicaragua, and exhausting water resources in El Salvador. In Turkey last year a suit was filed alleging that Coke ignored the intimidation and beating of union activists. Over the summer Coke has faced legal action of a different kind from a disgruntled former business partner in Uzbekistan, who accused the company of shady dealings with the country's authoritarian government. All allegations are denied.

At the very least, Coca-Cola has an image problem. Students in about 10 US universities have banned Coca-Cola drinks, many stirred up by the veteran labour activist Ray Rogers and his Killer Coke campaign. He has targeted universities in a strategy of whipping up anxiety about the firm's human rights and environmental record. An individual boycott "may pale in comparison to the revenues they still generate but students in particular are important," he said. "If a student gets hooked on a product, they've hooked a consumer for the next 40 or 50 years."

POSTAL WORKERS

New York University is the most prominent to sever ties with Coke—its 40,000 students voted in December to remove vending machines and clear cafeteria shelves of all its products. "There's a segment of the student population who felt very strongly about it," said Josh Taylor, an NYU spokesman. "We've taken Coke out of all our dining halls." Protests have also reached Europe and Canada, although the UK's National Union of Students recently voted down a similar ban.

But the campaign against Coke has spread beyond students. Postal workers in the US have urged the removal of vending machines from post offices, and teachers' unions in New York and California have passed resolutions calling for Coke's removal from schools.

In Britain, Coke has been promoting the launch of its latest brand extension, Coke Zero, a sugar-free version for men apparently too manly to buy something with Diet in the name. The company will hope the brand will perform a little better than its last big launch in the US: C2, a low-carbohydrate version of Coke that came on to the market just as the low-carb trend was beginning to wane.

Coca-Cola has drifted in the past decade, suffering from under-investment, heavy job cuts and management upheaval. It has lost almost a third of its market value since 2000 and was, symbolically, overtaken by PepsiCo in terms of market capitalisation in December.

The company has been wrong-footed by consumer trends after years of being the world's best-selling soft drink. Fizzy drinks sales are stagnant in developed markets but while its arch-rival Pepsi was launching energy drinks, bottled water and fruit juices to appeal to a new health-conscious consumer, Coke fell behind. The firm still relies on carbonated drinks for 85% of its sales.

How much impact have Coke's critics had on the firm's policies?

Success in developing markets—Coke claims it is sold in more than 200 countries—is crucial for growth.

Coke's critics are largely a ragtag bunch but the company has been unable to drown out the background noise, despite an annual marketing budget of $2bn. It began a campaign to counter what it dismisses as rumour, slander and urban myth. But it probably does not help that Coca-Cola is a symbol of America just as the superpower's role in the world has come under increasing scrutiny.

Ed Potter, Coke's head of labour relations, said: "We are probably the best-known brand in the world and so therefore we become a target . . . It has less to do with our practices than to make the point of an individual. If you ask why don't they do the same thing with Pepsi, it is because it has no cachet. The well-known examples of Colombia and Turkey fit into that category. There is no substance to the claims being made but the urban myth is more attractive than wanting to know what the facts are."

He said the company had "engaged more actively" with students, including a Washington DC summit last year, and was trying to respond more quickly to issues around the world when they do arise. It has put out its second social responsibility report.

In an effort to silence the drumbeat of criticism, Coke has engaged the International Labour Organisation to assess its practices in Colombia. It has also commissioned a study of its business in India, by a nonprofit organisation, the Energy and Resources Institute. It has taken out advertising in the US student press and signed up to the UN Global Compact in March—the world's largest voluntary corporate responsibility initiative. "The student campaign has stalled," said Potter. "There are not that many individuals involved—but they make a lot of noise."

Jeff Seabright, Coca-Cola's vice-president for environment and water resources, said he had been to Kerala twice this year, over a factory that notoriously closed two years ago after claims that it had depleted the local water table. "The high court in Kerala appointed a panel that found the cause was severe drought and that Coke had not been the cause," he said. "In fact, we have invested in rainwater harvesting." The issue, he insists, is one of perception.

He said Coca-Cola's volume had grown by 35% since 2000 but that more efficient processes had cut net water usage by 1%. He said it was unclear what had polluted the lagoon in Lagos but said the company would build a waste-water treatment plant as soon as the government allowed.

FEARFUL

Activists are critical of Coke's counter-PR campaign and unlikely to be silenced soon. War on Want's Joe Zacune has catalogued alleged abuses in *Coca-Cola: The Alternative Report* and went to India last year to examine the claims. Of Kaladera, Rajasthan, he said: "The people are very, very angry. Farmers took me to their wells to show me how water levels had fallen. They are so fearful of their livelihood and kept using the term 'dark zone' and said we'll end up abandoning this area."

Local people took him to see equipment that Coke installed to collect water and replenish aquifers. "There was one in the grounds of a college. They said Coke had set it up but there had been no maintenance and it had broken. The students had ripped it down and the metal girders were twisted. There is anger, resentment and complete frustration. This isn't stuff you can find out unless you visit these remote and inaccessible places," he said.

Jeremy Moon, a professor of corporate social responsibility at Nottingham University, suggested that Coke was perhaps going through the same growing pains as other multinationals. "Being a branded company clearly brings opprobrium," he said. "If you look at Nike or Reebok, probably they have better practices than anyone else in their supply chains but because they are branded, they are targeted.

"It's a paradox. In many cases these companies have become leaders in corporate social responsibility (CSR) . . . they come under criticism and then work to demonstrate that they are doing the right thing. They come under further criticism and lift standards still further. Nike's latest CSR report is a revelation for the amount of information they give."

Whether all the negative publicity will really have any impact on Coca-Cola sales is another question. Rita Clifton, head of the consultancy Interbrand, is doubtful. She reckons Coke is still the world's most valuable brand, ahead of Microsoft.

"It depends on how much people love the brand and how serious the issue is," she says. "If people like a product and it's convenient then they will probably carry on buying it. People are radical in research questionnaires and reactionary at the checkout . . . People like to carry on doing what they like doing."

IMAGE PROBLEM

Nigeria: Allegations that Coca-Cola killed fish by pumping untreated waste into a lagoon near Lagos

Italy: Protesters disrupt relay of Olympic torch on route to Turin winter games

India: Charges that drinks contain 27 times the permitted levels of pesticides and water reserves have been depleted Colombia, Guatemala, Nicaragua; Claims of ignoring anti-union abuses United States; Universities, postal workers and teachers vote to remove products

Turkey: Allegations of ignoring intimidation and beatings of union activists Uzbekistan; Linked to authoritarian government

ISSUE SUMMARY

Over the past century, the vast majority of what are now considered developed countries went through a period of laborintensive industrialization. The garment industries in New York and Boston paid notoriously low wages in the early 1900s. The situation was quite similar in other major international cities that are now relatively wealthy and sophisticated, such as London, Munich, and Tokyo. Journalist Thomas Larsson, in his book *The Race to the Top*, contends that poor labor standards are a national competitive disadvantage in the long run. Nations must therefore find a way to climb out of the low-wage category to attain a higher level of prosperity. A quick look at the most recent nations to ramp up their level of industrialization, such as Asia's four tigers, Taiwan, South Korea, Singapore, and Hong Kong, reveals a similar pattern of low wages followed by rapid economic growth. Many scholars contend that one key to progress is to encourage foreign investment and the valuable currencies that come along with it.

Sweatshops have arguably faded significantly from the global manufacturing landscape thanks to intense scrutiny by the media and international organizations in the past decade. Multinational firms have recognized that treating workers fairly creates a number of long-term benefits. With higher wage rates and better work conditions, turnover is likely to be reduced and motivation should increase. The potential damage to a firm's reputation is also a major factor that has led to an overall increase in global work conditions. Despite paying wages well above the local minimum wage, firms can still dramatically reduce manufacturing costs by contracting workers in developing nations to produce labor-intensive products.

Organizations such as the International Labor Organization (ILO), Global Exchange, and the Fair Labor Association have been instrumental in implementing formal workplace monitoring systems. The ILO's factory monitoring and improvement program is now viewed as a generally acceptable practice and firms that agree to participate can be reassured that their factories are up to international standards. While firms have been working hard to improve their images through aggressive corporate social responsibility strategies and practices, national governments have also been actively trying to clean up their reputations to increase the influx of foreign direct investment and high-paying jobs.

One final issue that falls under the realm of sweatshops is the use of children in the workplace. Although many nations have minimum-age laws for children to enter the workforce, these laws are often overlooked, especially in the poorest nations of the world. This presents a complex dilemma for multinational firms since many children drop out of school at a young age to support their families. Some firms have built on-site educational facilities, while others have promised jobs to children when they reach a certain age or complete a specified grade level in school. Nevertheless, firms must carefully balance the best interests of the child with the firm's long-term goals and reputation.

ISSUE HIGHLIGHTS

- The vast majority of multinational firms now pay workers at overseas contract manufacturing facilities above-average wages when compared to the prevailing wage rate in the local country.
- A number of international monitoring organizations have surfaced in the past decade to observe and audit work conditions around the world. Some of these organizations are funded by major manufacturing firms such as Nike, Reebok, and Gap.
- Some developing countries are embracing international standards in order to attract more highpaying manufacturing jobs from foreign firms.
- Nike has become a standard bearer in the global manufacturing community due to strict labor policies that were established by the firm after a few scandals in the early 1990s.
- New firms, such as No Sweat Apparel, have surfaced with a niche strategy focused on customers who purchase products that are made in a socially responsible fashion.
- One emerging theory is that nations must proceed through a "sweatshop" phase as a necessary evil to economic development.
- Many children have few viable options beyond working. Laying them off can often lead to tragic results.

CRITICAL THINKING

1. Wage rates are relative. Many multinational manufacturing firms pay workers in their Chinese factories between $5 to $10 a day. While this wage rate appears to be appallingly low by U.S. standards, it is substantially higher than the prevailing rate in China. Many workers in Chinese firms with no foreign affiliation are paid less than $2 a day, half of the rate that foreign firms typically pay. As a result of paying wages that are well above the local rate, multinational firms have experienced a major reduction in turnover in recent years.

2. The United States went through an Industrial Revolution in the early twentieth century, and work conditions, as well as wages, were extremely poor. Many scholars have argued that economic development cannot occur unless a nation passes through a low-wage, heavy manufacturing period. As more developing nations attract higher-thanaverage foreign wages, this can be seen as an initial step to the next level of economic progress. Moreover, when local workers earn higher wages, they tend to spend more locally, which in turn creates the momentum for economic growth.

3. Due to a number of scandals related to the misuse of workers in developing nations, multinational firms have begun to seriously embrace proactive strategies of corporate social responsibility. Firms have recognized that the negative effects of publicity surrounding their overseas manufacturing operations far outweigh the marginal wagerate savings. As a result, multinational firms have implemented a number of policies to ramp up the work conditions for their foreign subsidiaries and contract manufacturers. While some firms still employ questionable practices abroad, in many instances working for the foreign manufacturer in a developing country is possibly the best job in town.

ADDITIONAL READING RESOURCES

Elizabeth Becker, "Low Cost and Sweatshop-Free," *The New York Times* (May 12, 2005), page 1.

Maxine Frith, "The Ethical Revolution Sweeping through the World's Sweatshops," *The Independent* (London) (April 16, 2005), page 20.

Thomas Larsson, *The Race to the Top* (The Cato Institute, 2001).

Laura Smitherman, "Nike Gets a Good Report Card," *The Baltimore Sun* (August 19, 2005), page 1E.

A guide to ending sweatshops and promoting fair trade, http://www.sweatshops.org.

The Fair Labor Association monitors activities of U.S. manufacturers abroad among other activities, http://www.failabor.org.

What Are the Best Approaches to Minimizing Global Corruption?

Bribery has been a barrier to entry into foreign markets for centuries. The extent to which bribery and other forms of corruption are prevalent in a society tends to vary by country for cultural, economic, and other reasons. While multinational firms must strictly adhere to corruption laws in their home countries, behavior in host countries has been questionable due to less-stringent laws and cultural traditions. As a result, many firms have implemented formal codes of ethics as an attempt to regulate the actions of their managers and agents overseas. Some governments and international agencies have also instituted policies and signed agreements to help minimize corporate wrongdoings while operating in a foreign environment.

What is corruption? According to the German anticorruption organization Transparency International, corruption is defined as "the misuse of entrusted power for private gain." Corruption can take many forms such as bribery, extortion, insider trading, embezzlement, and falsifying official documents. Generally, when firms or managers abuse their power to either break laws or harm innocent stakeholders, some form of corruption has likely occurred.

A number of governments have attempted to minimize corruption in international business. The Foreign Corrupt Practices Act (FCPA) was passed in 1977 by the U.S. Congress to control the behavior of U.S. citizens while operating abroad. Essentially, if a U.S. manager pays a bribe to an Egyptian government official to secure a contract, that manager could be prosecuted under U.S. law. For 20 years, the FCPA was essentially the only international legislation, so U.S. managers often faced an uphill battle in highly corrupt nations since European and Asian counterparts didn't have to worry about government prosecution for bribery abroad. Then in 1998 the Organization for Economic Co-operation and Development (OECD) put forth an anti-bribery agreement that was essentially parallel to the U.S. act. Since 1998, all 30 OECD member nations and five additional nations (Argentina, Brazil, Bulgaria, Chile, and Slovenia) have signed the anti-bribery convention. One major factor in the OECD accord is the tax deductibility of bribes. Previously about one-half of the OECD member nations allowed bribes to be deducted from tax returns, yet with the new OECD agreement, this policy is no longer permitted.

In Transparency International's 2005 ranking of 158 countries on their Corruption Perceptions Index, only 40 countries scored 5.0 or higher on a 10-point scale (with 10 being the least corrupt). The vast majority of the countries in the highly corrupt category are extremely poor. Helping raise the income levels in the poorest nations of the world would significantly reduce the levels of corruption worldwide. Yet the United Nations Development Program contends that it would take close to $300 billion a year to move the poorest 1 billion people of the world out of their level of poverty. Moreover, the World Bank estimates that bribery alone totals over $1 trillion US annually.

A number of other organizations have also been working hard to reduce global corruption. The United Nations, World Bank, and International Monetary Fund (IMF) each have strong programs that are geared toward reducing corrupt activity in both the public and private sectors. The World Bank estimates that over 30 percent of all public investment is wasted due to bribery and corruption. IMF research pegs the cost of money laundering at over $500 billion US per year. By creating a cleaner business environment, banks and other international lending institutions can significantly reduce extreme risks and massive loan defaults that can be linked ultimately to corrupt activities.

In his article "Fighting Corruption Is a Global Concern," David Zussman discusses some of the anti-corruption agreements and measures that have recently been established by a number of multinational organizations. Specifically, Zussman cites the progress that the OECD and the United Nations have made, and he outlines some of the financial costs of corruption. In the article, "Renewed Interest in Overseas Bribery Law: A Q&A with White & Case's Owen Pell," an interview with attorney Owen Pell is presented with a focus on the Foreign Corrupt Practices Act. Pell responds to questions about the history of the FCPA and elaborates on why the number of cases filed in court has increased substantially in recent years. The third article, "Rules on Corporate Ethics Could Help, Not Hinder, Multinationals" by Kenneth Roth, takes a pragmatic look at the increasing pressure to establish clear ethical standards for multinational firms. Roth argues that the development of universal standards should help level the moral playing field while putting more pressure to obey rules on smaller firms that have historically slipped through the cracks. In his article about fighting corruption in Nigeria, Alex Brummer describes the courageous efforts of Nigeria's finance minister, Ngozi Okonjo-Iweala, and her attempts not only to combat curruption but also to alter the image of Nigeria in the international community. The final article, an OECD policy brief, provides a comprehensive summary of the OECD anti-bribery convention and goes into depth about the responsibilities of the signatory nations with respect to the enforcement of the convention's rules, regulations, and implementation standards.

ISSUE ARTICLES

David Zussman, "Fighting Corruption Is a Global Concern," *Ottawa Citizen* (October 11, 2005), p. A15.

Owen Pell, "Renewed Interest in Overseas Bribery Law: A Q&A with White & Case's Owen Pell," *PRNewswire* (February 9, 2005), posted online at http://www.prnewswire.com.

Kenneth Roth, "Rules on Corporate Ethics Could Help, not Hinder, Multinationals," The *Financial Times (London edition)* (June 21, 2005), p. 19.

Alex Brummer, "Courage of the Woman Fighting to Rid Nigeria of Corruption," *The Daily Mail, London* (October 27, 2005).

OECD, "Fighting Bribery in International Business Deals," *OECD Observer* (November 2003).

ARTICLE 3.1

Fighting Corruption Is a Global Concern

David Zussman

For a few days last month, Beijing was the site of a most timely conference on anti-corruption. In fact, it was the fifth anti-corruption gathering under the auspices of the OECD and the Asian Development Bank and was hosted by the Ministry of Supervision of the Peoples' Republic of China. The conference gives Canadians an opportunity to reflect on corruption as a global issue seen in the context of the soon-to-be-released Gomery Commission report, David Dingwall's resignation as CEO of the mint, accusations of conflict of interest among executives in Toronto city hall, and allegations of contract rigging in Montreal.

To set the context of the Beijing conference, Transparency International—which brings civil society, business and government together to combat corruption around the world—provided an overview report on the levels of corruption in the world and explained the value of public disclosure in keeping anti-corruption issues in the public eye. While there are acknowledged measurement issues, its work places corruption in an interesting global context. (Canada is ranked the 12th-least-corrupt country; Finland is ranked No. 1.)

Many countries and international institutions—such as the World Bank, the International Monetary Fund, OECD, Asian Development Bank and others—have been working for years on eliminating corruption in both the public and private sectors. Their motives are consistent regardless of levels of development or size of the economy. As a starting point, the World Bank estimates that about one-third of all public investment is wasted due to bribery and other forms of corruption. Moreover, more than 30 per cent of multinationals feel that corruption is a major or very severe concern to them in their investment decisions with countries around the world.

Looking at corruption from another perspective, the UN Development Program has cited that, "the total amount of bribes paid around the world is estimated by the World Bank at $1 trillion U.S. per annum, more than 10 times the total amount of development aid for needy nations." Added to bribery is the cost of money laundering, estimated by the IMF at about $500 billion U.S. per year. To put these numbers in perspective, the UNDP's Human Development Report projects that it would take about $300 billion U.S. a year to move the poorest one billion people out of their extreme poverty.

As a result, many countries are preoccupied now with anti-corruption efforts. First, corruption interferes with economic development and siphons huge sums of money away from the intended targeted public investment. Second, corruption diminishes citizens' quality of life by denying them access to services and products that were intended for them and perversely affects fairness and equity. Finally, it undermines people's trust in government and jeopardizes opportunities for creating effective partnerships between government, the private sector and non-governmental organizations.

What is the relationship between corruption and economic development?

The consensus that emerged from the conference is that there are at least four elements to the successful implementation of an anti-corruption strategy once a government has developed one.

First, there have to be adequate laws in place that deal with access to information, privacy, whistle-blowing, conflict of interest, post-employment behaviour and sanctions that signal that the governments are serious about eliminating the problem.

Second, all citizens—in particular, the leaders of the private and public sectors—must be aware of the rules so there can be no misunderstanding of the government's intentions and of the possibility of sanctions in those instances when problems arise.

Third, there must be aggressive implementation of the policies, with a clear signal that prosecutions will be a consequence of legitimate claims of corrupt activities.

Finally, and as usual the most important, is placing the right people in leadership roles who are above reproach and act independently of the government or the private sector in implementing the policies.

For Canada, these principles are burdened by additional considerations. In the last 10 years, there has been a steady increase in collaboration between the public and private sectors, as well as increased mobility of personnel between them. This has created many new "grey zones" where conflicts of interest can arise as people move between public-service careers—including political ones—and the private sector. Moreover, the recent federal government decisions to consolidate and modernize operations in service departments will attract large IT and management-consulting contracts (as they have in the defence industry) that are sure to test current policies and rules, since the stakes will be high for the competing companies.

Based on international comparisons, Canada is well-placed to continue to improve on current laws and policies that are designed to thwart corruption, in and out of government, despite some current reminders that it is difficult to anticipate ethical lapses in both the public and private sector. In fact, one Canadian initiative—the Global Organization of Parliamentarians Against Corruption (GOPAC), headquartered at the Parliamentary Centre in Ottawa—has singled out elected officials as the focus of their work. All of these kinds of efforts deserve the strong support of Canadians.

Renewed Interest in Overseas Bribery Law: A Q&A with White & Case's Owen Pell

Owen Pell

U S and non-US companies with listed US securities are increasingly targets for investigations under the Foreign Corrupt Practices Act ("FCPA"). In place since the 1970s, there has been a recent surge in FCPA investigations and harsh penalties have been meted out by both the Securities and Exchange Commission ("SEC") and the U.S. Department of Justice. The recent crackdown has affected a broad range of industries, such as defense contracting, aerospace, petrochemical, mining and pharmaceutical, but no industry doing business overseas is exempt from an FCPA investigation. White & Case litigator Owen Pell, who is handling FCPA investigations for companies, talks about what impact the increased scrutiny might have for public companies.

Q: What exactly is the Foreign Corrupt Practices Act?

OP: Investigations by the SEC in the mid-1970's revealed that more than 400 US companies admitted making questionable or illegal payments in excess of $300 million to foreign government officials, politicians, and political parties. The abuses ran the gamut from bribery of high foreign officials in order to secure some type of favorable action by a foreign government to so-called facilitating payments that allegedly were made to ensure that government functionaries discharged certain ministerial or clerical duties. Congress enacted the FCPA to bring a halt to the bribery of foreign officials and to restore public confidence in the integrity of the American business system.

The anti-bribery provisions of the FCPA make it unlawful for a US citizen to make a corrupt payment to a foreign government official for the purpose of obtaining or retaining business for or with, or directing business to, any person. As important, the FCPA also mandates that companies maintain books and records sufficient to reasonably assure that no such payments are made, including by their non-U.S. subsidiaries or affiliates. Violations of the recordkeeping provisions carry stiff penalties even where there is no evidence of illegal payments being made.

What is the underlying purpose of the Foreign Corrupt Practices Act (FCPA)?

The US Department of Justice and the SEC both investigate potential FCPA violations and take enforcement action against FCPA violations.

Q: What's driving federal authorities to increasingly investigate companies under the FCPA?

OP: A number of factors. First, there is the Sarbanes Oxley Act which was passed a few years ago in the wake of several large corporate accounting scandals and has increased the focus on books, records and internal control systems. Companies now must vouch for their internal control systems. Audit committees are expected to pay more attention to these systems, and if they find problems, often must disclose such information. Second, there is a belief that many recent corporate debacles were the result of recordkeeping failures.

How has the Sarbanes-Oxley Act led to more FCPA convictions?

Q: What other factors might contribute to the increased scrutiny?

OP: Other factors driving the renewed interest in the FCPA have been heightened concerns about money-laundering and terrorism, as well as anti-corruption efforts in China and the EU (particularly member states Germany and Poland). Also, the UN has recently completed a treaty that for the first time defines "corruption." If ratified by EU nations and Japan, this will only increase the impetus for FCPA-like regulations across Europe and Asia.

Q: What impact might an investigation have on public companies?

OP: The ramifications can be very serious. If companies are found to be in violation of the FCPA, they're opening themselves up to huge fines, in the hundreds of millions of dollars, potential criminal prosecution and law suits by irate shareholders.

Q: What can companies do to protect themselves?

OP: Both the SEC and DOJ have said that companies have a legal obligation to report improper conduct or breakdowns in internal controls relating to the FCPA, including in their non-US operations. So the first thing companies have to do is review their internal controls and procedures, including outside the US. For example, companies should be developing audit trails and budgets to track things like promotional activities, charitable giving, entertainment expenses, payments to middlemen or distributors in foreign countries—in short, how money is moving, to whom is it going, why is it going there and who knows its going there. It may sound bureaucratic, but really that's what this is all about—creating audit trails and making sure that things that you've probably been doing in the US or as part of your US operations are also being applied to your foreign operations. Companies also should institute training and compliance programs in their US and non-US operations to teach their managers and employees about the FCPA and to create and maintain a culture of compliance. This can mean a great deal if you ever find yourself dealing with a regulator on these issues.

Q: What does it mean to create a culture of compliance?

OP: A culture of compliance means raising employee awareness about the FCPA, and a company's zero tolerance for things like bribery or "grease payments." Companies should review their mission statements and company credos and determine if employees are being trained to understand that paying a little money under the table to help close a deal is not acceptable, even if such activities have been regarded as commonplace in the past in that market. Employees also must understand that skirting the rules on how money is spent is not acceptable, will get everyone into big trouble and is not something the company wants to see happen. One strategy that the US government is recommending is that companies set up hotlines so that employees can anonymously report potential FCPA violations.

Q: Any last recommendations?

OP: In today's stricter regulatory environment, the cost of FCPA non-compliance has simply become too high. The ramifications can be very serious. Forward-thinking companies are proactively reviewing their internal controls and beefing up training programs relating to the FCPA.

Rules On Corporate Ethics Could Help, Not Hinder, Multinationals

Kenneth Roth

Most multinational companies automatically oppose calls for enforceable standards of corporate social responsibility. Under growing public scrutiny of their behaviour, many western companies have adopted voluntary codes of business conduct. But for most, the notion of enforceable standards remains anathema.

Recently, however, some western companies have privately questioned this posture. They have begun to recognise it might be in their interest to operate under enforceable standards that apply to all their competitors, rather than under voluntary ones that, for all practical purposes, apply only to prominent companies.

Public pressure, whether from activists or the press, has largely driven interest in corporate social responsibility. But public pressure tends to focus on highly visible companies, which is fine if a company's competitors are all large public companies. But if competition comes from less prominent businesses that can operate under the radar screen of public attention—the competitive playing field tilts. Well-known companies, worried about the harm that misconduct could cause their reputation, must assume the costs of meeting broadly recognised standards of corporate conduct. For example, a big company might have to accept paying higher wages associated with employing adults rather than children, or permitting trades unions to operate freely in its factories.

By contrast, a no-name company, confident that the public will not notice its misdeeds, may not feel compelled to act so responsibly.

Only enforceable rules, applicable to all companies regardless of prominence, can avoid this double standard. To a limited extent, enforceable regulations already exist but their reach is spotty. Some stock indices, such as FTSE 4Good, require qualifying companies to comply with basic ethical standards. Certain international financial institutions make similar demands of their loan beneficiaries. Companies that are complicit in serious human rights abuses risk liability under laws such as America's Alien Tort Claims Act. And individual governments, sometimes prompted by trade agreements, increasingly demand that trading partners regulate certain corporate conduct. Still, this

Why have some executives of U.S.-based multinational firms criticized the FCPA as an unfair law?

patchwork of enforceable rules hardly leaves a competitive environment that is fair and predictable.

The issue of social responsibility is not the first in which corporations have recognised the advantage of broad enforceable standards. A similar dynamic emerged after the US government's adoption in 1977 of the Foreign Corrupt Practices Act, which made it illegal for companies operating in the US to bribe foreign officials. That law seemingly left US companies at a competitive disadvantage because their foreign competitors remained free to continue securing business through bribery.

After years of complaints, the Organisation for Economic Co-operation and Development in 1997 adopted a treaty requiring all its member states to criminalise such bribery. According to the OECD, its 30 members account for some 70 per cent of world exports and 90 per cent of foreign direct investment. China remains outside the treaty, but as its companies increasingly operate overseas its exclusion will become legally less tenable.

The OECD has already begun a similar process in the area of corporate social responsibility, but its guidelines for multinational enterprises are, so far, only voluntary.

Using the anti-bribery effort as a model, the OECD should adopt a treaty requiring member states to enact laws similar to its guidelines that would be enforceable under national criminal or civil codes, carrying penalties such as fines or in extreme cases, imprisonment. Like anti-bribery laws, this national legislation would bind any company operating in that nation's jurisdiction.

In addition, the United Nations, which has already drafted non-binding norms on corporate conduct, might provide a forum to negotiate a universally applicable treaty.

What would enforceable standards look like? One must await treaty negotiations to answer that question with certainty. In all likelihood, the purpose of enforceable standards would not be to preclude doing business in certain countries but to prescribe the minimum standards by which corporations should conduct themselves in all countries. In that sense, the standards would reflect recognition that while international commerce may help alleviate poverty in developing countries, it does so more effectively if grounded in positive corporate conduct.

In the human rights realm, for instance, enforceable standards would certainly include the widely recognised core worker rights: the right to organise and bargain collectively, and freedom from forced labour, child labour and workplace discrimination. Companies would have to ensure respect for these rights in their own operations and those of their suppliers. In some cases, such as China's refusal to permit independent trades unions, pragmatism may require interim best-practice standards, but those requirements should be upgraded to international standards as quickly as possible.

Certain industries would require special rules. For example, extractive industries, because they often contribute revenue well beyond ordinary taxation, should face special rules on fiscal transparency to maximise opportunities for public accountability.

Manufacturing companies might be obliged to avoid sales to a government once they learn it is using their product for human rights abuse.

Companies operating in conflict zones should be required to take reasonable steps to avoid complicity in arbitrary violence. Enforceable standards are unlikely to require a global minimum wage—a move some developing countries would decry as protectionism. Wage competition would remain appropriate as long as it is within the context of full respect for workers' rights to organise and bargain collectively. But governments and businesses would be prohibited from competing by undercutting workers' basic rights as a route to lower wages.

Few if any of the standards likely to appear in a treaty on corporate social responsibility would be difficult for most multinational companies to embrace. The only thing these companies have to fear is an end to unfair competition from less savoury competitors. It is time, therefore, for them to begin publicly advocating enforcement.

How can strict enforceable ethical standards help multinational firms?

ARTICLE 3.4

Courage of the Woman Fighting to Rid Nigeria of Corruption

Alex Brummer

Mention the words Africa and corruption in polite company, and those present might immediately assume you are talking about Nigeria. This sprawling country, with its enormous oil wealth and huge population, has become synonymous with all that appears to be wrong with the continent—from the waste of a great natural resource to human rights abuses and ethnic strife.

In a recent league table of the most corrupt nations on earth, Nigeria was sixth in a list of 159. However, despite its negative image, the country is changing fast.

Earlier this month, in an unprecedented action, the Paris Club of rich creditor countries agreed to cancel $16bn of outstanding debt. This is being seen as evidence that one of Africa's potentially prosperous states is on the mend.

The traditional Western image of Nigeria as crime-ridden provokes anger among members of its current reforming government.

When I put these charges to Ngozi Okonjo-Iweala, the charismatic finance minister, she rebuts them passionately.

"In the country now, 99.99pc of Nigerians are honest, hardworking people who just want to earn a living like everyone else."

She adds: "The point is, we should not be typecast because of the tiny few who have a bad reputation. It's like in the past saying that all Italians are mobsters. That's wrong."

"We are working very hard to do away with this reputation. We've got the three kingpins behind bars now," she exclaims.

The minister is resplendent in a green and red native costume, with a fine string of matching natural stones around her neck.

She was in London for a conference to encourage more private investment in Africa, and it was on the fringes of this gathering that our meeting took place.

Okonjo-Iweala gave up the comfort of the World Bank and a large home in the suburbs of Washington to take on the mission to reform her country.

What are some of the factors related to the evolution of a culture In Nigeria?

She is currently one of only two female finance ministers in the world—the other is Luisa Diogo, who combines the post with being prime minister of Mozambique.

It is clear that Okonjo-Iweala is already a star among Africa's economic and business elite.

In a panel discussion on how to encourage foreign investment, everyone else is ignored and the questions are directed at her.

As she steps down from the podium her fans follow her, eagerly plying her with more questions and seeking to make themselves known.

Even a slim, young black representative of Shell—Nigeria's partner in the country's energy extraction—thrusts a business card into her hand as she sweeps along, trailing yards of cloth behind her.

Okonjo-Iweala, a protege of former World Bank boss James Wolfensohn, joined President Olusegun Obasanjo's government in July 2003.

Since then, she has worked tirelessly in the face of personal danger to end corruption and bring order to Nigeria's chaotic economic management.

"We've identified which areas of corruption are the largest," she asserts. "We found that in public contracting it was five times higher than in neighbouring countries."

"In two years we have managed to save about $1bn by auditing all the contracts and putting them out to international competitive bidding."

Her clampdown is paying dividends, as Western private sector companies are now more willing to come knocking at Nigeria's door.

The telecoms sector has been deregulated and, as a result, some $2bn of investment has poured in from overseas. Among the investors is Sir Richard Branson.

"He recently invested in a new airline," says the finance minister with some pride. "It's called Virgin Nigeria. It attracted $25m of institutional investment from within Nigeria. It is flying internally, but also has a London route and has opened a gateway to Prague."

It is widely imagined that Nigeria ought to be a much richer country than it is because of its vast oil and gas resources.

And indeed, it would be much richer if cash from the oil industry had not been wasted or spirited away to Switzerland during the bad old days before the Obasanjo government took office in 1999. Okonjo-Iweala's contribution is to take a leaf out of Gordon Brown's book and put in place fiscal rules based around the price of oil.

"We have been fiscally prudent," she explains. "In the past, when we had high oil prices we had high spending. When the oil price fell we didn't have much."

"Now, for the first time, we've instituted an oil price-base fiscal rule, meaning we are delivering for the price at which it is budgeted."

"We budgeted at $25 a barrel last year and at $30 in 2005, and that has enabled us to accumulate some savings. We have gone to a surplus from an average deficit of 3.5pc of national wealth over the past five to ten years. This is a break with Nigeria's past. We had an oil boom in the 70s and 80s and a bit of the 90s, and we didn't save. We spent it."

Not only that, but Okonjo-Iweala has been leading the fight, with the president, to recover the lost billions. "We have recovered $2bn so far," she reveals. "We recently recovered a further $500m by fighting our way through the Swiss courts. We have been able to certify that $500m was legitimately Nigeria's money and was stolen from us."

Nonetheless, the minister points out that the surpluses are a drop in the ocean as far as development is concerned.

As the joint owner of the oilfields, Nigeria reinvests $5bn a year in further exploration and facilities. After this the country receives around $25bn net—a tidy sum.

But Okonjo-Iweala emphasises that Nigeria has a huge population of 130 million. "People should realise that even if oil prices were to double in real terms, Nigeria's average income per person would only be $600. We are just $320 now."

The most surprising thing about her stewardship of the economy of her native land is that it happened at all.

A handsome woman, she was born in the village of Raqwashiuku in the mid-West of the country. Both her parents were academics. Her mother had a PhD in sociology and her father a doctorate in mathematical economics.

The young Ngozi was sent to a Nigerian boarding school based on the British public school model, but financed by the state. There she sat her GCSEs and A levels before winning a place at Cambridge. But she went to Harvard because her mother was researching and teaching at the neighbouring Boston University.

She married a Nigerian medical student who trained in Manchester, where she joined him and two of her four children were born there.

Okonjo-Iweala joined the World Bank in 1982, journeying across the globe for 20 years from the Middle East to Mongolia.

After the election of President Obasanjo in 2000 she heard the call of her homeland and took leave of absence from the Bank before being persuaded to become finance minister.

Her new job keeps her apart from her husband, who has a private medical practice in the US and works at a local Roman Catholic hospital.

If there is anything she really regrets, it is her long-distance marriage. She says emotionally: "I miss him terribly, I have to say that."

As an executive vice-president of the Bank, Okonjo-Iweala earned $240,000 a year. Now, as Nigeria's economic supremo, her salary is just $9,000.

Financing her children's education has become a struggle, with one taking a year off from his medical studies to try to help. "It is not all sweetness and light for them," she says.

But her enthusiasm for development is as infectious as ever.

She declares: "We still have some way to go in terms of delivery of better water supply, better education and health. But it is power that will liberate people in rural areas. If they have power, women do not have to grind the corn and the pepper manually."

Despite all the odds against her, somehow Okonjo-Iweala seems to be on the right track.

ARTICLE 3.5

Fighting Bribery in International Business Deals

OECD

INTRODUCTION

Bribing public officials to obtain international business raises serious moral and political concerns, undermines good governance and economic development, and distorts international competitive conditions.

The OECD has played a leading role in the battle against bribery and corruption in international business deals for more than a decade. The fight gathered momentum in 1999 with the entry into force of the Convention on Combating Bribery of Foreign Public Officials in International Business Transactions ("the Convention"). The Convention makes it a crime to bribe a foreign public official in exchange for obtaining, or retaining, international business.

By the end of 2003, the Convention had been ratified and transposed into domestic legislation by all the original signatories—the 30 OECD member countries and four non-members (Argentina, Brazil, Bulgaria and Chile). Slovenia, which acceded in September 2001, is in the process of adapting its national legislation to the standards of the Convention. The OECD is now ensuring that all Parties fully implement the Convention.

The Convention represents a landmark in international co-operation to fight bribery and corruption. For the first time, the world's largest trading and investment partners, which together account for more than 70% of world trade and 90% of foreign direct investment, are acting in concert to halt the flow of bribes to foreign public officials in international business transactions.

The Convention embodies the result of an ambitious undertaking that began with the development by the OECD Working Group on Bribery in International Business Transactions of various instruments—the Recommendations of 1994, 1996 and 1997. The overall purpose of these instruments is to prevent bribery in international business transactions by requiring countries to establish in their national laws, the criminal offence of bribing a foreign public official, and to have in place adequate sanctions and reliable means for detecting and enforcing the offence. They also include non-criminal rules for prevention, overall

What role do organizations such as the OECD play in the global efforts to eradicate corruption?

transparency and co-operation between countries. In addition, parties are also required to deny the tax deductibility of such bribes.

But outlawing bribery is not enough. Businesses themselves must play a role, by changing the corporate culture that allows bribery to continue. The OECD Guidelines for Multinational Enterprises include a chapter on measures that enterprises should take to prevent bribery and addresses passive and active corruption. The OECD Principles of Corporate Governance, in calling for more disclosure and financial transparency, also provide a framework that discourages bribery.

The OECD's work in public governance addresses the broader issues of preventing, detecting and penalizing misconduct by public officials. Activities with non-member countries aim at assisting countries in domestic policy reform and in raising international anti-corruption standards. The OECD is also contributing to implementation of the Convention through its work on official export credits and credit guarantees, including an action statement that calls for members to take appropriate measures to deter bribery before export credits are granted. This Policy Brief focuses on the Convention, its implementation and enforcement.

Is bribery culture- or economic-based? Explain.

WHY FIGHT CORRUPTION?

Instances of corruption around the world are reported on an almost daily basis. There is no scarcity of scandals that illustrate the depth and pervasiveness of corruption: bribes to high-level officials for major export contracts in many countries, the plundering of national assets, and the endemic confusion between private and public funds in some developing and transition economies.

Corruption in awarding business contracts has social, political and economic costs, which no country can afford. If public officials take bribes when awarding contracts to foreign businesses for public services such as roads, water or electricity supplies, this inflates the price, distorts allocation of resources and undermines competition. It has a devastating effect on investment, growth and development. Furthermore, such corruption exacts an inordinately high price on the poor by denying them access to vital basic services. Increasing intolerance of these effects has led to mounting pressure from citizens and financial markets for an international fight against corruption. The Convention is one response.

HOW DOES THE CONVENTION COMBAT BRIBERY?

Countries that accede to the Convention agree to make bribing foreign public officials in international business transactions a criminal offence. They also accept the OECD Revised Recommendation on Combating Bribery in International Business Transactions (the "revised Recommendation"), which contains broader measures to prevent and combat transnational bribery. These measures include eliminating the tax deductibility of bribes, ensuring the transparency of book-keeping and auditing practices, and adopting preventive and repressive measures against corruption in public procurement systems.

The Convention provides that legislation making bribery of a foreign public official a criminal offence must apply to all persons (natural persons and companies) and that it must cover the offer or promise, as well as the giving of a bribe. It is an offence regardless of whether the bribe is done through an intermediary or whether the advantage is for a foreign public official or a third party.

The offence must prohibit all forms of bribes, including tangible or intangible as well as pecuniary and non-pecuniary advantages. The Convention covers bribery for the purpose of obtaining or retaining "business or other improper advantage in the conduct of international business." This applies not just to obtaining contracts, but also obtaining regulatory permits, or preferential treatment in taxation, customs, or judicial and legislative proceedings.

Bribery remains an offence even if the person concerned was the best-qualified bidder and should in any case have been awarded the contract purely on merit. And it does not matter whether the bribe achieved the desired result, or if bribery is tolerated or even widespread in the country concerned.

The Convention defines a "foreign public official" as any person holding a legislative, administrative or judicial office of a foreign country, whether appointed or elected; any person exercising a public function for a foreign country, including for a public agency or public enterprise; and any official or agent of a public international organisation.

In addition, the Convention requires each Party to:

- establish effective, proportionate and dissuasive criminal penalties for the foreign bribery offence. Where a country's legal system does not apply criminal responsibility to enterprises, they shall be subject to effective, proportionate and dissuasive non-criminal penalties;
- establish its jurisdiction over the foreign bribery offence when the offence is committed in whole or in part in its territory. Where a Party has jurisdiction to prosecute its nationals for offences committed abroad, it shall establish such jurisdiction over the foreign bribery offence according to the same principles;
- establish a money laundering offence in relation to the bribe and/or proceeds of foreign bribery if it already has such an offence for domestic bribery;
- prohibit accounting and auditing practices that make it easier to conceal foreign bribery;
- provide prompt and effective legal assistance to other Parties in the investigation and prosecution of foreign bribery offences. The bribery of a foreign public official shall be deemed an extraditable offence under the laws of the Parties and the extradition treaties between them.

To comply with the revised Recommendation, Parties also pledge to take a number of related measures to deter, prevent and combat international bribery.

These measures should:

- encourage the introduction of sound internal company controls, including standards of conduct. Companies responsible for bribing foreign public officials should be suspended from future bids for public contracts.
- ensure that procurement contracts funded by bilateral aid include anti-corruption provisions and promote the proper implementation of anti-corruption provisions in international development institutions. They also agree to work closely with development partners to combat corruption in all development co-operation efforts.

HOW ARE IMPLEMENTATION AND ENFORCEMENT MONITORED?

To ensure the effective implementation of the Convention and of the revised Recommendation, Parties adopted a monitoring process based on the OECD peer-review principles.

The monitoring process is divided in two main phases.

Phase 1 evaluates whether the legal texts through which State Parties implement the Convention meet the standard set by the Convention.

Phase 2 studies the structures put in place to enforce the laws and rules implementing the Convention and the Revised Recommendation and to assess their application in practice. This includes reviewing national investigations and prosecutions and conducting "on site" interviews with government and regulatory authorities and other persons concerned with application of the Convention.

The OECD Working Group on Bribery in International Business Transactions (the "Working Group") is in charge of monitoring the implementation of the Convention and the related instruments.

What responsibility should multinational firms hold for the actions of their contract manufacturers overseas?

The Phase 1 reviews, which began in April 1999 when the Convention was ratified, are almost completed, with 33 countries having been examined by the Working Group. These reviews have found that overall, national standards are in line with the Convention; where necessary, remedial measures were recommended. Several Parties have taken action to implement these recommendations. Others are in the process of amending their legislation.

The Phase 2 reviews started in 2001 and are scheduled to be completed for all 35 Parties to the Convention by 2007. At the end of 2003, eight countries, including four G7 countries, had been reviewed.

WHAT IS THE ROLE OF CIVIL SOCIETY AND THE PRIVATE SECTOR?

Civil society plays a key role in fighting corruption, and several civil society and private sector organizations work with the OECD in implementing the Convention.

Monitoring Enforcement of the Convention

Once the OECD has reviewed a country's anti-bribery legislation to ensure it conforms to the Convention (Phase 1) it turns its attention to how the law is being applied in practice (Phase 2). This involves reviewing each country's performance, publishing the results and following up to see whether the country is carrying out any recommended changes. The Phase 2 reviews also offer a chance to evaluate the successful prosecution of alleged foreign bribery cases.

The monitoring and follow-up for both the Convention and the Recommendation is carried out by the OECD Working Group on Bribery in International Business Transactions, made up of government experts from the 35 countries which are Parties to the Convention. The Working Group has developed a monitoring mechanism under which all Parties are examined according to a formal, systematic and detailed procedure that includes self-evaluation and mutual review.

The monitoring procedures are similar for the Phase 1 and Phase 2 examinations. For each country reviewed, the OECD secretariat prepares a draft report, based on information provided by the country under examination as well as information collected by the OECD Secretariat and two other countries from the Working Group who act as "lead examiners." In Phase 2, the information gathering includes an on-site visit to the country examined, during which consultations with representatives from various government departments as well as from the private sector, trade unions, civil society, journalists and practitioners such as lawyers and accountants take place.

The report of the review is put to the Working Group for final adoption, and is also shown to the country under review for comment. The country under review may express a dissenting opinion, which is reflected in the final report, but it cannot prevent the Working Group from adopting the report. The document, which contains an evaluation of the country's laws and practices to combat foreign bribery, is published by the OECD and is also posted on its website (www.oecd.org/corruption).

The examined country is required to provide within a year a detailed report to the Working Group on steps it has taken or is planning to take to implement the review's priority recommendations, and within two years it has to provide a detailed written report which is published as an addendum to the review.

The OECD Working Group on Bribery in International Business Transactions is committed to consulting regularly with non-governmental organizations and to providing information to the public on its work. Civil society, trade union and business representatives are invited to comment on the country reviews. They are in particular consulted during on-site visits by the OECD as part of the Phase 2 monitoring process. This enables examiners to check, for example, whether the law implementing the Convention is well-known to local firms. Feedback from trade unions, non-governmental organizations and journalists can provide an independent perspective on whether their government is doing enough, and can also put pressure on governments to comply with their commitments. All Phase 1 and Phase 2 reports are published on the internet which gives the public the opportunity to pressure governments for changes.

If the Convention is going to have any real effect, companies must become fully implicated in ensuring compliance with the Convention and with national anti-bribery laws. Some companies have established their own anti-corruption strategies, including the adoption of codes of ethical conduct that include provisions concerning bribery and extortion between the private and public sectors as well as between private companies. These codes express the companies' serious commitment to comply with international efforts to combat corruption, and are intended to modify the corporate culture and attitudes of its employees to reduce the risk of corrupt behaviour. They are often accompanied by the creation of management systems for monitoring and reviewing compliance.

In its chapter on combating bribery, the OECD's revised Guidelines for Multinational Enterprises (non-binding recommendations to enterprises made by the member countries), include rules for combating bribery of public officials, as well as for preventing the channeling of payments through the use of subcontracts, purchase orders and consulting agreements to public officials.

WHAT ABOUT THE TAX DEDUCTIBILITY OF BRIBES?

Until the mid-1990s, the bribery of foreign public officials was accepted as a normal cost of doing business by many OECD countries. Companies doing business with foreign countries often claimed that they had to pay bribes in order to be favourably considered for the awarding of contracts. Only half of the OECD countries disallowed the tax deductibility of bribes to foreign public officials as a general rule.

The OECD Committee on Fiscal Affairs (CFA) believes that the disallowance of the tax deductibility of bribes to foreign public officials helps to serve as a deterrent, especially when it is combined with the criminalisation of such conduct. It also feels that non-deductibility sends a strong signal to companies that bribery is no longer an acceptable business practice, and serves as a politically visible symbol of the common international commitment to combat bribery.

Since agreeing to the 1996 Recommendation, all OECD countries that had previously allowed the tax deductibility of bribes to foreign public officials have amended their legislation to disallow such tax deductibility. As with the Convention, the success of these legislative changes depends on their effective implementation. In 2002, the OECD designed a Bribery Awareness Handbook for Tax Examiners to help countries to implement their national legislation denying the tax deductibility of bribes. This handbook provides guidance on the techniques used for bribery as well as tools to identify bribes during tax examinations. It has been translated into several languages and disseminated in the tax administrations of OECD member countries as well as a growing number of non-OECD economies. In addition, the relevant tax laws are being examined by the Working Group on Bribery in International Business Transactions, in co-operation with the Committee on Fiscal Affairs, in the course of its Phase 1 and 2 examinations of Parties' implementation of the Convention and the 1997 Recommendation.

Table 1   Countries Having Ratified/Acceded to the Convention[a]

	Country	Date of Ratification
1.	Iceland	17 August 1998
2.	Japan	13 October 1998
3.	Germany	10 November 1998
4.	Hungary	4 December 1998
5.	United States	8 December 1998
6.	Finland	10 December 1998
7.	United Kingdom	14 December 1998
8.	Canada	17 December 1998
9.	Norway	18 December 1998
10.	Bulgaria	22 December 1998
11.	Korea	4 January 1999
12.	Greece	5 February 1999
13.	Austria	20 May 1999
14.	Mexico	27 May 1999
15.	Sweden	8 June 1999
16.	Belgium	27 July 1999
17.	Slovak Republic	24 September 1999
18.	Australia	18 October 1999
19.	Spain	14 January 2000
20.	Czech Republic	21 January 2000
21.	Switzerland	31 May 2000

(continued)

Table 1   (*continued*)

22.	Turkey	26 July 2000
23.	France	31 July 2000
24.	Brazil	24 August 2000
25.	Denmark	5 September 2000
26.	Poland	8 September 2000
27.	Portugal	23 November 2000
28.	Italy	15 December 2000
29.	Netherlands	12 January 2001
30.	Argentina	8 February 2001
31.	Luxembourg	21 March 2001
32.	Chile	18 April 2001
33.	New Zealand	25 June 2001
34. (accession)	Slovenia**	6 September 2001
35.	Ireland	22 September 2003

a. In order of ratification/accession received by the Secretary-General
** Slovenia has not yet enacted full implementing legislation.

WHAT LIES AHEAD?

The rapid entry into force of the Convention and its ratification and implementation is a clear signal of its success in advancing the fight against international bribery. But there is still much work to be done, not least completing the Phase 2 reviews for all 35 Parties to the Convention. If new countries join the Convention, the implementation and application of their laws will also need to be carefully evaluated.

In terms of future action, OECD ministers at their annual meeting in May 2002 asked countries to consider whether there are gaps in the Convention—for instance bribery relating to foreign political parties—and if so, how to close these gaps.

New questions might also require further consideration by the Working Group on Bribery in the future, including whether to extend the Convention to cover private sector bribery, strengthening its accounting and auditing rules and reducing obstacles to co-operation between police and judicial authorities of different countries.

The Convention has also set an international benchmark for non-OECD countries' reform efforts and it is essential that the OECD maintains its role as a driving force in the fight against international corruption. The Organisation is continuing its policy dialogue with non-members. Some of these activities have developed Action Plans, through which participating countries commit to analysis, self-evaluation and peer review and to undertaking remedial action in areas of concern. The Anti-Corruption Network for Transition Economies, which also includes the sub-regional Baltic Anti-Corruption Initiative (BACI) and a new initiative for seven NIS countries, the Stability Pact Anti-Corruption Initiative for South Eastern Europe (SPAI), the ADB/OECD Asia-Pacific Anti-Corruption Initiative as well as the Governance and Anti-Corruption Forum for Latin America will continue to help work towards meeting international anti-corruption standards and enhance the capacity of participating countries to fight corruption. These initiatives will also continue to bring together donors, governments, private enterprise and civil society to provide mutual support to share successful experiences and techniques to curbing corruption.

What role should the United Nations play in the development and enforcement of global standards for businesses?

For the fight against international bribery to succeed, it is essential that there is sustained political commitment and involvement of organizations positioned to play a key role. For this reason it is important to acknowledge the invaluable contributions made by many organizations. Several international bodies have become involved, including the United Nations, the International Labour Organisation, International Monetary Fund, the World Bank, the Asian Development Bank, the World Trade Organization and the World Customs Organisation. Regional organisations and inter-governmental structures include the Council of Europe, the European Union, the European Bank for Reconstruction and Development, and the Organisation of American States.

Non-governmental organizations, such as Transparency International and the Open Society Institute, as well as international aid providers, both governmental and private, help raise public awareness of the dangers of corruption and provide technical assistance to countries in designing effective anti-corruption strategies. The involvement of companies, business associations and trade unions remains essential. Likewise, the contribution of free and independent media is vital to exposing corruption and to encouraging accountability of public officials.

ISSUE SUMMARY

Corruption serves as a major barrier to entry in many national markets. As a result, economic development is often stalled as foreign direct investment is either postponed or redirected due to concerns about bribery and corruption. According to World Bank research, over 30 percent of multinational firms believe that corruption is a major or severe concern when faced with various investment options. Nations that embrace corruption reform are likely to experience an increase in interested foreign investors, which, in turn, should lead to positive economic growth in the long term.

Recent anti-corruption laws and pacts, such as the Foreign Corrupt Practices Act (FCPA) and the OECD anti-bribery convention, have aided in the development of global standards in the fight against corruption. Yet enforcement of these laws has been historically relaxed, and this issue must be addressed if significant anti-corruption progress is to be accomplished. Only 42 cases were prosecuted in the first 20 years of the FCPA, and over 90 percent of those cases were initiated in the United States. Moreover, thanks to the Sarbanes-Oxley Act of 2001, thorough audits and better transparency have triggered excellent momentum in FCPA convictions. Fines for FCPA violations can amount to tens of millions of dollars, so firms are beginning to pay serious attention to their actions overseas. Moreover, firms must now carefully monitor and audit the activities of formal partners that operate on their behalf in foreign markets. And as OECD member nations begin to enforce anti-bribery measures abroad, the variation in moral environments that international managers face should stabilize over time. The power and influence of the OECD convention should be felt worldwide since the signature contries account for 70 percent of world trade and 90 percent of global foreign direct investment.

The hard work of organizations such as Transparency International has also created serious optimism surrounding global corruption. Transparency International's annual Corruption Perceptions Index (CPI) is now in its tenth year, and 158 nations were included in the 2005 sample (compared to less than 50 participating nations in 1995). Although twothirds of the nations in the most recent CPI scored on the lower half of the corruption scale, the willingness to participate in the survey alone can be seen as progress. With nations such as Haiti, Cuba, and Nigeria opening themselves up to more international scrutiny, the potential for reform is likely to increase substantially. The potential for more nations to sign on to the OECD anti-bribery convention will also be a major factor in the future as nations agree to level the moral playing field by signing international agreements that have domestic legal implications.

Overall, the combination of three factors appears to be helping put pressure on nations to directly confront corruption and search for plausible remedies to chronic problems. First, many nations have passed anti-bribery legislation related to their international operations, and this has created a new global moral standard. Second, many multinational firms have implemented stricter codes of ethics to monitor and control the behavior of their managers overseas. And finally, organizations such as Transparency International and the OECD have been instrumental in publicizing global patterns of corruption and in developing legislation that is designed to curb patterns of corruption.

ISSUE HIGHLIGHTS

- A number of international organizations, such as the World Bank and United Nations, have recently passed anti-corruption measures.
- Transparency International, a German agency that tracks national patterns of corruption, publishes an annual Corruption Perceptions Index based on an analysis of over 150 countries.
- The Foreign Corrupt Practices Act (FCPA) has been a U.S. law since 1977, and it prohibits U.S. managers from bribing government officials in foreign countries to secure contracts.
- The Sarbanes-Oxley Act has generated renewed interest in the FCPA and has led to a number of new convictions.
- Corruption is seen as a major barrier to economic development, and countries with weaker anticorruption laws typically develop at a slower rate.
- Public pressure has initiated a wave of corporate social responsibility by multinational firms.
- The creation of global ethical standards should help level the playing field for large and small firms.
- In some nations, such as Nigeria, it has been difficult to shake off a perception of corruption, and this has been a major factor related to the inflow of foreign direct investment.
- The OECD anti-bribery convention has a number of domestic legal and policy implications. Signature nations have agreed to eliminate the tax deduction of bribes and also to make the payment of a bribe to a foreign government official a crime.

CRITICAL THINKING

1. The Foreign Corrupt Practices Act (FCPA) was passed in 1977 as an attempt by the U.S. government to prohibit bribery by U.S. nationals when working abroad. The FCPA is very specific in that it restricts only the payment of bribes to foreign government officials when attempting to secure a contract. Grease payments, or bribes to facilitate routine government processes, such as clearing goods from customs, are permitted under the FCPA. Although the FCPA and the OECD anti-bribery convention only forbid payments to government officials in certain situations, they are still significant steps in the right direction.

2. The costs of corruption to businesses and governments can be astronomical. Firms that are required to pay bribes to enter foreign markets must factor those costs into the price of their goods. This price increase impacts distributors, retailers, and ultimately consumers. The time, money, energy, and resources that governments dedicate to fighting corruption are extremely high as well. And if the $1 trillion that individuals and firms pay annually in bribes were to be spent instead on goods and services, governmental tax revenues would increase substantially.

3. Patterns of corruption are difficult to track over time, yet a few influential factors are often present. Typically the least wealthy nations tend to have high levels of corruption. While white-collar crimes may be more present in developed nations, bribery, kickbacks, and extortion are often common practice in the developing world. Government enforcement of laws is also a major contributory factor to the level of corruption in a society. Other factors include cultural traditions, the state of the economy, the impact of unofficial trade, the form of government, and the influence of foreign investors.

4. While many nations have agreed to sign on to the OECD Convention on Combating Bribery of Foreign Government Officials in International Business Trasactions, the challenge in the future will be enforcing the domestic laws related to the agreement. The Convention explicitly states that each member nation must have formal legislation that makes the payment of a bribe to a foreign government official a punishable domestic crime. the OECD intends to monitor and observe law enforcement in two distict phases. In phase 1, the legal situation in each nation will be assessed. In phase 2, the enforcement mechanisms in each nation will be examined. In addition, future signature nations will be held to the same standards and reviews.

ADDITIONAL READING RESOURCES

David M. Katz, "While Foreign Rivals Make Payoffs Routinely, U.S. Firms Face New Pressure to Root Out Abuses," *CFO Magazine* (January 2005).

Michael Goldhaber, "Dirty Companies for Sale," *The American Lawyer* (April 2005).

Robert E. Klitgaard, *Controlling Corruption* (University of California Press, 1988).

Raymond W. Baker, *Capitalism's Achilles Heel: Dirty Money and How to Renew the Free-Market System* (John Wiley & Sons, 2005).

Transparency International, http://www.transparency.org.

OECD, http://www.oecd.org.

World Bank, http://www.worldbank.org.

United Nations Office on Drugs and Crime, http://www.unodc.org.

U N I T 2

Operating in a Global Economy

Free-trade agreements have triggered falling trade barriers around the world, and globalization has become a hotly debated topic among many groups. Proponents of globalization contend that fewer restrictions on trade have led to an increase in the total volume of international trade, which in turn has helped fuel economic development worldwide. Opponents of globalization are concerned with the distribution of this new wealth, the loss of cultural identity, and a lack of concern for the natural environment. The articles selected for this section describe various pros and cons of globalization, highlight a number of recent free-trade agreements, and assess how new technologies are playing a role in the rapid growth of the global economy.

Issue 4: How Does Globalization Affect the World?

Issue 5: How Do Free-Trade Agreements Affect Multinational Firms?

Issue 6: What Are Some Key Strategies for Taking Advantage of Modern Technologies Related to Global Logistics?

How Does Globalization Affect the World?

The notion of "globalization" has been around for a long time. While most scholars and practitioners recognize the recent surge in global trade, few acknowledge the historical roots of this phenomenon. Indeed history books are filled with numerous examples of global traders and their attempts to establish international trade paths. The Portuguese, Spanish, British, and Dutch seem to have mastered global trading by the seventeenth century. Even the United States has been trading with India, Japan, and China for close to two centuries. So why has globalization received so much attention? It is the rate of global trade in recent years combined with the depth of globalization's influence on national economies that has brought this idea to center stage.

Globalization can be defined as a trend toward a more integrated economic and geopolitical system. The underlying principle of globalization is tighter integration worldwide. One recent definition of globalization incorporates a similar concept: "the internationalization of trade, services, investment and information-sharing" (Peters, 2005). As these definitions suggest, globalization is a phenomenon that is far-reaching and has the potential to touch the lives of people all over the world. Historically, global trade was all but restricted to governmental agencies and large multinational firms. Yet since the global economic boom that commenced in the mid-1980s, thanks in part to the birth of the information age, it has become much easier for firms of various sizes to enter into the global marketplace. The Internet alone has created endless opportunities for small firms and entrepreneurs to engage in trade with citizens from faraway lands. Moreover, recent advances in transportation and communications, as well as falling trade barriers, have made it more efficient and more profitable to engage in non-domestic commerce.

One of the major conduits to the globalization movement has been the World Trade Organization (WTO). One of the primary missions of the WTO is to help bring down trade barriers while encouraging free trade. A number of free-trade agreements have been signed in recent decades, which has led to a significant reduction in import and export tariff rates. For example, between 1946 and 2005, the average tariff rate in the United States has dropped from 40 percent to 4 percent (Hufbauer and Grieco, 2005). Using a number of different techniques, the economic impact of globalization on the United States has been estimated to be over one trillion U.S. dollars per year, or a gain of roughly $10,000 per household (Hufbauer and Grieco, 2005). Over one-quarter of U.S. corporate profits are now generated from work performed, or products sold, overseas.

Globalization has found many critics and supporters. The critics claim that globalization has triggered a loss of national identity while enlarging the gap between the rich and poor. Supporters, on the other hand, contend that globalization has created a sea of jobs in the developing world while stimulating higher educational ideals and economic growth.

The featured authors in this chapter take a look at globalization from a number of different perspectives. First, in his article titled "Myths of Globalization," Ralph Peters identifies a number of myths that surround the topic, including the claim that globalization is new and that globalization will lead to utopian peace. Peters takes a pragmatic view of globalization and identifies a number of potential pitfalls. In "Globalization and Its Discontents," Herman E. Daly breaks down the concept and roots of globalization while providing an assessment of the consequences of globalization. Daly identifies a number of negative outcomes that have resulted from the globalized and newly "integrated" world.

In their article "The Payoff from Globalization," Gary Hufbauer and Paul Grieco dissect some of the causes of globalization. This is followed by a detailed analysis of the economic impact that globalization has had on the U.S. economy. In "Globalization Is Doing a World of Good for U.S.," James Flanigan makes a case for why globalization has led to a surge in corporate profits. Flanigan also outlines how work performed outside the United States can have a positive effect on the U.S. economy. Chris Rowlands takes a look at "globalisation" from the British perspective. In particular, Rowlands looks into supply-chain efficiency maximization that has been caused by the opening up of world markets in his article "Puzzling over Globalisation."

ISSUE ARTICLES

Myths of Globalization

Ralph Peters

Every generation has its illusions. One of ours is that "globalization"—the internationalization of trade, services, investment and information-sharing spurred by the Internet—will shatter states and change humankind for the better. While globalization itself is real enough, the visions imposed upon it by idealists and con men alike only make it harder to grasp what's happening—and what isn't.

Among the many myths surrounding globalization, two stand out: The notion that this phenomenon is new and, more dangerously, the claim that globalization will lead to an age of utopian peace. Those who see globalization as unprecedented simply don't know their history. Those who imagine that greater understanding, courtesy of the Internet, will deliver an idyllic peace don't know humanity.

The first claim, that globalization is a wondrous child without historical parents, is the easiest to demolish. Greek culture of the age of Alexander influenced India's hairstyles, while eastern silks were sold in Caesar's Rome. Chinese porcelain and coins more than a thousand years old turn up in East Africa. Europeans of the Middle Ages paid a premium for pepper harvested a continent away. The Islamic world brokered trade between the West and the Far East. And it was before the discovery of the Americas.

There are more parallels with the past than differences. When Portuguese warships wrested control of the Indian Ocean from the Ottomans and their clients at the dawn of the 16th century, they provided a model of strategic hegemony that remains in place today. Then, Lisbo's caravels and carracks controlled the spice trade. Today, U.S. Navy carriers guarantee the oil trade. The commodities have changed, but not the strategic geography.

ROOTS GO WAY BACK

Globalization today may proceed at a swifter pace, generate greater wealth and touch more lives, but its essence is at least 2,500 years old. Over the centuries, the process has changed international relationships profoundly, but it has never changed human nature.

What are some myths related to the idea of globalization?

Which brings us to the second myth—one that also has ancient roots—that globalization will bring about peace. The human desire to believe in a worldly paradise is as old as it is understandable. And it always proves illusory, foundering on humanity's capacity for mischief, our deadly good intentions and our ineradicable selfishness. Just as hippie communes fell apart because somebody had to do the dishes, predictions that war will become "unthinkable" fail because they embrace a dream and ignore human reality.

Historical eras of relative peace never came about because competing cultures agreed to cooperate, but because both sides were exhausted by war or because a hegemonic power laid down the rules. No peace lasted.

Predictions that humankind "learned its lesson" echoed in every age. On the eve of World War I, Western thinkers said that European wars were a thing of the past, that new weapons were too terrible, that societies had grown too enlightened, that international trade made war economically suicidal and that workers of France, Germany, Austria-Hungary, Britain, Italy and Russia had too much in common to march against each other. August 1914 saw a euphoric embrace of war.

Likewise, the collapse of the Soviet Union meant the "end of history." Democracy would sweep the world and put an end to conflict. Russia itself would become a Jeffersonian ideal. Well, democracy may still triumph at some future date, but the wreckage of the USSR failed to produce the Age of Aquarius. Instead, we saw bloodbaths in the Balkans, civil wars and genocide elsewhere, and a flood of passions the Cold War had dammed up.

We need not celebrate the human taste for violent solutions, but pretending the appetite doesn't exist only makes conflicts likelier and deadlier. As 9/11 should have taught us, toda's hyper-globalization means the globalization of insecurity. Our new enemies think as internationally as any statesman or corporate CEO.

Every claim that globalization equals peace ignores the facts. Suggestions that the world is flat may be right, but not in the ways intended. The new flat-worlders aren't the information-age aristocrats rising above their fellow citizens. The're the millions of frightened believers who reject science and social change, while debasing religion to superstition. The inquisition is back.

TOOL FOR HATRED

That's the international phenomenon that should occupy our thoughts: The dynamic movements in world religions insisting their gods are intolerant and vengeful. If information is power, fanaticism is nuclear power. Far from uniting humanity, globalization has made billions of people newly aware of economic disparities. Globalization threatens inherited values and traditional societies. And the Internet, for all its practical utility, has been the greatest tool for spreading hatred since the development of movable type for the printing press.

Islamist fanatics, neo-Nazis and pedophiles now can find each other with startling ease. Those who hid in dark corners a dozen years ago are all but unionized today. The real global brotherhoods of the Internet age are conspiracies of hatred. This is an age of new possibilities for the most talented humans. Yet it is also an age of bigotries reborn, with digital propaganda as the midwife.

Yes, our future is rich with new possibilities, but it will take a firm sense of reality to maximize those opportunities. The latest edition of globalization may do many things, positive and negative, but it will not change human nature. Another enduring lie is that the future belongs to the dreamers. It belongs to those who go forward with open eyes.

What is the responsibility of government in the management of globalization?

ARTICLE 4.2

Globalization and Its Discontents

Herman E. Daly

very day, newspaper articles and television reports insist that those who oppose globalization must be isolationists or—even worse—xenophobes. This judgment is nonsense. The relevant alternative to globalization is internationalization, which is neither isolationist nor xenophobic. Yet it is impossible to recognize the cogency of this alternative if one does not properly distinguish these two terms.

"Internalization" refers to the increasing importance of relations among nations. Although the basic unit of community and policy remains the nation, increasingly trade, treaties, alliances, protocols, and other formal agreements and communications are necessary elements for nations to thrive. "Globalization" refers to global economic integration of many formerly national economies into one global economy. Economic integration is made possible by free trade—especially by free capital mobility—and by easy or uncontrolled migration. In contrast to internationalization, which simply recognizes that nations increasingly rely on understandings among one another, globalization is the effective erasure of national boundaries for economic purposes. National boundaries become totally porous with respect to goods and capital, and ever more porous with respect to people, who are simply viewed as cheap labor—or in some cases as cheap human capital.

In short, globalization is the economic integration of the globe. But exactly what is "integration"? The word derives from *integer*, meaning one, complete, or whole. Integration means much more than "interdependence"—it is the act of combining separate although related units into a single whole. Since there can be only one whole, only one unity with reference to which parts are integrated, it follows that global economic integration logically implies national economic *dis*integration—parts are torn out of their national context (dis-integrated), in order to be re-integrated into the new whole, the globalized economy.

As the saying goes, to make an omelet you have to break some eggs. The disintegration of the national egg is necessary to integrate the global omelet. But this obvious logic, as well as the cost of disintegration, is frequently met with denial. This article argues that globalization is neither inevitable nor to be embraced, much less celebrated. Acceptance of globalization entails several serious consequences, namely, standards-lowering competition, an increased tolerance of mergers and monopoly power, intense national specialization, and the excessive monopolization of knowledge as "intellectual property." This article discusses these likely consequences, and concludes by advocating the adoption of internationalization, and not globalization.

THE INEVITABILITY OF GLOBALIZATION?

Some accept the inevitability of globalization and encourage others in the faith. With admirable clarity, honesty, and brevity, Renato Ruggiero, former director-general of the World Trade Organization, insists that "We are no longer writing the rules of interaction among separate national economies. We are writing the constitution of a single global economy." His sentiments clearly affirm globalization and reject internationalization as above defined. Further, those who hold Ruggiero's view also subvert the charter of the Bretton Woods institutions. Named after a New Hampshire resort where representatives of forty-four nations met in 1944 to design the world's post–World War II economic order, the institutions conceived at the Bretton Woods International Monetary Conference include the World Bank and the International Monetary Fund. The World Trade Organization evolved later, but functions as a third sister to the World Bank and the International Monetary Fund. The nations at the conference considered proposals by the U.S., U.K., and Canadian governments, and developed the "Bretton Woods system," which established a stable international environment through such policies as fixed exchange rates, currency convertibility, and provision for orderly exchange rate adjustments. The Bretton Woods Institutions were designed to facilitate *internationalization, not globalization,* a point ignored by director-general Ruggiero.

How does the World Trade Organization stimulate globalization?

The World Bank, along with its sister institutions, seems to have lost sight of its mission. After the disruption of its meetings in Washington, D.C. in April 2000, the World Bank sponsored an Internet discussion on globalization. The closest the World Bank came to offering a definition of the subject under discussion was the following: "The most common core sense of economic globalization . . . surely refers to the observation that in recent years a quickly rising share of economic activity in the world seems to be taking place between people who live in different countries (rather than in the same country)." This ambiguous description was not improved upon by Mr. Wolfensohn, president of the World Bank, who told the audience at a subsequent Aspen Institute Conference that "Globalization is a practical methodology for empowering the poor to improve their lives." That is neither a definition nor a description—it is a wish. Further, this wish also flies in the face of the real consequences of global economic integration. One could only sympathize with demonstrators protesting Mr. Wolfensohn's speech some fifty yards from the Aspen conference facility. The reaction of the Aspen elite was to accept as truth the title of Mr. Wolfensohn's speech, "Making Globalization Work for the Poor," and then ask in grieved tones, "How could anyone demonstrate against *that?*"

Serious consequences flow from the World Banks' lack of precision in defining globalization but lauding it nonetheless. For one thing, the so-called definition of globalization conflates the concept with that of internalization. As a result, one cannot reasonably address a crucial question: Should these increasing transactions between people living in different countries take place *across national boundaries* that are economically significant, or *within an integrated world* in which national boundaries are economically meaningless?

The ambiguous understanding of globalization deprives citizens of the opportunity to decide whether they are willing to abandon national monetary and fiscal policy, as well as the minimum wage. One also fails to carefully consider whether economic integration entails political and cultural integration. In short, will political communities and cultural traditions wither away, subsumed under some monolithic economic imperative? Although one might suspect economic integration would lead to political integration, it is hard to decide which would be worse—an economically integrated world *with,* or *without,* political integration. Everyone recognizes the desirability of community for the world as a whole—but one can conceive of two very different models of world community: (1) a federated community of real national communities (internationalization), versus (2) a cosmopolitan direct membership in a single abstract global community (globalization). However, at present our confused conversations about globalization deprive us of the opportunity to reflect deeply on these very different possibilities.

This article has suggested that at present organizations such as the International Monetary Fund and the World Bank (and, by extension, the World Trade Organization) no longer serve the interests of their member nations as defined in their charters. Yet if one asks whose interests are served, we are told they service the interests of the integrated "global economy." If one tries to glimpse a concrete reality behind that grand abstraction, however, one can find no individual workers, peasants, or small businessmen represented, but only giant fictitious individuals, the transnational corporations. In globalization, power is drained away from national communities and local enterprises, and aggregates in transnational corporations.

THE CONSEQUENCES OF GLOBALIZATION

Globalization—the erasure of national boundaries for economic purposes—risks serious consequences. Briefly, they include, first of all, standards-lowering competition to externalize social and environmental costs with the goal of achievement of a competitive advantage. This results, in effect, in a race to the bottom so far as efficiency in cost accounting and equity in income distribution are concerned. Globalization also risks increased tolerance of mergers and monopoly power in domestic markets in order that corporations become big enough to compete internationally. Third, globalization risks more intense national specialization according to the dictates of competitive advantage.

Such specialization reduces the range of choice of ways to earn a livelihood, and increases dependence on other countries. Finally, worldwide enforcement of a muddled and self-serving doctrine of "trade-related intellectual property rights" is a direct contradiction of the Jeffersonian dictum that "knowledge is the common property of mankind."

Each of these risks of globalization deserves closer scrutiny.

1. Standards-lowering competition   Globalization undercuts the ability of nations to internalize environmental and social costs into prices. Instead, economic integration under free market conditions promotes standards-lowering competition—a race to the bottom, in short. The country that does the poorest job of internalizing all social and environmental costs of production into its prices gets a competitive advantage in international trade. The external social and environmental costs are left to be borne by the population at large. Further, more of world production shifts to countries that do the poorest job of counting costs—a sure recipe for reducing the efficiency of global production. As uncounted, externalized costs increase, the positive correlation between gross domestic product (GDP) growth and welfare disappears, or even becomes negative. We enter a world foreseen by the nineteenth-century social critic John Ruskin, who observed that "that which seems to be wealth is in verity but a gilded index of far-reaching ruin."

Another dimension of the race to the bottom is that globalization fosters increasing inequality in the distribution of income in high-wage countries, such as the U.S. Historically, in the U.S. there has been an implicit social contract established to ameliorate industrial strife between labor and capital. As a consequence, the distribution of income between labor and capital has been considered more equal and just in the U.S. compared to the world as a whole. However, global integration of markets necessarily abrogates that social contract. U.S. wages would fall drastically because labor is relatively more abundant globally than nationally. Further, returns to capital in the U.S. would increase because capital is relatively more scarce globally than nationally. Although one could make the theoretical argument that wages would be *bid up* in the rest of the world, the increase would be so small as to be insignificant. Making such an argument from the relative numbers would be analogous to insisting that, theoretically, when I jump off a ladder gravity not only pulls me to the earth, but also moves the earth towards me. This technical point offers cold comfort to anyone seeking a softer landing.

Describe some of the cultural side effects related to an increase in global trade.

2. Increased tolerance of mergers and monopoly power   Fostering global competitive advantage is used as an excuse for tolerance of corporate mergers and monopoly in national markets. Chicago School economist and Nobel laureate Ronald Coase, in his classic article on the theory of the firm, suggests that corporate entities are "islands of central planning in a sea of market relationships." The islands of central planning become larger and larger relative to the remaining sea of market relationships as a result of merger. More and more resources are allocated by within-firm central planning, and less by between-firm market relationships. Corporations are the victor, and the market principle is the loser, as governments lose the strength to regulate corporate capital and maintain competitive markets in the public interest. Of the hundred largest economic organizations, fifty-two are corporations and forty-eight are nations. The distribution of income within these centrally-planned corporations has become much more concentrated. The ratio of the salary of the Chief Executive Officer to the average employee has passed 400 (as one would expect, since chief central planners set their own salaries).

3. Intense national specialization Free trade and free capital mobility increase pressures for specialization in order to gain or maintain a competitive advantage. As a consequence, globalization demands that workers accept an ever-narrowing range of ways to earn a livelihood. In Uruguay, for example, everyone would have to be either a shepherd or a cowboy to conform to the dictates of competitive advantage in the global market. Everything else should be imported in exchange for beef, mutton, wool, and leather. Any Uruguayan who wants to play in a symphony orchestra or be an airline pilot should emigrate.

Of course, most people derive as much satisfaction from how they earn their income as from how they spend it. Narrowing that range of choice is a welfare loss uncounted by trade theorists. Globalization assumes either that emigration and immigration are costless, or that narrowing the range of occupational choice within a nation is costless. Both assumptions are false.

Why do domestic firms engage in trade with firms from other nations?

While trade theorists ignore the range of choice in *earning* one's income, they at the same time exaggerate the welfare effects of range of choice in *spending* that income. For example, the U.S. imports Danish butter cookies and Denmark imports U.S. butter cookies. Although the gains from trading such similar commodities cannot be great, trade theorists insist that the welfare of cookie connoisseurs is increased by expanding the range of consumer choice to the limit.

Perhaps, but one wonders whether those gains might be realized more cheaply by simply trading recipes? Although one would think so, *recipes*—trade-related intellectual property rights—are the one thing that free traders really want to protect.

4. Intellectual property rights Of all things, knowledge is that which should be most freely shared, since in sharing, knowledge is multiplied rather than divided. Yet trade theorists have rejected Thomas Jefferson's dictum that "Knowledge is the common property of mankind" and instead have accepted a muddled doctrine of "trade-related intellectual property rights." This notion of rights grants private corporations monopoly ownership of the very basis of life itself—patents to seeds (including the patent-protecting, life-denying terminator gene) and to knowledge of basic genetic structures.

The argument offered to support this grab is that, without the economic incentive of monopoly ownership, little new knowledge and innovation will be forthcoming.

Yet, so far as I know, James Watson and Francis Crick, co-discoverers of the structure of DNA, do not share in the patent royalties reaped by their successors. Nor of course did Gregor Mendel get any royalties—but then he was a monk motivated by mere curiosity about how Creation works!

Once knowledge exists, its proper price is the marginal opportunity cost of sharing it, which is close to zero, since nothing is lost by sharing knowledge. Of course, one does lose the *monopoly* on that knowledge, but then economists have traditionally argued that monopoly is inefficient as well as unjust because it creates an artificial scarcity of the monopolized item.

Certainly, the cost of production of new knowledge is not zero, even though the cost of sharing it is. This allows biotech corporations to claim that they deserve a fifteen- or twenty-year monopoly for the expenses incurred in research and development. Although corporations deserve to profit from their efforts, they are not entitled to monopolize on Watson and Crick's contribution—without which they could do nothing—or on the contributions of Gregor Mendel and all the great scientists of the past who made fundamental discoveries. As early twentieth-century economist Joseph Schumpeter emphasized, being the first with an innovation already gives one the advantage of novelty, a natural temporary monopoly, which in his view was the major source of profit in a competitive economy.

As the great Swiss economist, Jean Sismondi, argued over two centuries ago, not all new knowledge is of benefit to humankind. We need a sieve to select beneficial knowledge. Perhaps the worse selective principle is hope for private monetary gain. A much better selective motive for knowledge is a search in hopes of benefit to our fellows. This is not to say that we should abolish all intellectual property rights—that would create more problems than it would solve. But we should certainly begin restricting the domain and length of patent monopolies rather than increasing them so rapidly and recklessly. We should also become much more willing to share knowledge. Shared knowledge increases the productivity of all labor, capital, and resources. Further, international development aid should consist far more of freely-shared knowledge, and far less of foreign investment and interest-bearing loans.

Let me close with my favorite quote from John Maynard Keynes, one of the founders of the recently subverted Bretton Woods Institutions:

> I sympathize therefore, with those who would minimize, rather than those who would maximize, economic entanglement between nations. Ideas, knowledge, art, hospitality, travel—these are the things which should of their nature be international. But let goods be homespun whenever it is reasonably and conveniently possible; and, above all, let finance be primarily national.

What impact has globalization had on the competitiveness of domestic markets?

ARTICLE 4.3

The Payoff from Globalization

Gary Clyde Hufbauer and Paul L.E. Grieco

The battle over the Central American Free Trade Agreement (CAFTA) recalls some familiar themes. The "modern" debate over trade barriers can be traced to the 19th century. Then as now, the debate has been dominated by special interests (land barons vs. merchants in the 19th century; the AFL-CIO vs. the Chamber of Commerce today). There is no question that trade liberalization creates winners and losers. Affected citizens and companies have every right to plead their case.

But Congress should consider how freer trade affects the nation as a whole. Since World War II the United States has led the international quest to liberalize world trade and investment. With leadership from the White House, Congress has slashed the simple average tariff rate from 40 percent in 1946 to 4 percent today, and other industrial nations have done much the same. After a half-century of steady liberalization it is fair to ask, what do Americans have to show?

As it turns out, quite a lot. Using four different methods, we estimate that the combination of shrinking distances—thanks to container ships, telecommunications and other new technologies—and lower political barriers to international trade and investment have generated an increase in U.S. income of roughly $1 trillion a year (measured in 2003 dollars), or about 10 percent of gross domestic product. This translates to a gain in annual income of about $10,000 per household.

Unfortunately for the cause of continued liberalization, Americans do not receive this money as a check marked "payoff from globalization." Instead, the payoff is hidden within familiar channels: fatter paychecks, lower prices and better product choices (compare the telephones available now with the standard black model of 1980).

Nevertheless, each of our four methods uncovers a large payoff. First, we parse international data that correlate the expansion of international trade with economic growth. This shows that the increase in U.S. income sparked by more intense trade equates to 13.2 percent of GDP. In the second method, we calculate how lower tariffs stimulate U.S. productivity through competitive forces and bring greater product choices to U.S. producers and consumers.

From *The Washington Post*, June 7, 2005, pp. A23. Copyright © 2005 by Institute for International Economics. Reprinted by permission.

The estimate for these benefits comes to 8.6 percent of GDP. Third, we draw on a computable general equilibrium model to suggest how today's economy would react to the restrictive Smoot-Hawley trading environment of the 1930s. That exercise indicates an estimate of 7.3 percent more in GDP from liberal trade. Finally, we calculate the productivity benefits arising from use of imported components and find a benefit of 9.6 percent of GDP. While none of the four estimates is perfect, the broad result is clear: The benefits of trade and investment liberalization are positive and large.

Given the large gains from past liberalization, and today's low tariffs and modest investment barriers, skeptical commentators might say, "Been there, done that." But our estimates of future policy liberalization alone (excluding likely benefits from better communications and transportation) indicate that a move from today's commercial environment to global free trade and investment could produce an additional $500 billion in U.S. income annually, or roughly $5,000 per household each year. Much of the benefit would come from sectors of the economy that were effectively ignored during earlier rounds of liberalization: services, agriculture, transportation and trade with developing countries. No single trade or investment agreement can confer the entire range of benefits on Americans; instead, the prize requires steady liberalization—through agreements such as CAFTA and the World Trade Organization's Doha round, each providing a steppingstone toward the eventual goal.

Despite the huge payoff to the United States, maintaining political support for trade liberalization has never been easy. Poli Sci 101 gives the explanation: Large gains are widely dispersed, and much smaller private losses are highly concentrated. Surveying several estimates, we arrive at a middle-of-the-road figure of roughly 225,000 trade-related job losses per year. Most dislocated workers find new jobs in six months, many far sooner; but some are unemployed for an extended period. Even workers who are re-employed may face significant pay cuts. Taking these features into account, we estimate that the lifetime costs of a year's worth of trade-related job losses is roughly $54 billion, about $240,000 per affected worker. This is a huge loss on a personal level, but only about 5 percent of the annual national gains from liberalization. Moreover, a rough estimate of the adjustment costs to agricultural landowners suggests that the progressive removal of trade barriers and farm subsidies over a decade could lower agricultural land values by $27 billion a year. The strident opposition to CAFTA from sugar barons such as the Fanjul family confirms that this is a sensitive matter. Yet again, lower property values are a one-time private loss and a fraction of national gains.

America's national interest will best be served by staying the course of free trade and investment. At the same time, it is morally imperative to address private losses incurred by dislocated workers; as well, it may be politically necessary to cushion the blow to agricultural land values. The federal government spends less than $2 billion per year helping trade-dislocated workers. Over the past decade, the Organization of Economic Cooperation and Development

What has been the impact of globalization on the economy and employment levels in the United States?

estimates that U.S. government policy has boosted domestic farm incomes by an average $40 billion per year through direct subsidies ($23 billion) and trade barriers ($17 billion). Given the enormous dividends from international trade, more should be done for workers forced to bear the burden of economic adjustment. Meanwhile, U.S. farm subsidies should be spent in ways that help farm owners adjust, rather than encouraging them to fight liberalization with all their political energy.

Globalization Is Doing a World of Good for U.S.

James Flanigan

The news from the global economy is bullish: Major U.S. corporations are reporting sharply higher earnings thanks to surging profits from overseas.

Take General Electric Co., where rising profit from foreign operations pushed overall earnings up 25% in the first quarter. And last week Caterpillar Inc. in construction equipment, Intel Corp. in computer chips and EBay Inc. with an enormous rise in international auction trading all reported sharply higher earnings thanks to global growth.

Indeed, a quarter of all U.S. corporate profits, or about $225 billion, were earned outside the United States last year, according to the federal Bureau of Economic Analysis.

That figure seems sure to rise in coming years because developing economies, from Eastern Europe to China, are growing at about 8% a year, compared with 3% to 4% for the U.S. and scarcely any growth at all for Western Europe and Japan.

Businesspeople look at such growth in formerly poor countries and see opportunity and long-term promise.

"We are witnessing a revolution in the movement of capital," says economist John Rutledge, an advisor to President Reagan and the current Bush administration.

Many Americans, however, look at the same emerging economies and see only a threat to U.S. jobs. Whether it's computer programming being performed in India or manufacturing of such diverse products as cars and clothing in China, the popular images of the global economy are creating anxiety at home.

This is driving political moves in Congress and alarmist outcries on television and in a rash of new books that picture U.S. workers as a vanishing species.

But the alarms get globalization all wrong.

We've been here before. In the 1960s, the anxiety was over computers idling millions of workers. In the 1980s, the rise of Japanese industry was supposed to turn Americans into hamburger flippers.

What are some of the major factors that have spawned the surge in globalization in the past two decades?

The nightmare visions didn't come true then, and they certainly won't come true today.

Computers unleashed a huge new information industry, creating many thousands of jobs. And the competition from Japan pushed America into new frontiers such as technology and healthcare, where the U.S. now dominates.

Likewise, globalization is creating wealth for American companies and new jobs at home as well as overseas.

GE is a prime example of the way the world is turning.

"Globalization is an asset for us," is how GE Chairman Jeffrey Immelt puts it. He sees the developing economies of Eastern Europe, Russia, the Middle East, India and China as GE's aces in the hole.

Why? Because those countries are moving from village to city and farm to highway and therefore need GE's turbines for electric power plants, locomotives, jet airplane engines and water treatment and desalination plants.

More to the point, the GE example also demonstrates that growth abroad can lead to benefits at home. The company employs 129,000 people in the U.S., a number relatively unchanged in the last five years, and 98,000 outside the U.S., up 6% since 2000.

The non-U.S. employment seems sure to grow because foreign operations are now 49% of GE's $152 billion in annual revenue, up from 31% only three years ago. But work changes with technological advances, and the average job at domestic GE now pays double what it did 10 years ago, the company says. (In comparison, average weekly wages have risen only 30% over the same period, according to the Bureau of Labor Statistics.)

The truth is that modern work is increasingly shared across borders. GE, for example, makes jet engines in Evendale, Ohio, for new regional jets in China, with some parts made in China. Servicing of GE airplane engines is performed in Prestwick, Scotland. And lease financing on airplanes is done by its U.S.-based GE Capital Aviation Services.

The company employs advanced materials and technology to make gas turbines in Greenville, S.C., for electrical plants around the world, with some parts made in other countries. "The intellectual capital components are made here," a spokesman says.

Even intellectual capital development is becoming a cross-border operation.

GE in recent years has opened technology research centers in Bangalore, India; Munich, Germany; and Shanghai. That means some discoveries will be coming from abroad because the U.S. certainly has no monopoly on brains. GE today has 1,800 researchers in Bangalore.

The company also has invested $100 million to rebuild the venerable research lab at Niskayuna, N.Y., where GE's early geniuses Thomas Edison and Charles Steinmetz worked in the 19th century.

Whether the work is done in Bangalore or Niskayuna, if it makes profit for a U.S. company it benefits Americans. As companies make more profits overseas, those earnings form the basis of higher stock prices in markets. And

What role does foreign earned income play in the overall strength of the U.S. domestic economy?

that expands the wealth of Americans through their pension or mutual fund or individual investment accounts.

And not to be overlooked is the fact that growing profits finance expansion and new ventures everywhere for U.S. companies. GE has used its profit in recent years to expand into biotech, where it is teaming with Eli Lilly & Co. for research on Alzheimer's disease, and water desalination, where it is embarking on a major contact in Qatar. It has also acquired Universal Studios, combined it with NBC and is expanding both.

To be sure, the domestic jobs picture is clouded. U.S. employment growth in this economic recovery has been weaker than in previous economic cycles. And wages are not growing. A study by the Economic Policy Institute, a liberal Washington think tank, finds that productivity and profits have risen far faster than wages in the current business cycle, a reversal of the historic pattern.

Inevitably, some U.S. workers will be displaced. Management consulting firm McKinsey & Co. advocates special government and private industry insurance to finance retraining for employees.

Yes, a lot of work in the future will be done outside the U.S.—but a lot of work will be created in this country as well.

As the largest economy and the creator of most of the world's capital, the U.S. need not fear globalization. Instead, the American economy stands to benefit mightily from rising living standards for billions of formerly poor people.

ARTICLE 4.5

Puzzling Over Globalisation?

Chris Rowlands

Most manufacturers have at least made some inroads in the quest for lean manufacturing, applying the much heralded techniques to improve their factory operations. So, where should the search for world-class performance take you next? A fundamental question which has no simple one-stop answer. The answer is far-reaching, in fact global. It is to turn to the supply chain.

Every manufacturing business small and large has a supply chain, and each deals with it in a different way. Focusing on one aspect at a time helps, so business often looks at one of the largest spenders—purchasing. But this may be the wrong approach.

Mark Shaw, head of operations at business advisory firm Deloitte sets out the basic points: "It is not about purchasing," he says. "Lean has been the Holy Grail but it is not the end, it is just one piece of the jigsaw."

According to Shaw, complexity is increasing as the world is getting smaller. This complex jigsaw has some critical pieces; design, manufacture and service are just three of many. So when a manufacturer decides to up the ante and strive to gain competitive advantage in any of these areas, it has to optimise. Shaw says that he and his colleagues see that businesses that "wake up early" to this are becoming the best.

In fact, in a recent survey of 800 manufacturers, the ones that have optimised their global supply chain were seen to be up to 73% more profitable than those that have not. And these companies are not solely large automotive or US conglomerates. Over half the manufacturers spoken to come from Europe, and almost 90% are in sectors outside automotive.

The key is to optimise upstream and downstream, throughout the supply chain. Those companies which do not treat activities as individual islands are excelling. But this is a huge task for any company, and Shaw warns that companies doing this will encounter "organisational and cultural resistance". The skills to overcome cultural resistance are part of the DNA of great managers and leaders in industry, but the techniques to deal with organisational resistance can be learned.

From *Works Management*, September 2005, pp. 32–34. Copyright © 2005 by Findlay Publications Ltd. Reprinted by permission.

CONSIDERED APPROACH

Shaw believes that there are two types of organisational factors. Manufacturers are aware of most of the competitive factors when looking at the supply chain. These can include simply driving cost out, but he advises: "Understand raw material sourcing: don't screw suppliers as you will just screw yourself." As business moves more global, other competitive issues will come into play, too, including exchange rates and demands for energy or materials in developing economies.

The second group of factors, however, are not always understood. These are compliance factors and are often hidden beneath the surface of deals done globally. Economics run alongside environmental and tax considerations, and these factors need to be in balance for both parties in any deal. Shaw says that not only must businesses balance these two sets of factors, but before a physical move, firms must look at the short-, medium-, and long-term economic worth of going global. Building in a view of risk including infrastructure issues along with views on future possible conflict can all be added into the mix.

It can appear rather daunting. And perhaps this explains why, from Deloitte's survey, only about one in ten companies have launched initiatives to optimise the entire supply chain. But remember: the rewards can be immense. Optimising the global network can significantly reduce supply chain costs and risk, and boost growth and profitability. Manufacturers that manage their 'global value chain' most effectively are as much as 73% more profitable than others with a less capable value chain and/or less global networks.

So how do manufacturers actually do it? Shaw describes how larger companies often have a presence in the countries where they are buying or selling goods. Being in that market, and understanding what they want, means that a business can "apply rules in the UK safely—quality or compliance rules, for example—and make sure that what you are buying is what you need."

Smaller companies go about it the same way. Martin Baker is managing director of Devlin Electronics.... Devlin manufactures custom keyboards for any application. The processes at the plant in Basingstoke include PCB and mechanical assembly, and moulding (in two colours) of 'p-tops'—the item touched by the user.

Devlin's business demands that it is flexible in manufacturing. Flexibility and global supply chain solutions in the same manufacturing strategy? Baker says: "No single project is really high volume, so we must be flexible. After several UK attempts, we turned to a toolmaker and moulder in Taiwan." This toolmaker was introduced to Devlin as part of an existing partnership deal with Fujitsu Australia, and this supplier brought much to the party. "Costs in the UK could be between £100,000 and £150,000 for tooling, and the cost in the Far East is about a third of that. But they also deliver on time and to their promises," says Baker.

Devlin needed the first tools in around six weeks. Baker decided that a personal presence was needed, so he took his CAD designer to visit the moulder. "We sat down, and we asked them what would help the tool design to mould quicker, better and cheaper." Baker and his designer bounced ideas around with the supplier, went through a range of 'what ifs' and they came up with the tool design together. Baker believes that talking to the supplier and having a good attitude on both sides of the partnership is critical. "We're not always the best at everything, so we shouldn't try to teach our suppliers how to do their job," he says.

How does globalization affect people in developing nations?

After this success, custom cables were next for Devlin. It needed to get custom cables made more cost effectively, so developed another partnership with a Taiwanese company—a partnership which, according to Baker, is more of a friendship. For example, immediately after the events of 7 July in London, Devlin received an email from the Taiwanese supplier checking that nobody from Devlin was involved in the events, and offering a united supportive statement against terrorism.

Baker says that both the cable supplier and the moulder have now got operations in mainland China. The cable supplier he believes is a very responsible company, continually retraining its staff. He had tried a few different companies, but after a visit to this supplier he "got the right results."

Baker didn't hesitate about visiting these plants in Taiwan and China: "You need to see what they can do. Some things are no big deal to them, if you are blind to that you don't get the value." He talks of examples where side action tools are made at much lower cost by his Far Eastern supplier—and more quickly, too. And, he adds: "If you want to have faith in a supplier, you shouldn't think twice about spending £1,500 to fly out and visit them."

For Devlin Electronics, the toolmaker in the Far East is making three to four tools per year. Although not high volume, the cost enables tools to be made at this frequency. Typically, a tool is designed over about four weeks, made in around eight weeks, and goes into production in another four after that. The supplier is now moulding as well as manufacturing the tool. Although the price, when freight is included, is not vastly cheaper than that offered by UK suppliers, the service is very good. The supplier is now including small lots in the runs. Quality is not a concern either. Baker sent his quality manager to the plant. He was nervous about the trip, but once there, he rang Baker immediately to say he couldn't find anything wrong. Baker says that his supplier will turn around any tool corrections, unless a major metal on change, in "about a week."

RIGHT MODEL

So Devlin Electronics has a proven and successful model for its global supply chain. "If it fits the model, we would do it again, particularly for service and cost," says Baker. Fitting the model is indeed crucial: Baker has seen those that have failed. One power supply manufacturing company saw manufacturing in China as the solution. It was manufacturing only between 100–150 units per month, quite a custom offering, and for China says Baker, "custom is not the answer." The company is no more. So when Devlin Electronics now looks at its

PCB through hole and surface mount assemblies, these don't fit the model, so the company keeps control of this process. It can be a hard way to realise that going global is not the answer, says Baker, and "when you need to air freight items in, you lose all the cost savings."

Another company to benefit is Unicut Precision. Over 40% of its turnover is now created by components machined for Canada, Germany, Malta and the USA. Jason Nicholson, joint managing director, says that Unicut focuses on making it easy for its customers by providing all certification and arranging deliveries. Given the global supply that they are undertaking, Nicholson says: "It is most important not to bleat over currency fluctuations. That is our task to constantly monitor our costs and improve the way we supply these parts to off-set any changes to the value of the pound." It's a strategy that certainly seems to be working for Unicut—sales are up by more than 25%.

Currency, costs and delivery are all part of the competitive and compliance factors mentioned by Deloitte's Mark Shaw. But like Devlin Electronics, a personal presence in the area where parts are being sent is again highlighted. Charles Kenny, joint managing director of Unicut says: "We have made several visits to these different customers and they are all impressed by our consistent quality and delivery, and our ability to react to supply small batches of parts." One recent contract from the USA involves over four million small turned parts, in batches from 10 to 40,000.

Having a strategy to optimise globally is working for a variety of companies in the UK. Deloitte's survey looked at two measures, both global complexity (in how many countries they source, produce, develop or sell products) and the strength of capability for managing that global value chain.

Neither Devlin Electronics nor Unicut Precision would claim to be at the top of the tree in terms of global complexity, but they both clearly demonstrate strengths in managing their supply chain up or down stream. And what's more, for both of these companies, the result matches the findings of the global survey by Deloitte—great performance.

ISSUE SUMMARY

●

There are a number of causes or "triggers" that have led to the boom in global trade in the past two decades. Perhaps the most powerful factor that has spawned globalization has been the massive reduction in trade barriers worldwide. For many decades, now-formal international organizations, such as the General Agreement on Tariffs and Trade (GATT) and the World Trade Organization, have worked hard to bring down tariffs on goods and services that cross borders. A number of other regional trade agreements have followed suit, and free trade is now embraced by the majority of the world's economies. Another undeniable cause of globalization is the Internet, which has made it much easier for international communication and transaction processing. Transportation and shipping technology has advanced substantially in recent years and has certainly played a role in the acceleration of global trade. Other factors such as advances in cable television, air travel, telecommunications, and political cooperation have also assisted in the transition toward a global economy.

Proponents of globalization argue that the positives clearly outweigh the negatives when looking at the results of global trade. On the plus side, benefits include increases in income in developing nations, job creation in the developing world, and an increase in communication between nontraditional trade partners. Some scholars also argue that reducing trade barriers fosters open competition, which leads to more efficient markets and more affordable products and services for all. In the developing world, the creation of jobs through foreign direct investment directly leads to overall economic development. And as multinational firms raise the bar for worldwide manufacturing standards, issues such as health care and education should also improve in the poorest countries.

While there are a number of positive outcomes that have resulted from globalization, some opponents argue that the negative consequences are almost too much to bear. Some multinational firms have adopted environmental and social standards that are much lower in their non-domestic locations, which has led to an array of problems. Globalization has also triggered mergers among some of the most powerful firms in the world, which leads to semi-monopolistic power. The loss of national identity has been identified as a negative outcome of globalization due to the convergence of many cultural values around the globe. Infringements of intellectual property rights have also been problematic, with software piracy rates over 90 percent in certain parts of the world such as Vietnam (Business Software Alliance, http://www.bsa.org).

It certainly looks like globalization is here to stay. The days of strict protectionism appear to be history. In the future, leaders in government and industry must keep a close eye on globalization to ensure that the positive consequences can be maximized. While there will always be some drawbacks related to global trade, perhaps the key is to identify these problems and try to minimize the potential impact that they can have on society as a whole.

ISSUE HIGHLIGHTS

- The process of globalization has been ongoing for centuries yet the speed and impact has been much stronger in recent years.
- Some of the major causes of the recent spike in globalization are the Internet, a reduction in trade barriers, and more fluid transportation methods.
- Critics of globalization assert that many cultures are losing their identities and core values as a result of increased trade and exposure to foreign values.
- Proponents of globalization contend that increased world trade fosters economic development at all levels.
- Many firms have "gone global" to maximize efficiency and minimize costs in their supply chains.
- Globalization has had a positive economic impact on the U.S economy.
- One of the possible negative outcomes of globalization is more communication among people who want to disrupt world peace.
- One of the organizations that has served as a major catalyst to globalization is the World Trade Organization.

CRITICAL THINKING

1. A number of benefits and costs exist to both developed and developing countries as a result of globalization. As trade barriers come down, products and services become less expensive worldwide, which puts more disposable income in everyone's pocket. The creation of jobs in developing countries by multinational firms can also serve as a stimulant to economic development. The opening up of markets provides more opportunities for firms to sell their products or services. Yet as trade barriers fall, many cultural traditions and rituals also fall to the wayside. Also, some firms take advantage of lower social and environmental standards abroad, which, if not properly monitored, can have devastating effects.

2. The world has recently experienced a surge in global trade due to a variety of influential factors. While most scholars point to falling trade barriers as the number one cause of globalization, other factors cannot be overlooked. It is much easier today to transport goods overseas due to advancements in shipping technology. Many new forms of communication have also fostered growth in global commerce. Other factors, such as formal trade agreements, infrastructure improvements, and the ease of international advertising and promotions, have also played a significant role in globalization.

3. How new is globalization? Although the concept of globalization has been around for a long time, it can be argued that we are now experiencing a true renaissance in global trade patterns. The level of integration among nations is unprecedented. Trade barriers are at an all-time low.

It is difficult to pinpoint exactly when this new age of global trade began. Many scholars will argue that the efforts of the World Trade Organization, founded January 1, 1995, combined with the widespread presence of the Internet beginning in the mid-1990s, points to the end of the twentieth century as the beginning of today's breed of globalization. Others contend that the earlier efforts of GATT and the European Union could trace the rebirth of globalization back to 1980 or earlier.

ADDITIONAL READING RESOURCES

James E. Alvey, "Economics and Religion: Globalization as the Cause of Secularization as Viewed by Adam Smith," *International Journal of Social Economics* (vol. 32, no. 3, 2005), pages 249–267.

J. Buchanan and Y.J. Boon, "Globalization as Framed by the Two Logics of Trade," *The Independent Review* (vol. 6, no. 3, 2002), pages 399–405.

S. Leduc, "International Risk-Sharing: Globalization is weaker than you think," *Business Review* (2005), pages 20–25.

R. Gilpen, *The Challenge of Global Capitalism* (The Princeton University Press, 2000).

A. Rugman, *The End of Globalization: Why Global Strategy Is a Myth and How to Profit from the Realities of Regional Markets* (AMACOM, 2000).

World Trade Organization, http://www.wto.org

How Do Free-Trade Agreements Affect Multinational Firms?

The notion of free trade extends back decades if not centuries. In 1776 Adam Smith proposed the theory of absolute advantage in his classic book *A Wealth of Nations*. The theory of absolute advantage essentially argued that free trade was beneficial to a country and a necessary step in the quest for economic prosperity. Smith's arguments captured the concept of laissez-faire economics, which is an idea that represents the lack of government intervention in trade. While Smith's theory has made a significant impact on the academic world, the underlying principles of free trade have indeed been set into action by governmental leaders for many years as well.

What exactly is meant by the term "free trade"? According to Hill (2004), free trade is "a situation in which a government does not attempt to influence through quotas or duties what its citizens can buy from another country or what they can produce and sell to another country." Many nations have recently pursued free trade by signing free-trade agreements with other nations. Chile is a classic example of a nation that has accelerated economic development by maintaining a formal policy of free trade. In fact, Chile has signed 43 free-trade agreements— many with massive economies such as the United States, China, and Mexico.

Although many nations have embraced free trade as a general economic policy, protectionist barriers still exist in various parts of the world. Protectionism is when a government attempts to protect local business and industry by erecting trade barriers and restrictions such as tariffs, quotas, and embargoes. One of the major charges of the World Trade Organization (WTO) is to level the international playing field by reducing tariffs and other trade barriers worldwide. The WTO also works to reduce government subsidies of certain industries, which are seen as harmful to global competitiveness.

As one of the largest and earliest trade agreements in modern times, the European Union (EU) has paved the way for a number of other countries to embrace the idea of free trade. The EU began in 1957 with a trade pact signed by its six original members: the Netherlands, Belgium, Germany, Luxembourg, France, and Italy. By the year 2005, the EU had admitted 25 members, with the majority of its members using the euro as a common currency. The EU now contains a population of over 450 million people and a GDP of approximately $9.3 trillion.

NAFTA (North American Free Trade Agreement) went into effect in 1989 and in many ways is seen as the competitive rival of the EU. NAFTA has three members (the United States, Canada, and Mexico), a total population of about 420 million, and a collective GDP of $12 trillion. Critics of NAFTA argue that too many jobs have left the United States for Mexico, while proponents contend that free trade within North America has generated enough new exports to more than compensate for any job losses. The debate surrounding job gains and job losses is a heated one and is not unique to NAFTA.

The EU has not only expanded by adding new member nations but also by increasing the diversity of its population. In his article "Immigration: At the Gates" Christopher Dickey identifies and assesses the new face of Europe that has resulted from a recent rise in immigration. Specifically, he outlines the challenges that EU officials are facing with respect to immigrants from North African and sub-Saharan Africa. The 2005 riots in France by predominantly African immigrants suggests that the issue of how to best integrate immigrants into the EU must be more closely addressed in the near future.

Alan Field outlines some of the potential winners as a result of the recently passed Central American Free Trade Agreement (CAFTA). Field contends that U.S. exports, of products ranging from poultry to automobiles, to Central America should increase due to the elimination of excessive import tariffs. Meanwhile job creation in CAFTA member countries, such as Nicaragua and Guatemala, should increase as a result of a spike in foreign direct investment.

For more than a decade, leaders from the Western hemisphere have gathered at the Summit of the Americas meeting to discuss the possibility of enacting a free-trade area that would expand from Canada to Chile. Alan Clendenning highlights some of the key issues discussed at the 2005 meeting in Argentina. While 27 nations appear to be in favor of the Free Trade Area of the Americas, five nations (Brazil, Argentina, Uruguay, Paraguay, and Venezuela) have voiced dissent for a number of geopolitical and economic reasons.

In his article titled, "China, Chile and Free Trade Agreements," Jorge Heine, the Chilean ambassador to India, analyzes China's timid relationship with free trade and discusses how Chile, a free-trade veteran, managed to convince the Chinese to enter into an agreement. Heine also discusses China's growing interest in Latin America as both a target for raw material sourcing and as a potential market for the sale of consumer goods. Indeed, with rising incomes and a wealth of mining materials and natural resources, Latin America has begun to arrive on the global economic horizon.

The final article related to free trade is a summary of the 2005 WTO meetings in Hong Kong. David Armstrong assesses the global fight that has escalated with respect to subsidies by major economic powers, such as the EU, Japan, and the United States. Armstrong also takes an in-depth look at other recent WTO meetings and provides some colorful examples of small businesses that are affected by WTO-endorsed policies.

ISSUE ARTICLES

Christopher Dickey, "Immigration: At the Gates," *Newsweek* (October 24, 2005).

Alan M. Field, "After CAFTA," *Journal of Commerce* (August 8, 2005).

Alan Clendenning, "Summit of Americas Ends in Deadlock," *Boston Globe* (November 6, 2005).

Jorge Heine, "China, Chile and Free Trade Agreements," *The Hindu* (November 22, 2005).

David Armstrong, "Global Confrontation: World Trade Organization Meeting Galvanizes Protesters," *The San Francisco Chronicle* (December 14, 2005).

ARTICLE 5.1

Immigration: At the Gates

Christopher Dickey

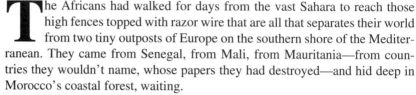

If Turkey joins the EU, how will the immigration issue change?

What are some challenges related to immigration in the EU?

The Africans had walked for days from the vast Sahara to reach those high fences topped with razor wire that are all that separates their world from two tiny outposts of Europe on the southern shore of the Mediterranean. They came from Senegal, from Mali, from Mauritania—from countries they wouldn't name, whose papers they had destroyed—and hid deep in Morocco's coastal forest, waiting.

When the moment came, they used cell phones to coordinate their assaults on the fences, rushing forward like human avalanches, hundreds of men at a time, some carrying ladders, some with gloves and loose clothes, cascading against the barriers erected around the Spanish enclaves called Ceuta and Melilla. Starting in late September, as Spanish authorities set about methodically raising the fence from three meters to six, wave upon wave of would-be immigrants made desperate attempts to clamber over. Spanish security forces, greatly outnumbered, haven't been able to hold all of them back. Moroccan security forces, first diffident, then excessive, have twice opened fire. At least 14 of the climbers have been killed. But if these tragedies have inspired pity and fear all over the European Union, it's not just because of the drama of the moment; it's because they are omens of greater troubles to come.

As the union's frontiers expand, drawing in countries that used to be buffers between First World prosperity and Third World poverty, the lines of demarcation between affluence and misery, democracy and extremism, become as sharp as razor wire. If Turkey eventually accedes, Europe will border Syria, Iran, Iraq, Georgia, Armenia and Azerbaijan. "Some say we should keep our buffer zone, and that Europe shouldn't be naive about what it is bumping up against," says Daniel Koehane of the Centre for European Reform in London. "Others say it would help the EU to shape those countries, similar to the way that it has successfully shaped the new member states in the east and even Turkey." But on the problematic frontiers like Ceuta and Melilla, the record is one of grand promises and stopgap measures that have utterly failed to cope with a burgeoning crisis.

Consider the French island of Mayotte, part of the archipelago off the coast of southern Africa that includes the Comoros. Some 55,000 of Mayotte's 160,000 people are illegal immigrants. About 97 percent are Muslim. The dominant language is a variety of Swahili. But social benefits and laws of citizenship that apply in Paris apply in Mayotte, too, making its allure almost irresistible. Any child born on French territory, including Mayotte, can potentially claim French—and European—citizenship. According to social workers, unwed mothers often risk their lives in rickety boats to get to the island, then give birth and sell the "rights" of fatherhood to the highest bidder. Mayotte's only maternity ward is the busiest in France, surpassing those of Paris, Lyons or Marseilles with 7,500 births a year. According to Mansour Kamardine, a member of the French National Assembly elected from Mayotte, the island expels some 8,000 illegals a year. "But it's like a boat taking in water, and the captain only has a saucepan to bail it out."

European leaders treat the situation along the southern shore of the Mediterranean with greater urgency, but their solutions aren't much more effective than Kamardine's saucepans. *L'Espresso* last week chronicled the humiliations suffered by illegal immigrants in the holding pen on Lampedusa, a small Italian island closer to North Africa than to southern Italy. Yet after the alleged beatings and abuses there, most illegal immigrants were sent to a larger facility in Sicily and, finally, just released to fend for themselves in Europe because the legal system couldn't cope.

A few days before the recent German elections, outgoing Interior Minister Otto Schily once again proposed setting up what amount to refugee camps in North Africa. French Interior Minister Nicolas Sarkozy met with Libyan leader Muammar Kaddafi earlier this month to ask for his help. Last year, after Italian officials paid similar visits, Libya reportedly signed an agreement to do just that, but the details were never officially made public, and the results haven't been encouraging. Libya's treatment of the third-country nationals it repatriated was criticized by human-rights organizations, while most of those illegal immigrants who come to Italy by sea still come via Libya. In fact, the numbers are rising dramatically: 15,300 reached the Italian mainland so far this year, compared with about 10,000 in all of 2004, according to the Italian Interior Ministry. The number reaching Sicily jumped from 1,800 to 5,000.

Is culture a barrier to further integration in Europe? How?

There are, to be sure, some examples of strong cooperation elsewhere. Joint Spanish-Moroccan naval patrols have helped cut by half the number of illegal immigrants arriving in the Canary Islands. Clandestine boat traffic across the Strait of Gibraltar is down as well. But like a balloon that's tied off in one place only to expand in another, the immigrants just keep looking for new points of entry like Ceuta and Melilla.

Most experts agree that over the long term better development programs are needed in North Africa and among the sub-Saharan countries where these new immigrants originate. "We know exactly what it takes" says Steffen Angenendt of the German Council on Foreign Relations in Berlin. But that would require opening up more EU markets to such countries, especially for agricultural products, and there's no strong support for such a move in Europe. Moroccan Communications Minister Nabil Benabdellah bluntly complained in Paris last week that Brussels has been promising tens of millions of dollars in aid for the last six years, which has never materialized. "Morocco cannot assume by itself the burden of all the misery on the African continent," said Benabdellah.

The American poet Robert Frost once wrote, famously, that good fences make good neighbors. But when the neighbors are as desperate as the Africans storming the concertina wire at Ceuta and Melilla, no fence is good enough.

After CAFTA

Alan M. Field

At ProNicaragua, the government investment agency in Managua, phones rang steadily during the last days of July. The reason: the impending vote in the U.S. House of Representatives on the Central American Free Trade Agreement.

"Once it became clear that CAFTA was going to pass, we had a record number of potential new investors visit us on fact-finding missions," said Carlos Sequeira, Nicaragua's chief negotiator for CAFTA. Some of those visitors, mostly in the apparel industry, later committed themselves to investing in Nicaragua after they received word that CAFTA had passed. It was a pleasant turnaround for Sequeira. He acknowledged that some investors had canceled planned investments in Nicaragua when rejection of CAFTA seemed likely.

North of the border, CAFTA's supporters see a quick payoff for U.S. companies that currently sell to the region. "There will be a very quick impact on trade in Central America," said John Hyatt, vice president at Irwin Brown & Co., a New Orleans customs broker and freight forwarder.

The agreement will immediately eliminate import duties on U.S. products that have been priced out of the market. For example, U.S. poultry exporters, long stymied by duty rates as high as 164 percent in Central America, will see their rates drop to zero. "It will make U.S. poultry competitive" Hyatt said.

Another major beneficiary, he predicted, will be U.S. automakers. Their exports to Central America, a region with no auto-assembly plants of its own, have been restricted as a result of local tariffs that range from 50 to 75 percent. Once those tariffs are eliminated, U.S. cars will more competitive against Asian vehicles.

It will be months before CAFTA takes effect. Although the governments of El Salvador, Honduras and Guatemala have already ratified CAFTA, three countries—Nicaragua, the Dominican Republic and Costa Rica—have yet to approve it. Sequeira expects Nicaragua and the Dominican Republic to ratify CAFTA within 60 days. He said ratification by Costa Rica could take two years. "The tradition is, Costa Ricans are the very last to jump," Sequeira said. Despite Costa Rica's absence, Sequeira expects CAFTA to formally go into effect by next January for the other six signatories. (The agreement allows the pact to take effect even before all signatories approve it.)

What impact will NAFTA have on the U.S. economy?

The real impact of CAFTA could take much longer, as multinational companies reassess their international supply chains and decide if they want to expand their presence in Central America.

Textiles and apparel are the industry most likely to benefit. A major appeal of CAFTA, Hyatt said, is that its preferences will be permanent, unlike those of the U.S.-Caribbean Basin Trade Partnership Act, enacted in 2000 to provide preferences from 24 U.S. trading partners that use U.S. materials and then re-export them to the United States. Hyatt said relatively few U.S. companies have taken advantage of the Caribbean act's preferences to invest and source in Central America. The reason, he said, is that the Caribbean act was only for eight years. By contrast, "CAFTA locks the preferences in stone."

After CAFTA takes effect, most of the new investments will be in low-value-added apparel assembly. "Right now, we are most interested in apparel because it employs a lot of people," Sequeira said. Nicaragua's population is growing rapidly, and the country must create 2.5 million new jobs over the next 15 years." Over the next 10 years, we hope to train our labor force, and jump into higher value activities. We have to look beyond low-value-added apparel into textiles and fabrics," he said.

CAFTA's benefits may not be enough to counter the overwhelming presence of China and other Asian countries in global markets, Hyatt said. "They will have to compete against China, India, Bangladesh and Indonesia, which are vertically integrated," he said. Nicaragua, the poorest country in Central America, offers the region's lowest wages, along with proximity to the U.S. market. But Sequeira admits that Nicaraguan labor productivity is poor, as is much of the region's infrastructure. He said the average speed of a truck traveling on a major Costa Rica-Guatemala route is only 15 miles an hour. "It's hard to compete against areas where it is 50 miles an hour," he said.

Greg Mastel, chief international trade adviser at Miller & Chevalier, a Washington-based international law firm and a former chief economist for the Senate Finance Committee, said that although apparel is a traditional starting point for economic development, Central America faces a tough challenge in that sector. "China has made such an impact, it will be hard for Central America to make a big dent," he said. "The numbers for China are pretty overwhelming."

Which countries are targeted to become members of CAFTA? Why do you think Costa Rica is taking its time with respect to joining this trade pact?

The long-term impact of any major trade agreement is harder to predict than its supporters or opponents usually anticipate, Mastel said. "My experience from NAFTA is that it is not a light-switch phenomenon that goes on instantly with companies," he said. "Many companies that have benefited the most from NAFTA were not deeply focused on NAFTA when it was approved by the U.S. Congress" in 1993, Mastel said. "Many electronics companies that now benefit from cross-border plants in both the U.S. and Mexico only vaguely thought about NAFTA at the time, and did not have such plants in mind."

He said industries besides apparel that could emerge in the region include agricultural commodities, and assembly plants for electronics, automobiles, chemicals and other products. Another possible winner is tourism, which hopes to take advantage of relatively low prices, pristine rain forests and beaches, and proximity to the U.S. market. Following in the footsteps of Costa Rica, which has carved out a major market in high-end eco-tourism, Nicaragua is luring hotel developers with a wide range of tax incentives, including 80 to 90 percent exemptions on income taxes, import taxes and value-added taxes. "CAFTA will put Nicaragua more on the map in the mind of U.S. investors," said Maria Rivas, Nicaragua's minister of tourism.

Rivas said U.S. investors already contribute nearly 40 percent of foreign investment in tourism. With assistance from Costa Rican experts, Nicaragua and Costa Rica are jointly developing and selling "eco-tours" that combine four days in each country at such luxurious "eco-lodges" as Morgan's Rock, on Nicaragua's unspoiled Pacific Coast. Hilton and Marriott will soon be opening hotels in Nicaragua. CAFTA will make it possible for hotel developers throughout the region to stock their hotels with a wide range of U.S.-made furnishings and consumer products that were previously subject to high duties.

All this will inevitably spark increased ocean-carrier services to the region. Carriers, however, are watching cautiously. When the Caribbean Basin Trade Partnership Act was enacted in 2000, some ocean carriers introduced new vessels on routes to the region, because they expected "exponential growth," Hyatt said. "With CAFTA, you will see some exponential growth, but the carriers got burned the last time around and they will take a wait-and-see" approach.

Mark Miller, spokesman for Crowley Liner Services, said his company will carefully assess how quickly trade expands as a result of CAFTA before making any moves to increase service. "With the passage of CAFTA, the stage has been set for market growth both southbound from the United States and northbound from Central America and the Dominican Republic," Miller said. He said Crowley, with more than 40 years in the Central American trade, has increased sailings and added services over the years as markets have developed. "We plan to take a similar approach to accommodate new customers and/or new commodities that may begin to move as a result of CAFTA."

ARTICLE 5.3

Summit of Americas Ends in Deadlock

Alan Clendenning

Leaders debating whether to revitalize talks on a free trade zone spanning the Americas ended their two-day meeting yesterday without an agreement.

A top negotiator said the summit's declaration would state two opposing views: one favoring the proposed Free Trade Area of the Americas, and another saying discussions should wait until after World Trade Organization talks in December.

The negotiator asked not to be identified because the declaration had not yet been publicly announced. Mexico, the United States, and 27 other nations wanted to set an April deadline for talks, but that was opposed by Brazil, Argentina, Uruguay, Paraguay, and Venezuela.

The United States says the proposed Free Trade Area of the Americas, stretching from Canada to Chile, would open up new markets for Americans and bring wealth and jobs to Latin America. The zone's main opponent, Venezuelan president Hugo Chávez, says it will enslave workers in Latin America. He came to the summit vowing to "bury FTAA."

Brazil, a key regional player with Latin America's largest economy, hedged at setting a firm date because it wants to focus on ongoing World Trade Organization talks aimed at cutting tariffs around the world and boosting the global economy.

"Anything we do now, before the WTO meeting, could confuse the facts and we'd be creating an impediment to the WTO," Brazil's president, Luiz Inacio Lula da Silva, told reporters during the summit.

Mar del Plata was calm yesterday after protesters opposed to President Bush's presence at the summit clashed in street battles with riot police, burning and ransacking businesses just 10 blocks from the theater where the summit opened.

Sixty-four people were arrested, but police reported no deaths or major injuries.

Protests have become commonplace at summits, especially those dealing with free trade and US policies. Friday's violence was on a much smaller scale than clashes in 2001 during the Americas Summit in Canada, when police detained 400 people and scores were injured.

What is the Summit of the Americas? What is the Free Trade Area of the Americas?

Rallies earlier Friday were peaceful, with Chávez declaring the deal dead in a speech to more than 20,000 demonstrators.

Yesterday, President Vicente Fox of Mexico expressed irritation with Chávez, saying: "This is a personal position of the Venezuelan president."

Fox also denied allegations by Chávez that Washington is trying to strong-arm the region into a free trade agreement. "No one has ever been forced into a free trade deal" he said.

The summit declaration was also expected to address key issues for Latin America, including job creation, immigration, and disaster relief for an area often devastated by hurricanes and earthquakes.

But the battle over the trade zone dominated the meeting, with Chávez pushing for an anti-FTAA formed just for Latin America and the Caribbean based on socialist ideals.

Fox argued that the 29 countries that want to forge ahead should form the trade on their own, even though that would dash hopes of creating a bloc that would eclipse the European Union.

While there were no immediate signs that protests would reignite yesterday, security remained tight at the summit site; a large downtown section of Mar del Plata remained closed by metal barriers and police and soldiers carried semiautomatic weapons.

Leftist activists also protested Friday in Uruguay, Venezuela, and Brazil— where Bush was headed for a much-anticipated visit with Silva. He travels today to Panama.

The violence was front-page news yesterday across Latin America, with dramatic photos of masked rioters smashing the glass storefronts of at least 30 businesses in Mar del Plata, setting a bank ablaze and battling riot police with slingshots and sharpened sticks.

Bush planned to spend the night in the Brazilian capital, Brasilia, and be Silva's guest at a barbecue today. The visit is aimed at strengthening relations with Silva, who was distrusted by Washington after becoming Brazil's first elected leftist leader in 2003.

Since then, Silva—a former shoeshine boy, grade-school dropout, lathe operator and radical union leader—has abandoned his leftist rhetoric and has stabilized Brazil's economy.

Why are some Latin American nations opposed to the Free Trade Area of the Americas?

ARTICLE 5.4

China, Chile, and Free Trade Agreements

Jorge Heine

On November 19, at the 21-nation APEC (Asia-Pacific Economic Cooperation) Summit held in Pusan, South Korea, Presidents Hu Jintao of China and Ricardo Lagos of Chile signed a Free Trade Agreement (FTA). With immediate effect, 92 per cent of Chile's current exports to China will enter that country duty free. The same goes for 50% of China's current exports to Chile. The significance of this FTA, however, goes way beyond the technicalities. This is not only the first such agreement between China and a Latin American nation; it is the first signed by China with a single country, as opposed to a regional grouping, anywhere.

Given that this was originally mooted by China—in June 2002 and the five FTA Negotiation Rounds took place in a record ten months, from January to October of this year—it raises a question. Why would China, an emerging global superpower, be interested in a trade agreement with a medium-sized Latin American country half way across the world whose GDP is one sixteenth ($100 billion) of its own ($1.6 trillion)?

Partly, because of booming bilateral trade. In the past five years, Chile's exports to China have more than tripled, from $958 million in 2000 to $3.34 billion in 2004, and Chinese exports to Chile have almost doubled, from $1 billion to $1.9 billion. With a total trade of $5.2 billion, China is now Chile's second largest trading partner, after the United States, and its third largest export market, after the U.S. and Japan. China's enormous appetite for raw materials and commodities—which Chile and South America more generally help satisfy—accounts for this. Minerals make for almost 80% of Chile's exports to China. The latter has become the world's largest consumer of copper, and close to half the copper it consumes comes from Chile.

Industrial products make up for some $626 million of Chile's exports, and agricultural products, some $43 million. Minmetals, a Chinese company, has entered into a deal with CODELCO, Chile's state-owned copper company and the world's largest, to secure its long-term supply of "red gold." Chinese consumption, which averaged one million tonnes a year in the 1990s, is projected to reach 4.4 million tonnes by 2010.

Far from being an isolated event, almost a fluke, in the broader scheme of international economic affairs, this FTA between Asia's and Latin America's most vigorous economies is the result of a carefully calibrated international trade strategy followed by both countries. It has paid high dividends to both.

China has for long realised that to sustain its emerging status as "the world's factory" it needs ever-larger amounts of raw materials and inputs—be it oil, copper, iron, wood and paper, soybeans. Much of this can be sourced in South America, perhaps the world's richest region in mining and agro-forestry products. Latin America's 33 countries and 530 million people, on the other hand, are an attractive market for Chinese manufactured products, which are doing very well there. In 2003, Chinese-Latin American trade reached $30 billion, ten times the trade between India and Latin America.

China has therefore actively pursued greater trade and investment links with Latin America. After the 2004 APEC Summit (held in Santiago, Chile, last November), President Hu Jintao visited Argentina, Venezuela, and Cuba, in a whirlwind tour that put China firmly on the region's diplomatic radar screens. Brazil, of course, is China's main Latin American trading partner. Brazil is now planning to build special dams in the heart of the Amazon region to cater to the energy needs of Chinese investment projects.

Why has Chile aggressively pursued a strategy of free trade? How did the Chilean government convince China to sign a freetrade deal?

For Chile, on the other hand, this is only the latest of 42 FTAs it has signed with most of the leading economies around the world including the U.S., the European Union, Canada, South Korea, and Mexico. No other country has signed more, and it has just been announced that negotiations for an FTA with Japan will be launched soon, and others with Malaysia and Thailand are in the offing. A Preferential Trade Agreement (PTA) with India is being negotiated.

Many economists have been leery of these FTAs, which they believe only create a "spaghetti-like" net of unwieldy bilateral deals, difficult to monitor, and are a suboptimal solution at best, compared to an overall, global trade liberalisation and lowering of tariffs. Yet, the obstacles faced within the Doha Round, to be addressed in the WTO Ministerial meeting to be held in Hong Kong in December, attest to the difficulties in making fast progress on such a topic when more than 100 nations are involved. To push for continuous trade liberalisation, the best alternative would seem to be to do so simultaneously on all fronts—multilateral and bilateral.

This is exactly what Chile has done. While participating actively in the Doha Round (as a member of the G-20+, led by Brazil and India), it has persisted in its bilateral efforts, especially in Asia.

For Chile—as for much of Latin America—its traditional export markets had been in the U.S. and Europe, and until the late 1980s most trade and investment promotion efforts were targeted there. Yet, in the early 1990s, it realised the world's economic axis was shifting towards Asia, and that unless it became a partner in the process of growth and change sweeping across the Asia-Pacific region, it would be left behind.

Chile thus joined APEC in 1994, the second Latin American country to do so. Over the past decade, Asia has become the region with which Chile trades the most. Twenty-seven percent of Chile's foreign trade is with Asia, as opposed to 25% with Latin America, 22% with Europe, and 16% with the U.S. and Canada. More than a third (34.9%) of Chile's exports, in fact, went to Asia in 2004. Of Chile's four largest export markets in 2004, three were in Asia—Japan with $3.7 billion, China with $3.2 billion, and South Korea with $1.8 billion.

Chile's success, based on an export-led, policy-driven strategy that relies on an open economy, sound macroeconomic management, and strong institutions, is at least partly related to this diversification of its export markets, in which Asia has played a key role. The Chile-South Korea FTA, the first between Asian and Latin American countries, in effect since April 1, 2004, is the best proof that these treaties do have a positive effect on bilateral trade. In 2004, it increased by $1 billion in relation to 2003, reaching $2.5 billion. In the first ten months of 2005, it has increased by 25% in relation to same period in 2004.

INDIA–CHILE TRADE

Yet, much as Chile followed a "Look East Asia" policy in the early 1990s, and is now reaping the benefits of it, it is now looking at South Asia, and especially at India, as "the next frontier" in its international trade and investment strategy. Bilateral trade has grown considerably over the past few years reaching $525 million in 2004. It should touch new, record levels by the end of this year, and, although the trade balance is largely favourable to Chile, India's export basket to Chile is much more diversified, including cars, pharma, chemicals, garments, textiles, and electrical machinery.

Still, these figures are way below those of some of Chile's East Asian trading partners. With the 90 per cent growth in the value of Chilean exports to India in 2004, India jumped from number 21 to number 17 among Chile's foreign markets—tangible progress, but still far removed from the East Asian levels.

Given India's infrastructure needs and the dynamism of its industry, its demand for raw materials and commodities should not lag far behind that of its East Asian neighbours in the near future. Indian companies are coming to realise that they have been missing out on much of the action in Latin America, and are finally targeting the region.

Essar has recently announced a $1.2 billion project, a greenfield steel mill in Trinidad & Tobago. Reliance has had long-standing business with Venezuela and Brazil, among other countries, and other Indian oil companies have been looking at offshore fields in Cuba, Ecuador, and Venezuela. In Chile, the recent takeover by Tata Consultancy Services of Cromicrom, a business process outsourcing company that has 70% of the bank checking business in the country, in a $23 million deal, may be the prelude for a strong business offensive by India's largest IT company in the region. Wockhardt recently landed the contract for supplying all of the insulin to Chile in 2006. The time is right for a major breakthrough in Indo-Latin American trade and investment.

Global Confrontation: World Trade Organization Meeting Galvanizes Protesters

David Armstrong

While trade negotiators haggled on the opening day of the World Trade Organization conference on Tuesday, a small group of protesters clashed with police.

Led by militant South Korean farmers, some protesters confronted police in a planned march some distance away from the convention center in Wanchai district.

Hong Kong police boats also intercepted scores of farmers who tried to swim to the harbor side of the convention center. Meanwhile on land, police pushed back protesters who tried to breach security lines some distance from the convention site.

Police in riot gear used pepper spray to scatter most of the militant protesters. A few protesters tried to set an anti-WTO float on fire but they were stopped by police in a scuffle that lasted a half-hour.

Television news showed one injured protester being carried away on a stretcher. Hong Kong media reported that nine people were injured, including two police officers.

Inside the cavernous convention site, the high-profile ministerial meeting of the WTO began with the global body's 149 member states deadlocked on how to reform international rules on services, manufacturing, intellectual property rights and, especially, agriculture.

INITIATIVE FOR GROWTH

The six-day meeting, which has attracted 5,800 national delegates, 3,200 journalists and more than 2,000 representatives of nongovernmental lobbying organizations, was scheduled to advance an agreement reached in principle four years ago in Doha, Qatar, by WTO trade ministers to use liberalized trade to jump-start economic growth in the world's poorest countries.

Little headway has since been made on exactly how to do that. This has lowered expectations that the Hong Kong meeting will produce a breakthrough, though top trade officials say they are determined to do as much as possible here to cut market-distorting agricultural subsidies in wealthy nations such as the United States, the European Union and Japan, and to increase market access around the world while slashing protective tariffs and quotas on imported goods.

In general, many advanced countries see free trade as a highly effective means of improving the economies of developing countries. By contrast, many developing countries fear that they will be swamped by powerful rivals in rich nations if they open their markets as asked and will remain in poverty as a result.

"In the coming few days, WTO members will have to make important decisions," the WTO's director-general, Pascal Lamy, said at the outset of the Hong Kong meeting. "Hong Kong is one of many steps along the road of a complex and lengthy negotiation. However, it is a step that should take us closer to our finishing line next year."

This meeting, the sixth ministerial round since the WTO, based in Geneva, succeeded the General Agreement on Tariffs and Trade in 1995, opened with a glittering ceremony in Hong Kong's convention center on the lip of Victoria Harbor.

INTENSE SECURITY

Tuesday's protests in Hong Kong were smaller in scale and largely free of violence compared with past WTO meetings. Past demonstrations by protesters who blamed the WTO for favoring rich countries over poor ones resulted in street violence in Seattle in 1999 and Cancun, Mexico, in 2003. An anti-WTO protest by South Korean farmers even prompted the suicide of a Korean farmer in Cancun.

Hong Kong has mustered 9,000 police to secure the convention site, which is patrolled by frogmen in inflatable craft on the water and armed police on land.

What can the WTO do to gain a higher level of international support?

In the first days of this gathering, protests have been largely colorful and peaceful, and Hong Kong police have responded with a reasonable degree of friendliness, answering delegates' questions and giving directions to tourists. Security netting draped over the open sides of central Hong Kong's many elevated walkways is festooned with cutout Christmas trees, snowflakes and candy canes.

HARD BARGAINING

Inside the soaring steel and glass convention center, nongovernmental organizations have for the first time been invited to sit in on some negotiations and attend press briefings. If WTO organizers have their way, this will be a kinder, gentler WTO. Still, hard bargaining is likely to be in the offing.

Prior to this meeting, the United States offered to make steep cuts in its generous agricultural subsidies, asking the EU to match them. At the behest of France, the EU has resisted this, contributing to the present impasse.

Agriculture's importance is underscored by the presence of U.S. Secretary of Agriculture Mike Johanns, who has accompanied U.S. Trade Representative Rob Portman to Hong Kong.

Officials from the U.S. Farm Bureau Federation and the California Farm Bureau Federation are also attending, and indications are that cotton and bananas will attract the early attention of trade negotiators this week.

Veteran WTO-watchers expect haggling and horse-trading to go on long into the night, and important advances are unlikely to be announced before the gathering concludes on Sunday.

"We need to make progress in the area of manufactured goods and services," Portman said when he arrived in Hong Kong for the talks. "After all, manufactured goods alone account for three-quarters of global trade, and developing countries have the most to gain here, too. Seventy percent of the tariffs paid by developing countries are paid to other developing countries.

"But we cannot avoid the hard choices needed to reach an agreement on agriculture, which from the start has been at the core of the Doha round," Portman said.

NUT FARMER FROM MODESTO

U.S. agricultural interests hope to see markets open up for their exports but would like to hold onto some protective barriers to protect American farmers from rivals in low-cost countries, too. This is by no means assured in free-wheeling negotiations.

Modesto almond and walnut grower Paul Wenger, who made the 14-hour flight from San Francisco to Hong Kong as part of the California Farm Bureau delegation, said U.S. negotiators in the past have been too willing to drop protections for specialty crops such as his, which are commonly exported and need U.S. protection to be competitive with overseas growers.

Even before the trade talks formally opened, the environmentalist group Greenpeace called for the talks to start all over again.

"Greenpeace wants developed countries to end all agricultural export subsidies immediately without attaching any conditions to such a move," the group declared Tuesday. Indeed, "Greenpeace is demanding that delegates to the WTO agree to a complete social and environmental review of the global trade system."

However, champions of free trade think the agenda should be quite different.

World Growth, a nongovernmental organization that advocates free trade, said Tuesday that trade negotiators should resist demands such as Greenpeace's in favor of opening markets and, if necessary, walk away from Hong Kong with no agreement in order to try again another day.

"No deal is better than a bad deal," said Alan Oxley, World Growth's chairman and a former chairman of the General Agreement on Tariffs and Trade. "Many studies by the World Bank and others show that developing countries gain by liberalizing markets."

What is the WTO's role in negotiating the reduction of government subsidies by wealthy nations? How do these subsidies affect developing nations?

Oxley said he hopes the WTO could negotiate real reform in Hong Kong so that the global trading system doesn't have to fall back on less comprehensive trade pacts between two nations or within a single region.

"The WTO is the piece of glue that allows the U.S., the EU, Japan and China to regulate trade with each other," he said. "Their ability to make bilateral agreements with each other is pretty low, due to political considerations in their home countries."

If the Hong Kong meeting does not go far enough toward moving the world trade body forward, the WTO's Lamy has already mentioned holding another meeting, perhaps in Geneva, in three months.

Even then, forging a comprehensive and concrete global pact could be tough. The WTO operates by consensus. Any one of the WTO's members— joined by Saudi Arabia over the weekend—can block any pact agreed to by the other 148 members.

ISSUE SUMMARY

———●

Trade agreements have flourished since the initial steps taken by the European Union in the 1950s. All over the world, multi-country and bilateral trade deals are signed every year. Governmental leaders have recognized the mounting evidence that supports the positive relationship between free trade and economic growth. As a result, many nations have worked hard to reduce onerous trade restrictions with the hope that their domestic products will become more competitive in the global marketplace. Moreover, free trade tends to bring down the costs of production and forces retail prices to be more competitive.

Yet, while most of the world's industrialized nations have enacted free-trade measures, to some extent many of the world's developing nations still maintain excessively high trade barriers. According to U.S. trade representative Rob Portman, "seventy percent of the tariffs paid by developing countries are paid to other developing countries." The WTO has been working hard to bring down these trade barriers that tend to make developing nations less competitive.

Multinational firms also pay very close attention to trade barriers and free-trade agreements. From a market analysis perspective, one major factor in deciding the ideal target export country is clearly the financial implications of cross-border tariffs. Oftentimes, high import tariffs will dissuade a firm from entering a certain market. Also, as more firms seek to reduce costs through their supply chain activities, the level and scope of trade restrictions will continue to play a pivotal role in the international manufacturing decision-making process.

There are a number of political and sociological implications that stem from free-trade agreements. Many nations lobby to protect some of their most successful industries prior to the signing of freetrade pacts, and international dispute settlement bodies, such as the WTO, play an instrumental role in the arbitration process. Signing trade pacts can often bring together nations that have traditionally had less than amicable relationships. Immigration is also a significant topic in many trade negotiations, and this phenomenon may have deep legal and cultural implications depending on the level of integration specified in the trade agreement.

While NAFTA and the European Union have garnered significant attention, there are numerous other influential trade deals that have been signed in the past two decades. In the Western hemisphere, MERCOSUR is a powerful group in South America with core members Argentina, Brazil, Paraguay, and Uruguay. The Andean Community, with its members Colombia, Venezuela, Ecuador, Bolivia, and Peru, is a growing and important free-trade zone that is also located within South America.

In Asia, the Association of Southeast Asian Nations (ASEAN) is a free-trade area that includes 10 nations from Southeast Asia (Indonesia, Malaysia, the Philippines, Singapore, Thailand, Brunei, Vietnam, Laos, Myanmar, and Cambodia). The Asia-Pacific Economic Cooperation, while not a formal free-trade agreement, is an organization that consists of 21 Pacific Rim nations, including economic powerhouses Japan, Russia, China, and the United States, that work to reduce tariffs and restrictions across the Pacific. Finally, trade pacts have been passed in Africa, such as the Economic Community of West African States, and the Middle East, the Gulf Cooperation Council, and Chinese officials have been negotiating a number of bilateral trade agreements since the start of the new millennium.

ISSUE HIGHLIGHTS

- The reduction of trade barriers has for many years been encouraged by world leaders as a mechanism for stimulating more international trade.
- The EU has expanded dramatically since its creation and now includes 25 member nations and a number of applicant nations.
- The EU faces a difficult challenge as many potential immigrants from former colonies attempt to enter EU member nations and obtain citizenship.
- At the Summit of the Americas meeting, the Free Trade Area of the Americas (FTAA) is continually discussed. The FTAA is a proposed freetrade zone that would cover over 90 percent of the Western hemisphere.
- The World Trade Association has a number of responsibilities, including monitoring and arbitrating over trade disputes among member nations.
- Regional trade agreements, such as ASEAN, MERCOSUR and CAFTA, have also garnered interest and respect in recent years.
- CAFTA membership, when fully implemented, will include El Salvador, Honduras, Guatemala, Nicaragua, the Dominican Republic, Costa Rica, and the United States.
- Chile is a classic example of a nation that has prospered as the result of free trade. Chile has signed 42 free-trade agreements and was the first nation to sign an agreement with China.
- The World Trade Organization has been instrumental in the reduction of global trade barriers and is currently working to reduce government subsidies by wealthier industrialized nations.

CRITICAL THINKING

1. Immigration issues are a complex aspect of free-trade areas. The EU has faced a significant influx of immigrants in recent years, and as the EU expands, opportunities for immigrants also increase exponentially. The challenge for large trade areas, such as the EU and NAFTA, is to balance employment needs with immigration standards. The U.S. government has contemplated a guest worker program, which would strike a reasonable

balance between full immigration and temporary visa holders. Massive levels of immigration not only alter the cultural mosaic of a country but can also affect the cost of social services.

2. In the Americas, a number of free-trade areas exist. NAFTA and MERCOSUR are currently the largest trade groups, followed by the Andean Community. The recent approval of CAFTA by the U.S. government, with the pending ratification by member Central American nations and the Dominican Republic, will make it the second largest agreement in the Western hemisphere. While each of these trade pacts plays an important role from a regional perspective, the proposed FTAA, which would cover over 95 percent of the hemisphere, could offer a massive competitive advantage to its member nations in the future.

3. The WTO was created to help reduce trade barriers worldwide and to increase cooperation among nations. In recent years, WTO conferences have been met with numerous protesters from a wide range of groups. One of the main themes of the protesters is that the WTO does not do enough to promote income quality. The ideas of income equality and income distribution are important factors in the free-trade debate. Another issue that the WTO has recently confronted is government subsidies of certain industries. While the United States has offered to reduce many subsidies, the EU has not been willing to follow suit. With continued pressure by the WTO, subsidies could eventually be reduced to a level where global competitiveness is less affected.

ADDITIONAL READING RESOURCES

Charles W.L. Hill, *Global Business Today*, 3rd ed. (Irwin/McGraw-Hill, 2004).

Adam Smith, *An Inquiry into the Nature and Causes of the Wealth of Nations* (Oxford University Press, 1993 edition).

Andrew Rose, "Do We Really Know That the WTO Increases Trade," *The American Economic Review* (March 1, 2004), pages 98–114.

Sushil Vachani, "Mavericks and Free Trade: Chile's Pivotal Role in the Formation of the FTAA," *Thunderbird International Business Review* (vol. 46, no. 30, 2004), pages 237–253.

Mario Carranza, "Mercosur and the End Game of the FTAA Negotiations: Challenges and Prospects after the Argentine Crisis," *Third World Quarterly* (March 2004), pages 319–337.

Washington Office on Latin America, http:// www.wola.org.

World Trade Organization, http://www.wto.org.

Asia Pacific Economic Cooperation, http:// www.apec.org.

Summit of the Americas, http://www.summit-americas. org.

ISSUE 6

What Are Some Key Strategies for Taking Advantage of Modern Technologies Related to Global Logistics?

One of the most important challenges related to attaining a competitive edge over rival firms in the global economy is obtaining an effective and efficient supply chain management system. The entrance of more firms, ranging from small family-owned businesses to large conglomerates, into the world of international trade has led to an increase in both the number of global logistics firms and the number of advances in new technology. Many multinational delivery firms, such as FedEx, now collaborate with local, domestic-only carriers to enhance their networks. Other firms, such as DHL, have opted to expand their range of services to broaden their customer base. The demand for new technology, such as international temperaturecontrolled shipping, has also prompted a variety of new ventures. As a result, the entrance of new players to the global marketplace has led to increased pressure placed on traditional firms, such as FedEx, to clearly define and defend their strategic positions.

With more and more firms from around the world entering the global economy, pressure to maximize supply chain efficiency has also increased. Issues such as just-in-time inventory systems, global positioning systems, and warehouse location have become crucial factors in the strategic analysis of many firms. Some companies, such as Deutsche Post, have begun to provide one-stop shopping services while also expanding size criteria options to accommodate packages ranging from small parcels to major freight shipments. A number of firms, such as UPS and TNT, have also formally signed agreements with local partners in order to facilitate a wider delivery network. It is not uncommon for major international delivery firms to assist in the formal support of document clearance at customs and to help with any other border crossing issues such as labeling requirements and tariff payments. And with new technology, such as the electronic tracking technology that has been developed by Kansas City SmartPort, the efficiency and speed of international transportation should be significantly smoother in the future.

According to a recent study by UPS Supply Chain Solutions, just one-third of CFOs believe their companies' strategic and operational plans are well integrated. The same study found that over 60 percent of CFOs believe that the supply chain is an important factor related to the achievement of corporate objectives. The supply chain situation in China, the world's hottest new market, is underdeveloped and ripe for modern advances. For example, management costs in 2004 related to logistics were 14 percent in China, much higher than the U.S. average of 3.8 percent. The rugged and undeveloped terrain combined with numerous players in the delivery network, and a lack of logistics efficiency, have resulted in numerous cost inefficiencies. From a more global perspective, transporting goods from China to Europe and North America includes strategic decision making with respect to the shipping paths that must be considered. Major revisions to the structure and pricing schemes of the Panama and Suez Canals must be factored in to any decision related to shipping across the Pacific or Indian Oceans.

In their article about the strategic decision by FedEx to maintain status quo, Adrienne Roberts, Dan Roberts, and Andrew Ward describe some of the pressures involved with new expansion methods in the global logistics industry. The case of FedEx is emphasized because while most of the major international players in this industry are expanding services, FedEx has decided to stick to its core competencies. In his article, "Prescription for Success," Ian Putzger outlines some of the new high-tech services that are being provided by international shippers. In particular, Putzger focuses on a joint venture between DHL Danzas Air & Ocean and Lufthansa Cargo that will provide an uninterrupted cool chain of service around the world. This service is of particular interest to drug-makers that have products that must be kept at a level cool temperature at all times.

In his article titled "Chinese Business: Logistics in China, a New Frontier," Roy Kheng identifies a number of major obstacles that multinational logistics firms are facing as they enter the Chinese market. Kheng discusses the major challenge of topography in China and how delivery firms will have to be more versatile to accomplish their objectives in this massive mountainous land. Perhaps in the future the technology that is discussed in R.G. Edmonson's article about the Kansas City SmartPort will be available on a more global scale. Indeed, having the ability to track shipments to exact locations will facilitate numerous supply chain efficiencies. The final article, by Peter T. Leach, discusses the new services, fees, and improvements that have been made to the Panama and Suez Canals. With the sheer volume of shipments that now take place between Asia and Europe or Asia and the East Coast of the United States, it is important to gain an understanding of how these strategically important canals play a major role in the transport of containers worldwide.

ISSUE ARTICLES

Adrienne Roberts, Dan Roberts, and Andrew Ward, "FedEx Dares to Keep the Status Quo," *The Financial Times* (October 20, 2005).

Ian Putzger, "Prescription for Success," *Journal of Commerce* (August 8, 2005).

Roy Kheng, "Chinese Business: Logistics in China, a New Frontier," *The Edge Singapore* (October 24, 2005).

R.G. Edmonson, "Royal Treatment: The Kansas City SmartPort Emerges as a Leader in Supply- Chain Security, Technology and Trade Facilitation," *Journal of Commerce* (March 6, 2006).

Peter T. Leach, "East and West: Carriers Plan New Services This Year Through Panama and Suez Canals," *Journal of Commerce* (February 20, 2006).

FedEx Dares to Keep the Status Quo

Adrienne Roberts, Dan Roberts, and Andrew Ward

G o behind the scenes at some of Manhattan's top restaurants and the revolutionary impact of FedEx can be found staring straight back at you—in the clear, glistening eyes of truly fresh fish.

Thanks to the company's global delivery network, gourmet chefs are increasingly bypassing the traditional fish market and sourcing their best fish directly from individual fishermen thousands of miles away.

Turning business models upside down in this way is something the express parcel carrier does quietly all the time. When Apple sold one million new iPod nano music players in 17 days last month, the customised models bought online barely saw the inside of a warehouse but were fed directly from factories in China into the FedEx delivery system.

The efficiencies made possible by such low-inventory supply chains even play a key role in the flexibility and resilience of the US economy—most recently lauded by Alan Greenspan, chairman of the Federal Reserve.

But while FedEx continues to change the world of business, a curious stasis is apparent in its own business model. Fred Smith, the former US marine who largely invented the overnight airborne delivery industry by founding Federal Express in 1971, is sitting out the latest revolution sweeping the package delivery industry.

The company's biggest rivals—United Parcel Service, Deutsche Post and TNT—are expanding into an ever-wider range of logistics services but FedEx remains doggedly focused on its core small package and light road-freight businesses.

While Michael Dell now sells printers and Bill Gates chairs a software company that produces games consoles, Mr Smith is a rare example of a successful entrepreneur choosing to stick to his knitting. "We have looked long and hard at whether we want to be a big player in the contract logistics sector," he says. "We have chosen not to do so because it is a low margin business and it is not clear to us that there is the type of synergies there that our competitors hope to find."

Mr Smith has never previously been one to cling to the status quo. So it is tempting to wonder whether, after 34 years at the industry's cutting edge,

FedEx is becoming a more conservative company, and Mr Smith, at 61, is losing his eye for the new opportunity.

Deutsche Post, which owns the DHL parcel delivery network, believes that in an era of complex global supply chains, there is an opportunity for it to provide a "one-stop shop" for all the logistics needs of its corporate customers. The group already has the capability, following a series of acquisitions, to deliver anything from the lightest package to the heaviest freight by land, sea or air anywhere in the world.

The German group's offering will be strengthened further if its Pounds 3.7bn agreed takeover of Exel, the British contract logistics group, is completed as planned. In addition to coordinating the movement of its customers' goods around the world, Exel does everything from managing warehouses to sub-assembling parts for manufacturers.

UPS, the largest US package delivery group, has been more cautious in its expansion. But its acquisition last year of Menlo Worldwide Forwarding, a global air and sea freight company, suggests it broadly shares Deutsche Post's vision.

TNT, the Dutch post and package group, has also developed a powerful contract logistics and freight forwarding business.

What can FedEx do to further build on its competitive advantage?

FedEx, in contrast, has limited itself to a small, home grown supply chain services division and Mr Smith says there are no plans for a large acquisition in the sector. The group's only serious exposure to heavier goods is through its domestic road freight division. But even that is limited to the so-called "less than truckload" segment, transporting relatively light loads over short distances.

Mr Smith believes the small package and light freight markets are fundamentally different from—and more attractive than—the logistics and heavy freight businesses being pursued by Deutsche Post, UPS and TNT.

The former, he says, are high-margin activities focused on delivering small, high-value products, such as iPods or Louis Vuitton handbags, to their point of consumption. The latter, by contrast, is a lower-margin business, typically involving lower-value, larger-scale goods destined for earlier stages in the production process.

While small package customers include many small and medium-sized businesses and consumers with weak pricing power, the heavier freight and contract logistics markets are dominated by large retailers and manufacturers with the leverage to squeeze margins. "We've seen no reason to get into that sector," says Mr Smith.

His scepticism about diversification is at odds, not only with FedEx's rivals, but also with many investors. Jon Langelfeld, analyst at RW Baird, says an acquisition by FedEx in the freight forwarding sector "would be well received by investors."

Why has FedEx decided to stick to its core strategy and not expand its portfolio of services?

Mr Smith has never been afraid to go against investor sentiment. But he insists he would not hesitate to change the strategy if the company started losing business because of its lack of logistics services. "If we start to hear people saying 'we want a one-stop shop, we're going to take away your small shipment business', then we'll have another look," he says. "But, so far, we've seen very little leakage."

Mr Smith is equally cautious in his approach to international expansion. FedEx remains, at heart, a cargo airline. As such, it eagerly snaps up every additional take-off and landing slot it can secure in the plum parts of Asia and Europe. But the group is more hesitant about acquiring assets on the ground.

While UPS recently joined DHL in offering a domestic parcel service in China, FedEx has stuck with imports and exports. In Europe, too, the group has shown little interest in competing domestically.

Mr Smith says the reason for the caution is simple: the inter-continental express market, with its high margins and strong growth, remains a more attractive business than either China's nascent domestic market or Europe's fragmented and fiercely competitive road-based markets.

Instead of sinking hundreds of millions of dollars into fleets of branded delivery trucks around the world, FedEx has in many places preferred to forge partnerships with local delivery companies. In the UK, for example, FedEx uses Business Post, a British courier company, to access parts of the country not covered by its own vehicles.

"We would not be afraid to invest Dollars 5bn–Dollars 6bn (Pounds 2.8bn– Pounds 3.4bn) (in an overseas acquisition)," says Mr Smith. "But we are not going to make any investments of that magnitude unless there were wonderful financial returns."

There are clearly risks to FedEx's take-it-or-leave-it approach to geographical and sectoral expansion. If Deutsche Post's one-stop logistics shop turns out to be a winning strategy, FedEx will have a lot of catching up to do. Likewise, opting out of European and Asian domestic markets leaves holes in its global network that DHL and UPS could exploit.

Until then, Mr Smith's simple strategy of using a hub-and-spokes air network to deliver packages with speed and reliability remains as effective today as it was when the first FedEx aircraft left a runway in Memphis 34 years ago.

When you have a model that produces results, says Alan Graf, chief financial officer, it is best not to tinker. "What we haven't done," he says, "is just as important as what we have done."

ARTICLE 6.2

Prescription for Success

Ian Putzger

Keith Kreider wants to know where his company's products are and what condition they're in from the time they leave plants in 22 countries until the time they're delivered to customers. Kreider is global procurement manager of Dentsply International, which makes dental products, many of which are temperature-sensitive.

Being able to check that shipments are kept at the right temperature throughout the transportation cycle is as important to him as an uninterrupted supply chain. Kreider wants to know of a problem in time to correct it immediately, and to identify where the problem occurred so that it won't be repeated.

Logistics providers sense rich opportunities if they can meet these needs. That's why DHL Danzas Air & Ocean and Lufthansa Cargo started a joint venture company called LifeConEx last April. The companies have provided logistics services to pharmaceutical and life-sciences customers for years, but decided that an integrated approach would work better.

"We are the first company to virtually integrate the operating standards of the airline, ground-handling and freight-forwarding service providers to create more value for shippers of life sciences products," said Robert Krautheim, chief executive of LifeConEx, based in Miramar, Fla.

The joint venture isn't targeting pharmaceutical and biotechnology shipments that do not require an uninterrupted cool chain and end-to-end temperature monitoring. "We concentrate explicitly on customers from the pharma and life-sciences industry who need temperature-controlled transportation and logistics processes," said Michael Vorwerk, the company's chief operating officer. "We only come into the picture where the customer needs cool containers, special packaging or monitoring along the supply chain." He said this covers 20 to 25 percent of the total pharmaceutical market.

Instead of developing hard-and-fast services, LifeConEx has mapped 75 steps in the flow of products from door to door. Of these, 45 are critical for temperature-controlled movement and monitoring. Customers choose packages with combinations of those elements according to their needs. The joint venture has selected 11 airlines besides Lufthansa and five handling agents it says can provide adequate service and monitoring capabilities. "We're carrier-neutral," Vorwerk said, although he said Lufthansa has first call on LifeConEx traffic.

What are come challenges related to the international partnering of delivery firms?

How are multinational delivery firms teaming up with local firms to expand products and services?

Initially, the joint venture is concentrating on the trade lane between the United States and Europe. The original plan was for a European branch to open next year, with Asia to follow by the end of the year, but the schedule has been moved up. Vorwerk now says the European operation will probably be launched this fall and that the Asian service also will start a few months early.

Kreider said LifeConEx has performed well. He said its most important service has been reporting of current temperature data throughout the shipment, but that he also likes the one-source aspect. "I can go to a single source and get exactly the information I need, regardless of where the shipment is," he said.

The market also has attracted other logistics companies. In June, forwarder Panalpina made a global deal with Envirotainer to provide temperature-controlled air-cargo containers for its new cold-chain management service for the health-care industry. This enables the logistics firm to offer pharmaceutical companies an integrated cold chain covering air and ground movements, said Peter Reinhart, vice president of Panalpina's Competence Center Healthcare.

Earlier this year, logistics provider Kuehne & Nagel teamed up with Dutch airline KLM to equip containers with special temperature-recording devices that transmit the data to the companies' computers. The temperature probes are not new, but until now they have not been accessible en route.

"The customer can always put a probe inside a shipment, but it's inside the box. The container is sealed, so the data is invisible to us until the shipment is opened again at the consignee's warehouse," said Marcel Fujike, vice president of business development and product management at Kuehne & Nagel.

For the first trial, the pair monitored a consignment of cholera vaccine, which must be kept at temperatures between 2 and 8 degrees Celsius, from Sweden to Canada. Temperature readings were taken at a number of milestones along the journey and transmitted to an Internet platform. Those milestones were defined by the process map for air-cargo shipments under Cargo 2000, a global performance-standard initiative in which KLM and Kuehne & Nagel participate.

"One-time shipments always go right because of the special attention everybody pays to them," Fujike said. This month, KLM and Kuehne & Nagel started regular trials between Basel, Switzerland, and New York. By October, Fujike expects to add two or three additional routes.

In June, express operator TNT launched a second-day service for clinical trial shipments from Asia to the United States. TNT named AirNet Systems, which operates a fleet of 128 aircraft, as its exclusive partner to move this traffic inside the United States. AirNet made history this spring with the first coast-to-coast transport of a human kidney using a special device that nourishes the organ to extend the distance it can be moved.

TNT projects that clinical trial shipments from Asia to the U.S. will double next year. LifeConEx executives are equally bullish. Since April, their traffic using the service has grown to 500 tons per month. Vorwerk expects it to hit 25,000 to 35,000 in two or three years.

How have many major international delivery firms expanded services to take advantage of new opportunities created by the global economy?

Two converging forces are driving pharmaceutical and biotech companies to look for temperature-controlled logistics solutions with full visibility.

First, legislative pressure is mounting on the pharmaceutical industry to be able to prove that adequate temperature ranges are maintained throughout the logistics chain. "The pharma industry as a whole is being driven toward increased awareness of the conditions its shipments are subjected to. We're being driven by the regulatory agencies," Kreider said.

Second, the pharmaceutical companies have a natural interest in maintaining shipment integrity. Temperature fluctuations may affect the effectiveness of products such as anaesthetics, destroy polymer chains or cut down the shelf life of a product, Kreider said. Vorwerk said inadequate transportation wastes millions of dollars a year in the pharmaceutical and life-sciences sector.

Kreider hopes to see the type of service that LifeConEx offers in other modes of transportation, particularly surface. "I would like to see the service extended at some point," he said.

Chinese Business:
Logistics in China, a New Frontier

Roy Kheng

Historically, China has always been on the cutting edge of technology as evidenced by the massive civil engineering work that was the Great Wall (214 BCE) and the colossal infrastructure project that was the Grand Canal (486 BCE). The Grand Canal linked the Yangtze River and Yellow River valleys and ran from north to south. This infrastructure project unified the north and the south of China and laid the foundation for an integrated national economy.

Infrastructure has always been the precursor for development. Most of the earth's early civilisations were birthed along major waterways like the Indus, the Nile and the Euphrates where the ease of communications and wealth of resources allowed for specialisation, trade and urbanisation. Even though global civilisations have used logistical procedures for thousands of years, the science that is logistics is a recent phenomenon. Supply chain management, just-in-time (JIT) inventory systems, the global positioning system (GPS), IT structures and containerised shipping are recent innovations that have transformed global trade and the movement of goods over long distances.

The total value of logistics to GDP in China is behind those of the US, Japan and developed nations in Europe. Last year, the proportion of the total cost of logistics to GDP in China was higher by more than 10%. This was because 57% of total costs went to expenditure on transportation. Management costs were 14% of the total cost of logistics, far higher than the 3.8% of US firms. It is easy to see from the differences in cost structures that the largest problem for logistics in China lies in the organisational structures and lack of managerial expertise in this industry. This reflects the need to improve.

MAJOR OBSTACLES

If money is the lifeblood of a financial system, infrastructure is the economic arterial network of any thriving economy. China plans to complete the construction of an 85,000km highway network in 30 years. The investment for the

16,000km of expressways under construction and the 40,000km planned will cost an estimated two trillion renminbi ($1 approx 4.79 renminbi), and that's without taking into consideration the value of time. All manner of transportation infrastructure, such as railways, highways, waterways and port facilities, has been upgraded, with further improvements being planned.

Even though infrastructure is being upgraded, some major obstacles hamper the growth of a comprehensive, countrywide logistics industry in China. Chief among them is the topography. Industry fragmentation and the lack of logistics companies of a national and international scale are also major concerns. Other problems are the lack of managerial expertise, severe inefficiencies and technical backwardness.

Most challenging is its topography. China is a big country, resulting in a variety of geographical dilemmas such as mountainous terrain and associated high altitudes to surmount, wide rivers to bridge and to control, and deserts of shifting sand to overcome. These issues are an infrastructural nightmare.

As it stands, China's transportation networks are highly splintered. Provincial and local administrations tend to shield local companies from competition by placing entry barriers like local fees, licensing requirements and inspections. The country is rife with regionalism—it occurs when the local government has a relationship with local companies. The procedure for obtaining the various licences and permits to operate a logistics company is not just difficult; it is prohibitively expensive. Few licences have been issued for countrywide services. Third-party logistics solution providers have emerged as a viable answer because the few holders of licences face stiff resistance and protectionist action from the provincial and lower levels of government.

In terms of management and legislation, the logistics industry has lagged behind other industries in the country since its transition from a command economy to a free-market economy. Due to China's historical dependence on state-owned enterprises (SOEs) in this sector, managerial structures are inflexible and inefficient practices dominate. In the course of adapting to a free-market economy, the reform of managerial systems had fallen behind because of an adherence to traditional ideas and rigid mindsets. Despite reforms enacted at the highest levels of government and a prioritisation of these reforms, there has been resistance to change.

In terms of technology and technical innovation, China still lags behind more developed nations. There is a serious lack of managerial expertise and a dearth of skilled labour. Current systems are set up for the transportation of bulk goods like coal and grain. There has been a serious lack of adoption of modern logistical practices like the integration of comprehensive information systems, integration with GPS and inventory tracking. The industry is also poorly positioned to handle goods that are time-sensitive or perishable. Some foreign firms such as Haagen-Dazs use their own expertise to ensure the safety and quality of their products. Unfortunately, not all manufacturers have the resources. This is where third-party solution providers come into play.

What are some of the major challenges that logistics firms face when doing business in China?

THIRD-PARTY LOGISTICS PROVIDERS

In the West, consumer goods are normally shipped to retailers and consumers via third-party providers (3PLs). In China, even though the share of 3PLs in the overall logistics industry is small, there is a growing need for them and even fourth-party logistics providers (4PLs, normally local companies that sub-contract logistical jobs from 3PLs). There is room for 3PLs to fulfill a multitude of roles in the Chinese logistics industry, for example, the supply chain management of manufacturers can be subordinated to 3PLs, driving down costs, streamlining production and increasing efficiency.

Over 90% of foreign-funded enterprises in China outsource their logistics needs to 3PLs, while SOEs see logistics as a key cost centre and are in the process of outsourcing their logistical needs. Supply chain management, JIT inventory, inventory management and tracking, and bar codes are many of the innovations that will revolutionise the industry.

China's 3PL firms can be broken down into four broad categories: big SOEs, medium-sized domestic logistics companies, the logistics divisions of manufacturers and retailers, and foreign logistics providers.

SOEs like Cosco, Sinotrans, China Post (EMS), CMST and China Rail have comprehensive transport, warehousing and licensing assets. They have widespread national coverage and good relations with both central and local governments. Some have initiated restructuring efforts to evolve into value-added 3PLs. Their key advantage would be their extensive asset bases and wide networks.

Medium-sized local logistics companies are mostly privately owned. They tend to focus on regional markets or specialise in one or two aspects of logistics like warehousing and road transport. They are well positioned to take on the role of a 4PL because of their familiarity with the provincial or local area. Examples would be ST Anda and Guangzhou-based PG Logistics.

The logistics divisions of domestic producers are another part of the market—firms like Haier Logistics not only meet the supply chain management needs of their parent firms but are considering entering the logistics market and becoming independent entities.

Some foreign logistics providers are registered as wholly owned foreign enterprises. There are multinationals and smaller niche companies that operate in China as well. Many are actively expanding their operations in China by cooperating with domestic firms. Some examples would be DHL and United Parcel Service. These firms have the technical expertise, modern equipment and good managerial practices.

Domestic and international 3PLs face a dilemma in China's rapidly growing economy. SOEs need technology and managerial expertise; foreign firms need local experience and contacts to navigate the quagmire of local government. There will be many growing pains as this industry develops, but as manufacturers outsource more logistical functions, both producer and consumer alike will reap the benefits of the industry's development and consolidation.

MARKET SEGMENTS TO CONSIDER

Producers and consumers have found there are several major problems with domestic logistical solution providers. Costs are high, service is often unreliable and there is a lack of transparency. Furthermore, loss, damage and pilferage commonly occur. External or internal parties may consider the following market segments.

The domestic market will be a goldmine for companies that are able to navigate the myriad of local barriers. They will have no trouble getting business if they implement lean and efficient workflows, integrate IT and hire dependable staff. A reliable less-than-truckload or full-truckload domestic transport service definitely has the potential to become a major profit centre.

Another segment worth exploring is for smaller firms that focus on providing expertise in logistical solutions. Firms that provide hardware and software solutions that complement, improve and streamline logistical processes also have a market as companies ranging from SOEs to small and medium-sized enterprises scramble to modernise their systems.

The integration of procedural solutions offers opportunities for consultancy firms. Many domestic producers and retailers still use dated inventory control systems; professionally implemented supply chain management will greatly enhance their competitiveness.

In conclusion, the logistics industry in China is lagging behind its industrial development and there is much room for investment, development and profitability. Regionalism and red tape have to be dealt with but overall, the indicators are positive, with the government actively developing this sector and SOEs being restructured. It is heartening to know that the central government has designated logistics as a strategic industry. China's current role as the world's largest factory needs to be complemented by a comprehensive logistical system encompassing domestic and international trade.

What is the relationship between newly industrialized countries, global trade patterns, and the need for modern logistics systems?

Royal Treatment: The Kansas City SmartPort Emerges as a Leader in Supply-Chain Security, Technology and Trade Facilitation

R. G. Edmonson

The next step in supply-chain security and trade facilitation may come straight from the Heartland. Kansas City SmartPort, a nonprofit economic development agency, is testing security on a north-south axis. It has tested electronic technology to track a truck's location and the integrity of the freight from Kansas City, Mo., to destinations in Mexico.

More than that, "We're soon going to be home to the first inland U.S.-Mexico customs facility in the United States," said Chris Gutierrez, SmartPort executive director. He said U.S. and Mexican customs authorities can clear Mexico-bound exports in Kansas City, seal the truck with an electronic or bolt seal, and track and trace it all the way to the border, using technologies that the Smart-Port is testing. "We'll know where that truck is, and that the driver got there in the designated amount of time, and it can move into Mexico without any further inspection," Gutierrez said. The joint facility should be in operation by year-end.

SmartPort wants to test a mix of technologies. So far, Electronic Data Systems, which purchased the data-integration unit of the Black & Veatch engineering company, has tracked four truckloads on the Interstate 35 corridor between Kansas City and Laredo, Texas. Two of those were tracked on to their destinations in Guadalajara and Veracruz, Mexico, Gutierrez said. The objective has been to create clarity in the supply chain, and the project has tested a number of technologies, including global positioning satellite, cellular telephone and radio-frequency identification technology.

"We did one shipment where the company averaged 10 to 14 days to get their freight to the customer in Guadalajara. We did it for them in three," Gutierrez said. "The Mexicans are very committed to this. They see it as a great opportunity to relieve congestion at the border. The U.S. and Mexico have both said that this project has to have a technology component to track and trace and secure the freight. They're very excited about what we're doing, because we already have funding to do it."

What are some new technologies that will help track and control the international shipment of goods? How can these technological advances assist small entrepreneurial firms in their quest to enter foreign markets?

Kansas City SmartPort has received no funding from the Department of Homeland Security. Instead it has a $6 million grant from the Department of Transportation's Intelligent Highway Systems program. It also has a $500,000 grant from the Department of Commerce to promote exports to Mexico. Gutierrez said security is an objective, but it's a byproduct of greater supply-chain visibility. "What we're looking at is security in the supply chain, and visibility to the customers, whether that's the shipper, the carrier or the government."

It's no coincidence that the SmartPort project sounds like the Secure Freight Initiative that Homeland Security Secretary Michael Chertoff and Deputy Secretary Michael Jackson announced last year. Homeland Security has yet to put form to the Secure Freight concept, but Kansas City is ready whenever the Department of Homeland Security is, Gutierrez said. "Chertoff and Jackson are talking about the Secure Freight Initiative, and we hope that this is the ideal corridor to test this technology."

Other projects are testing tracking and tracing technology, but the Smart-Port project is taking that one step farther. Gutierrez said data the project is collecting will feed into a "data fusion" center that will analyze and distribute information to shippers or government security officials. Tracking systems are "great, but where does the data go?" he asked. "How does Homeland Security analyze risk, and shippers want to analyze risk. How do you provide data to the right people, and how do you protect it?"

Some trade groups are resisting the Secure Freight idea, because their members will not hand over proprietary information to anyone outside the government. It's a question SmartPort wants to address: Who would own the data? "Great question," Gutierrez said. "That's something that needs to be explored when we do these pilots." Cost savings from greater efficiency could cover the costs of data collection and storage. Another possibility is the "Visa-Master-Card model" for merchants. Businesses that want to offer credit-card services pay a fee to the issuers, and pay to access the data. Maybe a nonprofit company such as SmartPort could manage the data center for everyone, since it has no vested interest in the information.

Gutierrez said the projects depend on no specific technology or manufacturer. "The system we want to build here in Kansas City is open source. We're not going to dictate technology or equipment, but we're also active in the standardization process. We're not going to have nine different e-seals out there; that will add to costs."

SmartPort and its partners have representatives, for example, at the World Customs Organization's discussions of criteria for security and trade facilitation. It's conceivable that one day, a protected container can be tracked through a secure supply line from Kansas City through a seaport such as Houston, to any foreign country.

Another question: What should be the roles of the government and private sector in supply-chain security? "Homeland Security has stated it very well: The private sector is the group that's moving the freight and owns the data,"

Gutierrez said. "The government needs to see certain data if it's going to protect the supply chain. We agree with what Homeland Security is saying, (that) the Secure Freight Initiative is where we're going, but the private sector needs to take the lead and develop it." The government's role may be supplying seed money to get private-sector pilots under way, but ultimately it has to be a public-private partnership.

The next stage of the SmartPort project will begin to track containers on railcars, using Kansas City Southern Railway's line that extends to the Mexican Pacific port of Lazaro Cardenas. Hutchison Port Holdings, the port operator, is expanding container capacity from 200,000 containers in 2005 to 2.5 million in the near future, Gutierrez said. Kansas City is at the center of a port-to-port access that also extends north to Hudson's Bay at Churchill, Manitoba. Some planners are considering Churchill as terminus of an Arctic Ocean container route from Murmansk, Russia.

What are some new technologies that have led to increased precision in global delivery services?

SmartPort is one of a growing network of inland ports that want to use ocean routes to Churchill, or Lazaro Cardenas, or other ports to relieve congestion on the West Coast. For more than a century, Kansas City boosters have pointed out that the overland distance is shorter to a Mexican port than any West Coast port. The north-south routes would not likely supplant Los Angeles or New York–New Jersey, but the inland ports working together can provide some benefits for warehousing and distribution.

"The idea is that there is a network of interested parties that recognize there is some synergy within these inland ports, linking Canada, the U.S. and Mexico together," said Greg Dandewich, director of economic development for Destination Winnipeg, the northernmost partner in the inland network.

ARTICLE 6.5

East and West: Carriers Plan New Services This Year Through Panama and Suez Canals

Peter T. Leach

The growing popularity of all-water routes from Asia to the U.S. is raising two big questions this year: Can the Panama Canal squeeze out enough extra capacity to handle the new services? Or will the capacity crunch force more container lines to choose the more-expensive and slower route via the Suez Canal?

The answer to both questions is, "Yes."

Container carriers have been able to secure fixed-day reservations for at least two new all-water services through Panama that will start this year. Without such reservations they could not schedule new liner services. And carriers also are planning to launch as many as three new Suez liner services late in the year.

The Panama Canal's locks can accommodate ships with up to 13 rows of containers across their decks. With no locks, the Suez can accommodate the largest container ships afloat.

Deliveries this year of super post-Panamax container ships—vessels with up to 22 rows of containers across their decks—will free up enough smaller but still larger-than-Panamax ships to make up the strings of 10 or 12 ships that the new Suez services will require. There are already at least two round-the-world container services that call at Hong Kong on their way to the U.S. East Coast via the Suez Canal, but no direct services yet from China to the U.S. East Coast.

Except for the two round-the-world liner container services, there are no direct services from China to the U.S. East Coast via the Suez Canal. One new China service via Suez is planned to start later this year. There are six regularly scheduled eastbound liner services to U.S. East Coast ports via the Suez from ports in India, Pakistan and Sri Lanka. Two more are planned later this year.

The Panama Canal continues to be the most important transit point for all-water services to the U.S. East Coast. There are 15 regularly scheduled westbound liner services to East and Gulf Coast ports.

Opinions are split on whether the Panama Canal has enough capacity to handle the growth of all-water services. Drewry Shipping Consultants, which completed a study for APL Ltd. on the outlook for the Panama Canal last year, is pessimistic. But Global Insight, which also last year conducted a study of

Why are the Suez and Panama canals so strategically important? What are some key differences between the two canals?

how the Panama Canal Authority can finance its ambitious expansion plan with its third set of locks, is more optimistic.

The Panama Canal is "within four to five transits a day of capacity right now, which is essentially what the Drewry study says," said John D. Bowe, APL's regional president, Americas, who was in Panama this month. Bowe said APL has already addressed the issue of a possible capacity crunch by putting larger ships into the two all-water services it operate with partners.

Bowe said APL will participate in the joint all-water service that the Grand and New World alliances are scheduled to launch by midyear. It is not a new service, because it replaces the one that the Grand Alliance had with P&O Nedlloyd, which pulled its vessels out this month following its acquisition by Maersk Line. But the change will give APL additional capacity through three sailings per week from Asia to East Coast ports.

The Panama Canal Authority has taken several steps this year to increase canal transits. "We have been working on many small projects that will give us additional marginal capacity to accommodate the growing number of Panamax ships that want to go through here," said Jorge Quijano, the authority's director of maritime operations.

The canal authority has opened a new tie-up station on the east side of the Gaillard Cut that reduces idle time at the Pedro Miguel locks and will allow one additional daily transit by a Panamax ship. Another tie-up station being built on the west side of the locks will handle two Panamax vessels and eliminate the idle time altogether. The two stations will allow the canal to handle an additional three Panamax vessels per day, or 30 million to 40 million tons of cargo annually.

In addition, the canal has increased the number of reservation slots for container ships from 21 to 23 per day and is illuminating the locks so that Panamax ships can transit the entire canal except for the Gaillard Cut at night.

"This will give us the ability to handle the growth in transits that have been forecast for the next four to five or maybe six years," Quijano said. "It all depends on the mix of vessels, which we do not control," he said.

"The canal has a capacity ceiling on scheduling transits that is going to impact the carriers in the fairly near future," said Mark Page, Drewry's research director and author of its Panama Canal study. "There is an impending crunch, not just because of what's happening in the container trade, but what's happening in all the other trades as well." He said the canal's capacity is being squeezed by the growing size and number of ships of all types that are transiting the canal.

But Page admits that it's difficult to measure the canal's capacity. "It's hard to pin down exactly what the canal's capacity is, because capacity is a movable feast at the canal," he said. "There's no such thing as a fixed capacity."

The canal authority has been working hard to eke out every TEU and ton of transit capacity that it can. "The canal has extended the window during which the ships with bookings can transit the canal, so there are more bookings available during the week," said Ben Hackett, Global Insight's executive managing director for international trade and director of the study of expansion financing.

"The shipping lines that have fixed-day schedules tend to come through at the same time, so they are working more closely with the canal authority to go through during periods of low congestion," he said. "My general feeling based on the work we've done is fairly optimistic that they do have capacity, if the shipping lines can cooperate and spread their sailings so that they don't all bunch up."

One thing is for certain: It's going to cost more to ship goods from Asia to the U.S. via the Panama or Suez canals. Carriers will have to recover the rising cost of tolls and bunker fuel. The Panama Canal, which has been increasing tolls on container ships by 69 percent in three stages through 2007, will probably have to finance its expansion through still more toll increases.

"The positive sign is that the Panama Canal Authority realizes the problem and is thinking of expanding the canal," said Gao Weijie, chairman of Cosco Americas and the former vice president of Cosco Group in charge of its shipping and logistics operations. "They will have to raise tolls to pay for the expansion. But they will also have to come to a compromise with users about how much they are willing to pay in tolls to support construction of another set of locks."

Cosco Container Lines is planning to add two new all-water services through the Panama Canal this year. The first will be a fixed-day weekly service in a partnership with Evergreen Marine Corp. It will start in mid-May with nine vessels in the 2,200- to 3,300-TEU range. Cosco will provide four ships and Evergreen, five. The port rotation will be Shanghai, Yantian, Hong Kong, Colon, Savannah, Miami, Colon and back to Shanghai.

In advance of the full launch, the two lines will exchange slots on three consecutive weekly sailings starting on March 11. Cosco will provide one vessel and Evergreen, two for these initial sailings.

Cosco is also planning to launch another new all-water service via Panama together with the CKYH alliance with "K" Line, Yang Ming and Hanjin/Senator. That service is "on the drawing board," according to Gao. The service, which would be named AWE-5, would be the fifth operated by the CKYH group.

Howard Finkel, senior vice president of trade at Cosco North America, said Cosco is still looking at starting the service this year, but that nothing is "firm." Cosco is not looking at starting any Suez services this year, Finkel said. He said Cosco had operated a service via Suez several years ago, long before it had come into vogue, but had discontinued it.

"Cosco was one of the first to start a Suez service to the East Coast, but it didn't work out," said Drewry's Page. "It was using ships in the 2,000- to 2,200-TEU range, but you've got to use bigger ships. If you use smaller ships, you've got no economies of scale, but just extra cost as compared to Panama."

Now the situation has changed because of "the likelihood of recurring congestion at the West Coast ports, the expansion and deepening of East Coast ports, especially New York, and the fact that capacity of ships is becoming less valuable as overtonnaging hits," Page said.

He said all these factors will come together to make the Suez route a more economical route. "It's a higher cost operation than Panama, but you can put big ships in there and get economies of scale," he said.

"Ship time is becoming less valuable as ship capacity goes up," Page said. "You can afford to put 10 ships on a Suez service as opposed to seven on Panama, which does start to narrow the gap between Suez and Panama. We would expect Suez to become a more prominent part of the trans-Pacific trade over the next couple of years. At the moment, it's a very minor footnote."

ISSUE SUMMARY

———————————————————————————————●

The pattern of falling trade barriers around the world has led to the entrance of numerous new firms into the realm of international business. This increase in globalization has, in turn, led to higher demand for services provided by global logistics and delivery firms. Yet as technological advances and demand have resulted in a spike in global services by many firms, FedEx has elected to stick to its traditional core strategy. According to Fred Smith, the CEO and founder of FedEx, "We have looked long and hard at whether we want to be a big player in the contract logistics sector. We have chosen not to do so because it is a low margin business and it is not clear to us that there is the type of synergies there that our competitors hope to find." For the time being, it looks like FedEx will stay away from the contract logistics business and will attempt to defend its strong market share in the high-margin small-parcel delivery sector. There is no doubt that demand for global delivery services will increase in the future as more nations embrace global trade. The key for firms such as FedEx will be to continuously monitor and adapt, if necessary, their competitive strategies.

The complexities involved with global delivery services and supply chain management can be best observed by taking a deeper look at the dynamic and growing Chinese economy. As Roy Kheng points out in his article, "China is a big country, resulting in a variety of geographic dilemmas such as mountainous terrain and associated high altitudes to surmount, wide rivers to bridge and to control, and deserts of shifting sand to overcome." These topographical challenges are exacerbated by a lack of managerial competence and aging technologies. Throw in the need for guanxi, a cultural tradition where people with connections have a much better chance at fulfilling their tasks, and a massive need for logistical services, and the Chinese market becomes even more complex. Moreover, the challenges related to international shipping from China to the rest of the world are immense. Firms must constantly analyze alternative shipping routes and the incremental changes that are being implemented in the world's most strategically important canals: the Suez and the Panama.

A number of factors and strategies exist related to global logistics systems. Partnering with local delivery firms has been one strategic maneuver that has garnered some success. FedEx's use of a British courier firm, Business Post, is a successful example of an international courier firm teaming up with a local delivery firm in order to create a broader geographic range of service. The need for an ideal location has also surfaced as an essential ingredient in the development of a global supply chain network. Other factors, such as joint venture agreements for certain services and the option of offering one-stop shopping must also be considered when assessing global logistics strategic options. Finally, new technologies, such as global tracking systems that can pinpoint specific locations of containers, will clearly add to the speed and efficiency of the international transport of goods in the future.

ISSUE HIGHLIGHTS

- While many firms have expanded services to become more competitive, FedEx has elected to stick to its strategic core and focus on smallparcel delivery, the firm's traditional strength.
- Many multinational delivery firms have formally arranged partnerships with local domestic firms in an attempt to expand their geographic coverage.
- Modern technology has played a significant role in the creation of new opportunities for global logistics firms. One example is the temperature-controlled shipping that DHL and Lufthansa have teamed up to provide in the future.
- The Chinese market is extremely complex, and the logistics network is expensive and ripe for a number of technological advances.
- International shipping for China to Europe and to the East Coast of the United States typically includes crossing either the Suez or Panama Canals, and it is important to analyze strategic options related to the crossing of these canals.
- The Suez Canal is much wider than the Panama Canal and can accommodate much larger ships because it has no system of locks.
- New tracking systems have been developed to help identify the exact location of containers that are being shipped between countries.

CRITICAL THINKING

1. The FedEx strategy of status quo is somewhat controversial at this point in time. While other major international delivery firms, such as UPS, Deutsche Post, and TNT, are expanding services, FedEx has decided to maintain and defend its traditional core strategy of delivering only small parcels. Yet given the projected growth in the smallparcel sector and the higher margins, this strategy may be a real winner in the future.

2. The recent Joint Venture agreement by DHL Danzas Air & Ocean and Lufthansa Cargo is a classic example of two firms from different countries teaming up to create and provide a new line of service. The new service— temperature-controlled international deliveries—came about as a result of an increase in demand by the global pharmaceutical industry. While this venture is initially focusing only on trade between the United States and Europe, as the process is formalized, service to Asia will follow. In the future, this new technology is likely to spawn additional competitors in the industry, yet the DHL-Lufthansa venture will retain its first-mover advantage for a number of years.

3. The decision related to securing the ideal supply chain facility location is an essential component in maximizing supply chain efficiency. As more firms aspire to trim costs, the supply chain has been looked to as an area where significant savings can be found. Strategic decisions related

to location decisions such as regional interdependence, consolidation of logistics and distribution, larger multiuse facilities, intensifying security and surveillance, and locating facilities at strategic choke points can make a major impact on the bottom line of a multinational firm.

4. As international shipping costs increase due to rising fuel prices, it will become even more important to maximize efficiency in the global logistics process. Many East Coast U.S. ports, such as Savannah (Georgia) and Miami, have recently enhanced technology and can now receive larger deeper ships. International shipments between China and the U.S. East Coast are therefore likely to increase in the future, and the efficiency and cost structure of crossing the Panama Canal will become a key factor in minimizing transportation costs.

ADDITIONAL READING RESOURCES

James A. Cooke, "Circumnavigating the Choke Points," *Logistics Management* (October 1, 2005).

William C. Copacino, *Supply Chain Management: The Basics and Beyond* (CRC Press, 1997).

Ben Worthen, "The ABCs of Supply Chain Management," *CIO Magazine Online* (accessed February 14, 2006).

Susannah Patton, "Cracks in the Pharmaceutical Supply Chain," *CIO Magazine* (January 15, 2006).

Christopher Koch, "Making It in China," *CIO Magazine* (October 15, 2005).

http://www.fedex.com, The official Web site for Federal Express.

http://www.manufacturing.net, Web site that contains information and links related to various manufacturing, logistics, and supply chain issues.

http://www.cscmp.com, Council of Supply Chain Management Professionals.

UNIT 3

Managing in a Foreign Environment

Living abroad can be an incredibly valuable experience for a manager. Yet the challenges associated with an expatriate assignment are often cumbersome, stressful, and time-consuming. Managers who prepare well for their foreign assignments tend to adapt faster and perform at a higher level, and are less likely to return home prior to the target completion date. The articles selected for this section cover some of the major challenges that expatriates face while abroad and upon their repatriation back to their home countries. A specific focus is also placed on cultural differences, often considered the most significant challenge to expatriate adjustment. Finally, an analysis of strategic options related to competing in foreign markets is presented.

Issue 7: What Are the Major Challenges That Face Expatriates While Living Abroad?

Issue 8: Why Is It So Important to Understand Cultural Differences When Working Abroad?

Issue 9: What Are Some Key Approaches Related to Competing in Foreign Markets?

ISSUE 7

What Are the Major Challenges That Face Expatriates While Living Abroad?

Countless managers pack their bags and are shipped off to foreign locations at the company's request every year. As the world becomes more globalized and as trade barriers continue to fall, the number of expatriates living abroad will likely increase in the future. One of the most challenging events a manager can face is an extended stay in a foreign location as an expatriate. While living abroad can oftentimes be stressful and time-consuming, the potential social and professional benefits are tremendous.

U.S. managers have been traveling the world for a number of years, keeping track of local operations for foreign-based subsidiaries. Globalization has spawned numerous export opportunities, and it is no longer uncommon to find strategic alliances, joint ventures, and mergers across borders. These trade relationships have helped generate more opportunities for expatriates to live abroad.

An expatriate is defined as "a citizen of one country who is working abroad in one of the firm's subsidiaries" (Jones, 2003: 459). Expatriates typically spend more than one year abroad, yet their tours of duty can range from a few months to three or more years. When an expatriate fails to complete an assignment and returns home early, the event is classified as "expatriate failure." Culture shock, or the uneasy feeling that an individual faces when attempting to adapt to a foreign culture, is a major factor in expatriate failure. When managers do eventually return home, they go through the repatriation process, or the process of readapting to one's home culture. Some managers also face reverse culture shock when they return home, especially if they have been away for an extended period of time.

The cultural distance, or perceived gap in cultural values between two countries, is generally looked to as a potential source of culture shock. Managers can prepare for a foreign assignment, thus reducing the impact of culture shock, in a number of ways. Language training is often essential to facilitate strong assimilation into the local culture. Attending a training program that reviews the laws, customs, rituals, and culture of the target destination can also be extremely helpful. Making contact with managers who have recently completed an assignment abroad is a worthwhile endeavor as well.

While the United States is the top destination for non-U.S. expatriates, tens of thousands of U.S. managers work abroad every year. U.S. managers tend to return home early at a higher rate than their European and Japanese counterparts. This trend is due in part to a lack of prior international experience, which has led to U.S. expatriate failure rates of approximately 25 percent from developed countries and 70 from developing countries (Jones, 2001). Other reasons for expatriate failure include language difficulty, family problems, and the specific job responsibility. The cost of this failure can range from $250,000 to $1 million depending on the nature of the assignment (Jones, 2001). And when managers return home, many will end up leaving their firms, regardless of whether or not they completed their assignment. Close to one-third of U.S. managers quit their jobs less than 2 years after returning home (Nelson, 2005). Reasons for this transition include better opportunities elsewhere, poor repatriation programs, and not being able to use new skills learned while abroad.

There are a number of factors to consider when evaluating a foreign assignment. The four articles in this chapter look at living and working abroad from a variety of perspectives. In her article "Preparing for Global Expansion: A Primer," Gail Reinhart assesses factors such as compensation, benefits, tax implications and the local culture from the Canadian expatriate's point of view. Reinhart also discusses the importance of understanding and maintaining the firm's corporate culture while abroad. Rebecca Knight highlights the financial challenges and options of a Scottish manager living in Dubai in her article "Use Your Offshore Status," The importance of properly managing investments back home is pivotal to Knight's article.

In the article "The Benefits of a Formal Repatriation Program for the Organization and the Expatriate" by Jan Nelson, a number of important issues related to returning home after living abroad are addressed. Nelson asserts that "there are several ways an organization can help an employee stay and feel connected while abroad," which is an essential ingredient in the repatriation process. Finally, Frederik Balfour and Dexter Roberts discuss a new phenomenon of expatriate managers jumping ship to work for local firms in China in their article "Stealing Managers from the Big Boys." Balfour and Roberts discuss how this trend came about and analyze a few specific recent examples of managers and executives who have left their U.S. firms for high-level Chinese jobs.

ISSUE ARTICLES

Gail Reinhart, "Preparing for Global Expansion: A Primer," *Canadian HR Reporter* (March 14, 2005).

Rebecca Knight, "Use Your Offshore Status," *Financial Times* (London Edition) (November 6, 2004).

Jan Nelson, "The Benefits of a Formal Repatriation Program for the Organization and the Expatriate," *Employee Benefit News* (November 1, 2005).

Frederik Balfour and Dexter Roberts, "Stealing Managers from the Big Boys," *Business Week* (September 26, 2005).

Larry Werner, "Helping Homesick Brits," *Business Insider* (August 8, 2005).

ARTICLE 7.1

Preparing for Global Expansion: A Primer

Gail Reinhart

PENSIONS, BENEFITS, TAXES AND A HOST OF HR ISSUES

Thousands of Canadian corporations with international operations are relocating employees overseas on a regular basis. But even the most seasoned international relocation managers can be taken by surprise if they, their companies and their relocating employees aren't fully informed and prepared.

For firms looking to branch out internationally for the first time, the issues can seem daunting. Extensive research may be required in regards to local hiring practices, the availability of skilled labour and employment regulations.

Just as HR professionals need to know the legal requirements on compensation, benefits, employment contracts and labour relations here in Canada, they will need to know how to incorporate the new country's laws and practices into their companies' operation. Finding in-country advice about local practices certainly makes the job easier.

Organizations should try to find someone who is specifically knowledgeable about how things work in the country they are researching. Lawyers, accountants and HR professionals are all good sources of information.

China is an example of where it is critical to know how to proceed. Developing relationships with government officials and local business people is a requirement for anyone attempting to set up an operation in China. It can take years of relationship building before a company becomes successful in opening a new venture. And don't rely on Canadian staff to be knowledgeable about how things work in another country. They are Canadian experts, after all.

Assisting Canadian employees and their families relocate overseas is one important aspect of going global. Most crucial is the need to ensure the individuals selected to work in the new location understand the organization's business strategy and corporate culture.

A heavy load rests on these employees; not only must they ensure that the business is profitable, but they will also represent the company in a different country and culture. Their ability to be accepted by the local staff, government officials and business people can make or break the overseas venture's success.

As many organizations have experienced, just because an individual is successful in one country does not mean that he will be equally as successful in another. If these Canadian representatives fail to be accepted into the local culture, they put their company's reputation at risk, which could make it very difficult to conduct business there. A relocation manager should be prepared to offer up the right tools to assist in identifying the most potentially successful candidates.

WHAT STAFF WILL WANT TO KNOW ABOUT HR'S ASSISTANCE

Employees who are considering an international assignment will want to know how working and living in another country will impact their compensation, benefits, and taxes and what kind of relocation assistance they will receive. While there are different ways to tackle all of these issues, the right strategy depends on the organization's corporate culture as much as anything. However, there are generally accepted practices within the international relocation industry that support the fair and equitable treatment of expatriate employees.

What are some difficulties that expatriates face when initially adjusting to living abroad?

For example, the balance sheet approach to compensation ensures that the employee retains a similar level of savings as in the home country, and does not have to pay more for the cost-of-living or taxes in the host location. Attempting to remunerate an employee in a foreign location at the same level as a peer at that location may reduce the standard of living of the expatriate and family. This type of localization can also be a severe cultural shock for the employee and could prevent a successful integration into the new work environment.

Benefits can also present difficulties if not investigated and managed correctly. Most domestic benefit providers have limited coverage for out-of-country expenses, and provincial health-care plans may not allow the expatriate and family to remain as part of the plan.

Reimbursing employees' benefit and dental expenses from an international location can be seriously delayed due to differences in language and currency, so finding an administrative solution is extremely important. For example, there are international benefit providers that not only set up an international benefit plan, they can also receive and pay employee claims.

As pension regulations differ from country to country, it would be wise to know the exact implications around a company's pension plan contributions. Verify whether Canada has a treaty regarding CPP and other government-mandated contributions. If the contributions are not processed correctly, the employee's future pension and CPP earnings may be put at risk.

Perhaps one of the most critical issues not to overlook is the tax implications of living and working in a foreign country. In many cases, Canada will have a tax treaty with the destination country. Such a treaty likely means that the employee has to pay tax only in one jurisdiction, not both. Always consult with a tax expert. Tax providers can also assist employees with completing their tax returns on an annual basis.

LAST BUT NOT LEAST AMONG TOPICS TO RESEARCH: IMMIGRATION REGULATIONS

Allowing employees to enter a foreign country without proper immigration papers can put both the company and the employee at significant risk. Not only could the employee be arrested and put in jail, the company could be blacklisted by immigration authorities, preventing any future employee's entry into the country. In some cases, even corporate representatives who knowingly allow or permit employees to enter foreign jurisdictions without proper documentation could be held personally liable for such actions. For most corporations just starting out, this is an area that generates significant pressure on HR, particularly as business managers are pressed to get relocating employees and families to the new location as quickly as possible.

In conclusion, a strategic and proactive HR professional ensures that she is involved in the process as soon as she first hears rumblings about "going global." The research may be painstaking and difficult, but the efforts will pay off handsomely when she is able to assist the organization in making the right business decisions.

Why do some expatriates return home early before their assignment is complete?

HOUSES AND SPOUSES

Firms Can Do More to Make Relocation Attractive, New Study Shows

With Canadian companies relocating 110,000 employees annually at a cost of about $1 billion there's a lot at stake financially. Unfortunately, elements that improve the chances of a successful move are sometimes missing, a study of 100 Canadian firms by Royal LePage Relocation Services shows.

The report, Emerging Trends in Employee Mobility notes the average Canadian company invests almost $20,000 to move a single employee to another location in the country, while large companies (with more than 1,000 employees) typically spend almost double that figure. But there are a number of employee benefits and services that are being overlooked.

According to companies surveyed, certain benefits are often still not available to relocating employees. The report yielded the following rather surprising results, notes Royal LePage:

- one out of five companies does not pay for legal fees;
- one in three does not pay for mortgage discharge penalties and land survey costs;
- one in three companies provides employees with a guaranteed home price plan;
- more than half of the employees surveyed do not provide employees with any assistance for duplication of housing costs (if the relocating employee is temporarily carrying the costs of two houses);

- four out of five companies pay the spouse's expenses;
- one out of every five companies does not pay for the spouse's airfare;
- fewer than one in four provide job counselling for the spouse;
- two per cent of companies help compensate for lost spousal income;
- one in four companies pay for baby-sitting and pet boarding while the parents are away on a house-hunting trip;
- three per cent of companies provide elder-care support during a house-hunting trip....

What are the most important benefits that should be negotiated prior to an expatriate assignment?

ARTICLE 7.2

Use Your Offshore Status

Rebecca Knight

Gary McLean, an accountant from the Scottish Highlands who lives and works in Dubai in the United Arab Emirates, is basking in the expatriate life.

A financial controller at an international steel company, McLean earns a salary of Pounds 40,000 a year and a bonus of Pounds 10,000.

The 29-year-old is entitled to a Pounds 12,000 housing allowance, a company car, country club membership, health insurance and education benefits—he is doing a company-sponsored MBA with Warwick University.

"With no income tax and expatriate benefits, the only things I spend money on are food and drink and travel," he says. "Plus Dubai is an excellent city. It's quite multicultural and there are lots of great restaurants."

McLean has Pounds 42,500 of savings and investments. He owns two mortgaged buy-to-let properties in Edinburgh. Both are loss-making.

The first—a two-bedroom ex-council flat valued at Pounds 120,000—he bought in the summer of 1998. "It's not in very good condition, it's got a leaky roof and I'd be happy to sell it," he says.

The second—a one-bedroom flat built in the 1870s and valued at Pounds 220,000—he purchased over the internet in 2003. "I bought it because I knew that I'd need a nicer place to live when I eventually move back." After all, he admits, there's no place like home. "I do miss the UK, especially British culture like radio, newspapers and theatre."

McLean's main concern is making the most of his expatriate status. He is domiciled in the UK but deemed a non-resident for tax purposes. What are his options?

Gillian Cardy, a certified financial planner at Professional Partnerships, says McLean should investigate offshore funds because his non-resident status means he is not liable for UK income and capital gains tax on non-UK assets.

"The range of offshore investments is wide and Gary should be able to find an offshore fund which can take monthly contributions or lump sums over a period of years," she says.

"McLean will benefit from the greater investment flexibility afforded by offshore funds—regulation is different, and potentially more lenient."

But Cardy cautions that when researching offshore funds, McLean should ensure that charges are fair and do not eat up the tax benefits.

"Gary should also be careful of offshore products sometimes badged as 'offshore pensions' which are nothing more than savings schemes—rather like endowments—and can often be extremely expensive."

If McLean returns to the UK, he can keep the funds invested offshore, but he may then become liable to income or CGT on the proceeds.

"He should therefore think carefully about when he plans to return and make sure that his investments are rearranged—especially gains realised on property and other investments—before he becomes subject to the UK tax regime again."

Allan Harragan, a certified financial planner at JBW Associates, agrees that McLean would be best served investing in offshore accounts.

But he warns: "Being an expatriate, Gary may receive the offer of advice from companies operating in the jurisdiction in which he is working. Gary should be aware that if he deals with an adviser, even if that adviser is British and the company the adviser represents is not based in the UK, he will not have any of the protection afforded by the UK investor protection legislation."

McLean is also unsure about what to do with his buy-to-let properties. With mortgage payments and rental agency fees, they are costing him Pounds 12,060 a year, Pounds 1,160 more than he is making in rental income.

"My two Edinburgh flats have increased in value," McLean says. "But I realise that my investments are probably too heavily weighted in property. In some ways, I feel that I should invest in the stock exchange now since the market is recovering."

Peter Nellist, of solicitors Clarke Willmott, recommends that Gary commission a surveyor's report on his two property investments.

"Next I suggest that Gary sells the two-bedroom flat on the basis that it has the poorer investment return. He should then use the Pounds 20,000 in proceeds to add to his Pounds 35,000 cash and reduce the mortgage on the other flat."

Harragan agrees, noting that if Gary continues to let the one-bedroom property, he will achieve a positive net yield of 2.23 per cent a year.

"Still not as good as if you put the money on deposit, but at least he keeps the place in which he wishes to live and sees some positive notional return, although with current inflation rates the true return is still negative."

As for the stock market, Harragan says Gary would be smart to consider collective investments.

"They offer a spread of risk and the option to select active investment management. He could consider using a growth-orientated fund of funds or manager of manager service. Such arrangements can be slightly more expensive than holding funds directly, but he will have sub-contracted fund selection, monitoring and management to a professional who will aim to deliver attractive long term returns."

If McLean fancies himself a gambling man, Nellist has a suggestion.

What are some of the major financial concerns when living and working abroad?

"If Gary wanted a flutter and was prepared to give up a guaranteed income return from a cash deposit, he could look at premium bonds," he says.

"If he wanted something more, then National Savings Certificates may be very boring but they offer a lot of security and a guaranteed return."

Cardy says that while Gary should be investing his surplus income in the stock market, he needs to be realistic. A guarded approach is necessary, she says.

"Gary's relative wealth arises mainly from his expatriate status, and if this were threatened for whatever reason, this would have a serious effect on his financial position, and an over-emphasis on equities could make him vulnerable."

The Benefits of a Formal Repatriation Program for the Organization and the Expatriate

Jan Nelson

Every year, thousands of Americans and their families return to the United States after completing overseas assignments. While the process may appear straightforward, repatriation can actually be quite complicated and stressful for all involved if the sponsoring organization does not have a formal repatriation program in place or doesn't partner with a relocation provider to ensure that the transition goes smoothly.

Reverse culture shock is real and, for many, feeling out of place in a setting that should be familiar can be quite challenging. In fact, almost one-third of repatriates end up quitting their jobs within two years of returning from abroad. Many of the reasons for leaving stem from not being properly prepared to return to their work and personal environments back in the U.S., and not being able to utilize skills that were learned abroad. A formal repatriation program is essential to prepare employees and their families to reintegrate into their professional and personal lives, as well as to ensure the investment that was made to send the employee overseas does not walk away to the competition upon the expatriate's return to the U.S.

FIRST THINGS FIRST

Repatriation is essentially running the relocation tape backwards; in other words, the steps that were taken to transfer an employee abroad happen in reverse when they come back to the U.S. There are several necessary first steps to relocate employees and their families back home, and many of them must happen simultaneously.

The family must first begin disengaging from their housing abroad, making any necessary repairs to the residence and recovering related security deposits. The process of disengaging children from their schools must also start, including obtaining school records, transcripts and health certificates that are required to register for school in the U.S. Discussions surrounding the moving of household goods must also begin, including details regarding shipping logistics and the weight limit allocated in the organization's relocation budget for the return shipment.

Another key element for those that have been aboard for more than three years is to check on, and in many cases re-establish, their credit history in the U.S. This can impact the purchase of a home, and with escalating home prices, many expatriates not only suffer from "sticker shock," they may also require assistance securing the best mortgage for their financial situation. On top of this, expatriates are also likely to have dual country tax complications at least a year after returning to the U.S., and will likely require tax assistance to ensure that everything is handled properly.

While approaching this process six months in advance is ideal, it is more often at three months that the wheels are set in motion; any time frame less than three months can lead to a hectic, stressful transition. For these reasons and more, including the fact that many organizations do not have the staff to support these concurrent activities, a relocation provider can be a cost-effective resource for ensuring that each step happens as needed.

What can firms do to ease the repatriation process?

WILL I HAVE A JOB?

Surprisingly, many expatriates are not guaranteed a position with the company upon their return to the U.S. Yet, even when they are, expatriates should stay in close contact with the organization's human resource department to begin the planning process and ensure there is an open position available upon return. Organizations also need to be aware that providing a position where the expatriate can make use of the skills learned while abroad is an important step to ensuring the employee's continued satisfaction with the company.

An organization risks losing all of the money it has invested to send the employee abroad if the repatriation process is not handled smoothly and the employee leaves the company. New faces, office politics and business procedures are just a few of the things that can equate to the employee walking into an overwhelmingly different culture.

There are several ways an organization can help an employee stay and feel connected with others while abroad. An informal mentoring program, conference calls that utilize video conferencing, regular visits back to the U.S. office, and sending additional employees to the foreign location all serve to keep the expatriate informed of changes in the corporate structure and mission.

THE IMPORTANCE OF STAYING IN TOUCH

It is very important for the employee and the family abroad not to slip into feeling isolated. Many HR departments don't stay closely involved with the expatriate family while they are overseas. One of the valuable aspects of working with a relocation provider is the use of a counselor who not only helps the family move abroad, but stays involved with the family while they are on assignment. The counselor can assist with adjustments to the foreign culture, such as setting up language lessons, and also acts as a liaison with HR providing valuable updates and information, such as notification of exchange rate changes that could affect the family's housing or cost-of-living allowance.

Readjusting to life in the U.S. is not as easy as one might think, and employees who are not offered repatriation training for themselves as well as their families can experience reverse culture shock that contributes to their decision to leave the company. If the family is not helped to reintegrate back into the U.S., the family's own disappointment and disillusionment can undermine the employee's commitment to staying with the company.

REPATRIATION TRAINING

Many organizations overlook this important aspect of repatriation, but providing the family with a one-day repatriation "training" program allows them to deal with all of the issues surrounding reverse culture shock. This training helps every member of the family understand what they have learned, the value of their overseas experience and the impact it will have on their life going forward. Each individual emerges from repatriation training with an action plan of what they can do to re-enter mainstream American life.

Whether offered through the organization or by a relocation provider, a formal repatriation program is a solid investment to help assist expatriates with every step of the transition process and optimizes the organization's chances of retaining these valuable employees.

ARTICLE 7.4

Stealing Managers From the Big Boys

Frederik Balfour and Dexter Roberts

What motivates managers to leave their firms while working as expatriates for jobs with local firms?

By just about any measure, Aaron Tong was a success. He was pulling down $100,000-plus as a senior manager of Motorola Inc.'s cellular division in Beijing and had worked in Singapore and the U.S. But two years ago, when TV-and-phone-maker TCL Corp. asked if Tong might accept a position as vice-president, he jumped at the chance. Although the modest salary hike and stock options were welcome, that wasn't what really attracted him. "They were offering me a more challenging job," says Tong, 42. At "a Chinese company, you can do a lot more important things than with a multinational."

Tong isn't the only Chinese manager being poached from the global giants. Tang Jun, president of NASDAQ-listed online gaming company Shanda Interactive Entertainment, served as president of Microsoft Corp.'s Chinese operations. Jean Cai, head of corporate communications at Lenovo, is a veteran of Ogilvy & Mather Worldwide and General Electric Co. Telecom equipment maker Huawei has hired people away from Motorola and Nokia, while Haier (appliances), China Netcom (telecoms), and Brilliance China Automotive Holdings have lured staffers from consultants McKinsey, A.T. Kearney, and Boston Consulting Group. "We spend a lot of time advising multinationals on how to hold on to their best people," says Bill Henderson, managing partner for China at headhunters Egon Zehnder International.

This migration is a big change from five years ago, when no self-respecting white-collar worker in China would have dreamed of quitting a foreign company to join a local outfit. These days the turbo-charged growth, global aspirations, and deep pockets of China's ambitious private companies are looking better all the time. In 2000 locals made up just 20% to 30% of the managers recruited in China by headhunter Heidrick & Struggles. Today that figure is 60% to 70%. Local companies are "cherry-picking the best talent," says Steve Mullinjer, managing partner for China at Heidrick. He should know. One of his top consultants recently jumped ship to work as chief financial officer for a Heidrick client.

Managers say working for local companies lets them take on more responsibility and make a greater contribution. That's what made Wu Xianyong, a 34-year-old native of the southern province of Yunnan, quit flogging Crest toothpaste and Pringles potato chips for Procter & Gamble Co. In 2004, after nearly nine years at P&G, he jumped at the chance to serve as vice-president for marketing at Li-Ning, China's top athletic-shoe maker and sports apparel marketer. He has since taken on oversight of international business as well. "Li-Ning can provide me with a much better platform to play on," says Wu, who also snagged a 50% raise plus generous stock options. "I'm not just managing a brand. I do sports marketing, events, and PR, and I manage research." In fact, Li-Ning is chock-full of multinational alums: The vice-president for sales formerly worked at Avon Products Inc., the vice-president for footwear came from Nike Inc., and the chief financial officer left news wire Reuters Group PLC.

Much of the shift stems from global aspirations. By hiring execs with experience at multinationals, the Chinese figure, they'll have a leg up when they go abroad. For instance Gome, China's No. 2 retailer, has ambitious plans to expand. So in January it recruited Weng Xiangwei, a 37-year-old former vice-president in Morgan Stanley's mergers-and-acquisitions team, as its strategy chief and financial guru. "When a company grows to a certain size, it needs to think about more than just where to open its next store," says Weng, a Shanghai native with a PhD in biophysics from the University of California at Berkeley.

Some managers take a pay cut when they jump ship—although stock options often fill in the gap. That trend will accelerate as more private Chinese companies list on overseas stock markets. Deng Kangming, for example, saw his salary drop by 20% when he left his job as head of human resources at Microsoft in Beijing for a similar job at Net auctioneer Alibaba Technology, but he was granted a generous dollop of options. Two years ago, 27-year-old Zhou Donglei took a 35% cut when she left Japan's Softbank Infrastructure Fund in Beijing to run business development and investor relations at Shanda. "What drew me was the opportunity, definitely not the salary," says Zhou.

Yet salary can play a role in many searches, especially for sought-after talents such as finance. One veteran of the Bank of China saw his pay jump in just six months from $70,000 to $180,000 after a bidding war broke out for his talents among a foreign bank and two Chinese companies, according to Heidrick & Struggles: The manager ended up as CFO for a local valve maker.

China's state-owned giants are also likely to pay a premium to woo talent. For instance, Ping An Insurance Group, China's second-largest life insurer, has hired managers away from Canadian Imperial Bank of Commerce and American International Group—often upping their pay by as much as 50%. Ping An just hired a manager with five years of experience at an international bank for $65,000 per year—a huge sum in China, and 40% more than he was making at his old job.

Most telling of all, Chinese companies are even starting to look overseas for talent. Michael Zhang, a 37-year-old native of Sichuan province, worked for four years at medical device maker Guidant Corp. before being recruited as CEO of Microport Medical (Shanghai) Co., which makes stents used in unblocking arteries. He, in turn, hired 33-year-old Zhao Ruilin, who had joined rival device-maker Medtronic Inc. in Minneapolis after earning a PhD from a Harvard University/Massachusetts Institute of Technology joint program in health sciences and technology, as well as an MBA from the Wharton School. Zhao now serves as Microport's vice-president for business development and strategic planning. He earns just $60,000—a bit more than half what he made at Medtronic, though he also gets free housing. Still, he says, the greater responsibilities he has, coupled with Microport's hypergrowth—sales this year are expected to triple, to $30 million—make up for the pay cut. "Working for this company is so much fun," Zhao says. "Now I'm interacting with bankers, private equity shops, lawyers, and accountants."

The drive for talent by China's best companies feeds into the boom for middle and upper managers at both multinationals and local firms. One recruiter estimates managing directors at Chinese state-owned companies can earn up to $300,000 a year plus a car and housing, while middle managers with the right skills pull down $70,000 or more. Annual raises of about 13% to 14% are necessary to hold on to employees, while poachers offer pay jumps of 20% to 30%, according to Hong Kong recruiting firm Bo Le Associates. "For mid-level management, the market is really hot," says Bo Le managing director Louisa Wong Rousseau.

And don't expect things to cool off anytime soon. China will need 75,000 globally capable execs in the next five years but has fewer than 5,000 today, estimates McKinsey. As long as multinationals in China train locals to run their operations, there's likely to be no shortage of mainland rivals eager to snatch them away.

Many managers will leave their jobs after completing a foreign assignment and returning home. What are some of the motivations for this career move?

Helping Homesick Brits

Larry Werner

His love for a Minnesota woman led Brendan Ryan to the Twin Cities from England. His love for things British led Ryan from his corporate job to a home-based business that provides a variety of services to fellow transplants from the United Kingdom.

Ryan, founder and president of a company called Brits in America, is projecting $500,000 in revenue this year from a business built on the notion that the transition from England to America isn't as easy as people might think. His business, which began as a simple website in 1999, offers expatriate Brits a connection to their culture in the United States and offers U.S. businesses his contacts in England.

"It's a misconception that not only Americans have, but British have, that when we move here we don't see any cultural differences," Ryan said in the basement office of his south Minneapolis home. "When you come in as an outsider, the culture smacks you in the face and you see things people living within that culture don't necessarily see. As relatively intelligent people we can take those things we see and turn them into a business."

The business, which provides Ryan with a salary of $55,000, started out as a hobby for a transplanted real estate agent who was nostalgic for England after settling in Minneapolis. While working for a Twin Cities relocation company that bought houses from corporate transferees, Ryan put together www.britsinamerica.com. The website contained information on real estate for British immigrants and eventually added sections on entertainment, sports and TV programming of interest to Brits.

Soon, companies were buying advertising on the site, and by the time he quit his corporate job last December, he had built a network of people across the country who shared his passion for helping people make the U.K.-to-U.S transition. Most of the revenue came from fees paid by more than 200 British real estate agents around the country who get clients through Ryan's website. With revenue of about $120,000, Ryan quit his job with the relocation service last year and took on two partners.

One, Michael Belfield, is a real estate agent who coordinates the company's real estate services, and the other, Simon Dawson, a food-company marketer,

What are some cultural differences that have frustrated some British expats in the United States?

coordinates marketing services for U.K. companies seeking U.S. consumers and American companies who want help making contacts in England. Belfield and Dawson, who also emigrated to the Twin Cities from Great Britain, have kept their day jobs while Ryan pursues new revenue streams for the little company.

"I met Brendan through the website," said Belfield, who moved here 12 years ago because he, like Ryan, met a Minnesota woman who is now his wife. "As Englishmen, everyone thinks we speak the same language and it's very easy to move here. We found there's a definite need for people moving from England to the U.S. to help them with their real estate needs."

It wasn't long before visitors to the website suggested other ways Brits in America could help with the cultural transition.

"One of the things we struck on was the desire to get into the entertainment industry," Ryan said.

THE SOCCER CONNECTION

The entertainment services included information about U.S. tours by British musical groups and TV programming that would be of interest to expats. Another opportunity that emerged was connecting Brits in America with their favorite sport. After Ryan put together a trip to Chicago for a soccer match between the English national team and the United States team, he got an e-mail testimonial from a Twin Cities father, who wrote: "My son thinks I'm the best father in the world. Little does he know all I did is telephone you."

The company also takes British immigrants to Twins games for a taste of America's past time.

Ryan said event management won't be a big money-maker for his company, but television production might be. He said American TV networks don't understand the tastes of viewers who grew up with British television. Because he does understand it, he approached the Fox cable network with an idea for a reality show based on the adventures of an English professional soccer team in the United States. Ryan was surprised when the Fox Soccer Channel asked him to put together budgets and scripts.

"I was expecting them to say, 'We don't accept submissions,' " Ryan said. "But I was put through to the director of programming for the network, and he gave us a submission agreement. We're now going after production companies asking for bidding for this TV show."

Other services being planned by the company are tours for British immigrants in partnership with a travel company and an expanded, full-service website that the owners envision as Yahoo with a British accent.

BRANCHING OUT

Ryan and Belfield said their cultural-connections business has led them to think about launching similar websites that connect expatriates from other European countries. And while they love their home country, they are convinced that the United States is a much better place than Great Britain for entrepreneurs and their wild ideas.

"Back in the U.K., if we went to the corporate people with these ideas, we'd have been walked out by security," Ryan said.

Belfield said, "The opportunities here are endless. I don't know if it's that way anywhere else in the world. I think Americans in general are just more open-minded to ideas."

The expert's opinion: John McVea, an assistant professor of entrepreneurship at the University of St. Thomas College of Business, said Brits in America is an example of a startup whose strategy emerges over time.

"Traditionally, we think of the startup process in terms of 'ready, aim, fire,' "said McVea, who grew up in Ireland and worked in the United Kingdom. "However, on many occasions, it is possible to take a 'fire, ready, steer' approach, where the entrepreneur starts with what unique resources they already have—in this case a knowledge of expatriate frustrations—and asks, 'How can I make a business out of this?' "

In using this approach, McVea said, it's critical to keep overhead low at the start and to stay flexible while customers and other stakeholders guide the development of a strategy.

McVea said the would-be entrepreneur might ask: "What do I know that no one else does?"

"I would be wary of trying to translate unique knowledge of the British expatriate experience into other expatriate cultures, which may have entirely different demands," McVea said. "It might be less risky to continue to grow the British theme in new directions."

How would an "Americans in England" business help U.S. managers adapt to U.K. culture?

ISSUE SUMMARY

Managers that agree to serve in an overseas capacity for an extended period of time face an array of challenges before, during, and after their experiences as expatriates. Prior to moving abroad, it is important to prepare as much as possible for the journey. Language and cultural training are essential components to successful adjustment. It is also recommended that contact be made with employees who have had prior experience in the target foreign destination. Studying the local laws, political situation, and economic conditions also aid in the process of cultural adaptation. Prior to departure, managers should also fine-tune financial details, such as accounting for any salary adjustments and additional benefits and expenses that will be incurred while out of the country. Gail Reinhart recommends the balance sheet approach to expatriate compensation, which ensures that similar savings levels are maintained as if the employee were working in the home country.

One major point of transformation that most expatriates experience is culture shock. Culture shock can hit people differently depending on their prior experiences, emotional maturity, and the cultural distance between the home and host country. As Reinhart points out, it is important to work out all of the compensation and benefits details prior to arriving in the foreign location since legal and costof- living differences can add additional stress. Building relationships is a significant, yet important, challenge in some cultures, such as China, and a vital ingredient in the cultural adaptation process. Managers should also realize that they are ambassadors for their firms, and maintaining a high-level reputation is essential.

The repatriation process is a very important phase of the international work experience. According to Rebecca Knight, expatriates must manage their investments back home to assure a smooth transition. Putting aside enough funds to assist with mortgage payments and keeping retirement contributions at a reasonable level are key strategies. Knight asserts that balancing investments across real estate, mutual funds, and retirement accounts can be a challenging but worthwhile endeavor.

Firm's can help ease the effects of reverse culture shock by implementing repatriation programs. A typical repatriation program will assist workers with housing problems, school-related issues for children, and tax complications stemming from time spent abroad. It is also imperative that the employee and employer communicate regarding available positions in the home office.

Expatriates become valuable commodities, and if firms don't cultivate strong relations with their workers, there is always a chance that someone could jump ship for another firm. Nelson contends that over 30 percent of expats leave their jobs after returning home. Balfour and Roberts correctly point out that some highly qualified managers may leave their firms while abroad and take a job with a local firm. Sending a manager to work abroad is a major investment, and the entire expatriation process, from pre-departure to return home, must be carefully monitored to maximize the experience for all parties involved.

ISSUE HIGHLIGHTS

- Preparing for time spent abroad is a crucial component in the potential success of an expatriate.
- Compensation for expatriates is often adjusted due to differences in tax rates and cost of living.
- It is important for expatriates to understand that they are reflections of their firm's corporate culture while working abroad.
- Managing investments and savings while living overseas can be complicated.
- Many managers experience both culture shock and reverse culture shock.
- Firms can assist a manager's adjustment to the home office with a strong repatriation program.
- Many managers leave their firms during and after the expatriate experience.
- Some firms, such as Brits in America, have leveraged cultural differences to help expatriates adjust to new locations.

CRITICAL THINKING

1. A number of challenges exist when a manager is faced with the opportunity to live abroad. Preparing for cultural and standard-of-living differences can be time-consuming. Finding a house that is amenable to a manager's lifestyle can also be difficult. Understanding the local work habits and actual differences in job responsibilities is an essential step in successful adjustment to the foreign assignment. The thread that cuts through the multitude of overseas challenges is the emotional maturity of the expatriate manager. Moreover, prior international experience is extremely helpful in the adaptation process.
2. Culture shock and reverse culture shock are stages that an expatriate may face depending upon the assigned country and the manager's prior experience abroad. The extent to which an expatriate faces culture shock depends primarily on the cultural distance between the home and host culture. Language and cultural training can help alleviate some of the effects of culture shock. Many managers experience an uneasy feeling when they return from their overseas assignments. This reverse culture shock can be minimized through repatriation training programs.

3. Sending a manager off on an international experience is a major commitment for an organization. The financial costs of expatriates are extremely high to firms because of a number of expenses that are typically part of a manager's compensation and benefits package. Firms will typically pay a cost-of-living adjustment or hardship premium on top of base pay to adjust for local market conditions. Other benefits often include housing allowance, tuition reimbursement for children, club membership dues and flights home for the entire family. Training and developmental costs can also be high which is why many organizations are extremely careful when deciding which manager to send off on a foreign assignment.

ADDITIONAL READING RESOURCES

C. Christopher Baughn and Mark A. Buchanan, "Cultural Protectionism," *Business Horizons* (November- December 2001), pp. 5–15.

Charles W.L. Hill, *Global Business*, 2nd ed. (McGraw- Hill Irwin, 2001).

Jennifer Joan Lee, "Tax Relief in Sight for Expats; Working in France," *The International Herald Tribune* (December 13, 2003), p. 11.

Andrew Taylor, "London Is Europe's Dearest City for Expats Cost of Living," *Financial Times* (June 20, 2005), p. 4.

Joanne Wojick and Sarah Veysey, "Expatriate Health Coverage Often Hard to Coordinate," *Business Insurance* (January 26, 2004), p. 10.

http://www.actionamerica.org

http://www.oecd.org

Why Is It So Important to Understand Cultural Differences When Working Abroad?

O ne of the greatest challenges for managers operating in foreign environments is developing an ability to cope with cultural differences. A number of factors can lead to cultural misunderstanding, such as a lack of experience abroad, inability to speak the local language, and inadequate preparation and training. Cultural distance, or the perceived gap in values between two distinct cultures, also plays a significant role in a manager's ability to adjust to a foreign environment. It is certainly easier for an American manager to adapt to British culture (low cultural distance) than to Vietnamese culture (high cultural distance). Nevertheless, culture is an important factor when conducting business abroad, and the development of a comprehension of the various complexities involved with doing business in a foreign land can become an excellent strength for a manager.

What is culture? Culture is generally defined as the values, beliefs, rituals, and attitudes held by a certain group of people. Cultural groups can bridge multiple nations, and most nations have multiple cultural groups, or subcultures, within their borders. Culture can be broken down into a number of distinct components such as religion, language, aesthetics, customs, and traditions. Moreover, each of these components of culture can typically be segregated even further. Take language, for example. Languages tend to vary by country, yet each country often has its own dialect. The English spoken in Australia varies from the English spoken in Canada. Within Canada, French and English are both official languages. In India, there are more than 15 official languages and over 100 dialects. Many managers around the world default to a *lingua franca*, or a common international language, when doing business with foreigners. In recent years, English has taken the lead as the primary lingua franca, yet French, in Africa for example, and other languages, such as Spanish and Chinese, still carry significant levels of regional importance.

Cultural values tend to vary along a variety of dimensions. Researcher Geert Hofstede developed five cultural dimensions named uncertainty avoidance, power distance, masculinity, individualism, and Confucian Dynamism. These dimensions were designed to capture cultural beliefs about ability to cope with ambiguity, respect for authority and power, assertiveness, group versus individual orientation, and perception of time. The United States, for example, was found to be highly individualistic, while Japanese culture embraces more collectivistic values. Further, in the United States, people cope with uncertainty quite well, while in Japan people tend to avoid uncertainty using structured planning as a coping mechanism.

In her article, "Found in Translation: Consultant Bridges Cultural Differences," Deborah Willoughby assesses the situation that a young consultant from Alabama faces when confronted with a job as an intermediary between U.S. and South Korean firms. Issues such as language, mannerisms, and workplace traditions are discussed. Keith Bradsher, in his article "Disney Tailors Hong Kong Park for Cultural Differences," describes a number of the policies that have been considered by Disney for its new Hong Kong theme park. Disney has instituted a number of measures, such as offering local food items and requiring workers to speak in two Chinese dialects, that are geared toward cultural adaptation. Robert Matthews describes the recent results of a cultural perception experiment in his article. The results reaffirm that Eastern and Western perceptions are culturally based and vary significantly when faced with different contexts. Moreover, Matthews asserts that Asians tend to place more emphasis on the context of a situation when compared to Americans.

In her article about culture shock in Italy, Emma Bird describes the challenges that she faced when she moved to Milan as an expatriate. Bird examines issues related to relocation assistance and companionship, and she outlines some effective strategies for adapting to a foreign assignment. Rick Vecchio takes a good look at the dynamic and transitioning culture in Peru in his article "From Presidency to Pop to Supermarkets, Andean Culture Blossoms in Peruvian Society." A number of underlying cultural complexities ranging from racism to poverty to history are addressed in the context of today's society in Peru. While developing a certain level of cultural literacy takes a significant amount of time and effort, the articles provided here should be useful as an overview of some of the major issues that a manager is likely to face when working in a foreign environment.

ISSUE ARTICLES

Deborah Willoughby, "Found in Translation: Consultant Bridges Cultural Differences," *Montgomery Advertiser* (August 14, 2005).

Robert Matthews, "Where East Can Never Meet West," *The Financial Times* (October 21, 2005).

Keith Bradsher, "Disney Tailors Hong Kong Park for Cultural Differences," *The International Herald Tribune* (October 13, 2004).

Emma Bird, "Culture Shocks Abroad," *The Guardian (London)* (January 29, 2005).

Rick Vecchio, "From Presidency to Pop to Supermarkets, Andean Culture Blossoms in Peruvian Society," *The Associated Press* (January 4, 2006).

Found in Translation: Consultant Bridges Cultural Differences

Deborah Willoughby

Jay Townsend, an Alabamian in Asia, was starting to feel homesick. After years of teaching English and managing a factory in Korea, he was thinking about coming home. Then he started reading about Hyundai building an automotive plant in Montgomery. Hmmm.

"Of all things, this place where I spent so much of my life happened to be investing in Alabama," he said. "For me, it was the neatest thing in the world. That definitely was fate or some kind of divine guidance."

Townsend moved to Montgomery and opened Balhae/USA Business Consulting in January. Balhae (pronounced ball-hey) is the name of an ancient kingdom that was in Korea and northeast China, places where Townsend has lived and worked.

With Balhae, Townsend is smoothing the cultural and business interactions between American companies and Korean, Chinese and Japanese companies.

"I am helping executives with communications strategies with an emphasis on Alabama culture," he said.

One example: "The Korean language is very flat," Townsend said. As a result, some Southerners who are accustomed to the cadences and extra syllables of Southern English can mistakenly think a Korean businessman is being unfriendly or cold just because of the way he talks.

"To have good relations with Southerners, let your voice go up and down," he tells clients. "You'll come across as more friendly."

Townsend also works with U.S. companies during multinational business meetings.

"A lot of Koreans prefer to have a native speaker of Korean be in meetings as an interpreter. It makes them comfortable. The English-speaking side likes to have me around. There are nuances—'Is he going to follow up on what he said?'—that I can explain. I can debrief them about body language after meetings."

Lisa McGinty, director of small business programs for the Montgomery Area Chamber of Commerce, said Townsend's consulting business is a perfect example of how the business community is adapting as the multicultural landscape changes.

Why is learning the language such an important window into the local culture?

"Jay is another example among many of the talent that we raise here," McGinty said. "He has gone out and experienced so many things in the world, and he has brought his talents back to Alabama."

Michael B. O'Connor, managing partner at Slaten & O'Connor PC, already has experience with the kind of assistance that Townsend can provide.

"At my law firm, we work with many of the Korean suppliers and vendors who come into this state. When I was over in Korea meeting with my clients, he was able to help me tremendously, not only on the language part but on the culture," O'Connor said. "He was able to explain to me that what people think of as the Old South—the respect for elders and history and those types of things—are very similar to Korea's culture."

O'Connor is excited by the international business relationships being built in Montgomery.

"Think about what (Korean manufacturers) are doing for Alabama. They chose my home state. They've given a gift to the state of Alabama, which is an opportunity for people like Jay and for the guy or woman who is working on the line," he said. "Jay is able to take everything he learned and put it to use for himself, but just as importantly, he's able to help his home state. He took a very long journey to come back to Alabama."

Townsend's sense of adventure has taken him far from Alabama, and back. Some stops included:

- Birmingham. After receiving his bachelor's degree in French language and literature from Davidson College in North Carolina, Townsend worked at Birmingham Southern College—in his hometown—as director of its language lab.
- Montpelier, France. While an undergraduate, Townsend spent a year abroad. "That was my first exposure to the outside world. It motivated me to see the world," he said.
- Tuscaloosa. A master's degree in teaching English as a second language, and a master's in business administration, both from the University of Alabama, were his tickets to finding jobs in far-flung places.
- Abu Dhabi, United Arab Emirates. "I was looking for something exotic, and I found it," he said of his year teaching English in the Middle East.
- Pusan, South Korea. Townsend taught English for three years at Pusan National University. "I had heard the students were hardworking. They showed me so much respect," he said.
- Fushun, Manchuria, in northeastern China. Townsend taught English for six months and in the process got a preview of the economic power-house China would become. "These engineers I was teaching in 1997 had hardly any money, but they were motivated to make money and learn about America," he said.
- Daegu, South Korea. For three years, Townsend was general manager of an American-owned manufacturing plant.

"Nobody in the company spoke a lick of English," he said. "I was communicating with company headquarters about Korean culture and business practices and to the Korean employees about American culture and business practices, and negotiating between the two."

Ultimately, there were a lot of compromises and combinations of business styles.

"At almost all Korean companies, lunches are provided by the company. A local restaurant brings in the food. It was unthinkable for the Koreans to do it a different way. That was not negotiable, and Korean culture won," he said. "The company has a stellar reputation for quality, and it has unique business practices that are competitively advantageous techniques. That was easy to teach to the Koreans."

What are some workplace traditions that tend to vary by culture?

ARTICLE 8.2

Where East Can Never Meet West

Robert Matthews

E ast is meeting west like never before. Yet as those on either side of the table often find, it is not always a meeting of minds. The gulf is wider than mere differences in how to address the boss and what food to serve at meetings.

Research is revealing fundamental differences in perception, logic and even models of reality between eastern and western cultures, with implications for business people trying to bridge the divide.

It is almost a cliche that people from south-east Asian countries think more holistically than those in the west, who focus more on specifics and details. Now psychologists at the University of Michigan have shown that this difference extends to how those in each culture see the world around them.

A team led by social psychologist Richard Nisbett compared the eye movements of groups of Chinese and American students as they studied pictures of objects placed within surroundings—such as a tiger in a forest. The researchers found that the American students focused on the central object while the Chinese students spent more time scanning the background, putting the object in context.

According to the researchers, the different strategies for observation reflect deep cultural differences developed during childhood and encouraged by parents anxious that their offspring fit into society. "East Asians live in relatively complex social networks with prescribed role relations," say the researchers, whose results were published last month in the proceedings of the National Academy of Sciences. "Attention to context is, therefore, important for effective functioning. In contrast, westerners live in less constraining social worlds that stress independence and allow them to pay less attention to context." In other words, people raised in the east literally see the world differently from westerners. But the effects extend to more abstract issues, such as perceptions of cause and effect. With their focus on the individual, westerners tend to view events as the result of specific agents, while those raised in the east set the events in a broader context.

For example, an analysis of reports of crimes in English- and Chinese-language newspapers by Michael Morris of Stanford University and Kaiping

What is meant by cultural context? How do cultures vary with respect to context?

Peng at Berkeley found that the former tend to focus on the personality traits of the perpetrators. In contrast, reports published in Chinese newspapers stressed context—such as the perpetrators' background and relationships.

According to Prof Nisbett, this emphasis on traits instead of context can make westerners more prone to fall for the so-called "fundamental attribute" error—in which, say, an anxious interviewee is deemed nervous by nature and thus unsuitable for high-stress posts. "Easterners are more likely to notice important situational factors and to realise they play a role," says Prof Nisbett.

Cultural differences also pervade beliefs about how the world around us is put together. In a series of experiments at Keio University in Japan, researchers presented groups of Japanese and Americans with pyramid-shaped objects made from cork, whimsically called "daxes". They presented the groups with two trays: one with cork objects in different shapes, the other with pyramid-shaped objects made from other materials. When asked which tray contained more "daxes", the Americans pointed to the objects with the pyramidal shape, regardless of the fact they were made of different materials. In contrast, the Japanese went for the tray with cork objects, regardless of their shape.

What are some important components of culture beyond language?

This, say the researchers, hints at basic differences in perceptions of the world. The "analytic-minded" Americans perceive a world full of different-shaped objects, while those from "holistic-minded" Japan perceive it in terms of related substances. Thus where westerners see a road made of tarmac, the Japanese see tarmac in the form of a road.

The two cultures differ on their view of logic. Research by, among others, Profs Nisbett and Peng shows that westerners have a deep-seated distaste for contradictions, while those raised in the east see them as valuable in understanding relations between objects or events. Both responses have deep roots: Aristotle, the founder of western logic, ruled contradictions as inadmissible, while eastern philosophers had no such qualms.

With psychologists investigating and finding more differences between the two cultures, it is natural to ask who has the most successful approach—or, at least, it is natural for westerners struggling with the idea that both approaches could be best, depending on the context.

In his book *The Geography of Thought* Prof Nisbett argues that the growing links between east and west are likely to spawn new perceptions of how the world works, with benefits for both cultures. In the meantime, westerners struggling to break the ice with their business counterparts in the east can try out one of Prof Nisbett's tests: chicken, cow and grass—which two go together? If you pair the chicken and the cow, chances are you are one of the object-obsessed Occidentals hoping to do business with the relationship-savvy people on the other side of the table.

ARTICLE 8.3

Disney Tailors Hong Kong Park
for Cultural Differences

Keith Bradsher

Walt Disney is taking a series of steps to address local cultural sensitivities as the company prepares to open Hong Kong Disneyland a little more than a year from now, its president said here Tuesday night.

The theme park, long controversial here because of lavish investment in it by the local government, will include local food and music and provide services not only in English but two forms of Chinese, said Robert Iger, Disney's president and chief operating officer. He described these steps as part of a broad effort by the company to recognize national differences around the world.

"We know if we're too U.S.-centric, the products won't be too relevant to those markets," Iger said. "That's particularly true as it relates to Hong Kong Disneyland."

Esther Wong, a Hong Kong Disneyland spokeswoman, said that the company had rotated the orientation of the entire park by several degrees in the early design phase after consulting a master of feng shui, a Chinese geomantic practice of seeking harmony with spiritual forces.

On the master's advice, the company also designated part of one kitchen as an area where no fire would be allowed, so as to maintain the proper balance of forces there, she said.

"This is essentially an American product, but it's a question of how we tailor it to an audience in this part of the world," Wong said. "Disney is an American brand, and our guests, our potential guests, believe in this product."

As Disney prepares to open the park, including the broadcast of the first television ads in Shanghai starting Thursday, there are some signs of growing anti-American sentiment here. A survey of nine Asian countries and territories released Monday found that 47 percent of residents here held a negative opinion of the United States, second only to Indonesia.

Gallup and TNS, a London-based market information company, conducted the survey, which reported that the poor opinion had been shaped mainly by U.S. foreign policy, with residents still holding a much higher opinion of the American economy.

The survey did not include mainland China, where simmering nationalism has most recently been directed against Japan, but where anti-American protests did erupt five years ago after the accidental bombing of the Chinese Embassy in Belgrade.

Eden Woon, chief executive of the Hong Kong General Chamber of Commerce, which was the host for Iger's speech, said that he saw very little chance of any anti-U.S. protests here and doubted that any such sentiments here would hurt Hong Kong Disneyland.

"China always is conflicted between accepting foreign things and trying to maintain its own culture," he said.

The park is being built with 22.45 billion Hong Kong dollars, or $2.88 billion, in investments by the Hong Kong government. The government provided the land and is building road and rail links to it, although some of the road and rail costs might have been incurred even if the theme park had not been built.

The government owns 57 percent of the park, and Disney owns the rest. The government also holds subordinated shares that would convert to ordinary shares, raising the government's ownership as high as 75 percent, if the park does much better than originally envisioned.

How did Disney alter its Hong Kong theme park to adapt for the local culture?

Many here were upset after the deal was signed by the disclosure that Disney was in separate talks to open another theme park in Shanghai. Disney has not concluded any deals in Shanghai, however, and has said that any park there would not open before 2010.

Iger said that Disney already employed 1,000 people in Hong Kong, and would employ 5,000 by the time the park opens. Many theme park employees will speak both Cantonese, the language of southeastern China, including most Hong Kong residents, and Mandarin, the mainland's main language and the language of school instruction.

An unemployment rate of 6.9 percent helped prompt 5,000 people here to apply recently for 500 jobs as "cultural representatives" who would go to Walt Disney World in Florida in January and stay there for training until next summer. They will then return to Hong Kong to train other workers for the opening of the park.

What are some factors that led to Disney's conclusion that a theme park in Hong Kong would be successful?

While Iger said that the park would open in roughly a year, Disney executives have been careful to say that opening day could come in either late 2005 or early 2006.

ARTICLE 8.4

Culture Shocks Abroad

Emma Bird

I already spoke Italian fluently and had lived in six European cities. Moving to Milan on my own was going to be a breeze, wasn't it? Well, it wasn't. And judging by other people's experiences, I'm not the only one so blinded by the thrills of being paid to go abroad that I failed to read the small print.

Expat discussion forums are a popular meeting point for young workers abroad who clearly aren't enjoying themselves as much as they thought they would be. "Help, I'm bored to death," writes a 24-year-old in Rotterdam. "I moved to Rotterdam in October and all the expats I've been meeting so far are older than me."

International work is no longer the province of a few select senior managers, but has become everyday enough to cross the desk of juniors, too. More and more graduates are increasingly opting to study, live and work outside of their home countries in pursuit of professional success and adventure along the way.

"On the surface, they know lots of people, are sociable and have great jobs," says author Margaret Malewski about the people she calls GenXpat. "But on a deeper level, it's really, really hard. They make acquaintances but not really friends and end up living a lonely life out of suitcases and five-star hotels."

Margaret knows only too well what expat assignments involve. She has just written *GenXpat: The Young Professional's Guide to Making a Successful Life Abroad* which will be published this spring by Intercultural Press. In 1992 she left her native Montreal to study at the University of Warsaw before joining Proctor & Gamble in 1998. Margaret worked in Geneva and Tel Aviv before repatriating back to Vancouver in 2002 where she lives today.

But beware. Margaret, now 29, makes the challenge of perennial city hopping in search of spirit and adventure seem easy. However, unless you are well-prepared and have a good expat package, it can turn into little more than misery and a constant longing for friends, family and fried breakfasts.

When I moved to Milan, I thought I had the basics covered but now that I am a corporate relocation consultant I realise my support package was nonexistent. Never having sent anyone on international assignment before, my bosses had no idea just how difficult it is to get things done in Italy.

No relocation agency was used and I was left to sort out everything, from looking for a place to rent and contacting the utility providers, to finding a hire car all the while making contacts and interviewing fashion and textile personalities for the magazines who had hired me.

Jon Perry, a GenXpat originally from Wimborne, Dorset, works for a City law firm. A few months after joining he was sent to Singapore on a short-term assignment but he admits he never really integrated. Now, three years on, the former Oxford student has just been relocated to Hong Kong and is conscious he needs to make this experience work.

"My career is at a more important stage," says Jon, 27. "I no longer feel I'm going on an extended holiday and three years is definitely long enough to miss home. At the same time, the security of having a 'gang' isn't there so I was worried the first months might have been a bit lonely. Being single, I can see that the experience would probably be less daunting if I had moved out to Hong Kong with a partner."

Overseas postings can be lonely for everyone but for young single professionals especially. As happened to me, often the only thing set up for GenXpats when they go abroad is their work: they get a desk, a boss and a new job to prove themselves at. Meeting people in a foreign setting and in a foreign language is a challenge for everyone and even the most outgoing types often suffer from chronic shyness and inhibition.

When you don't know anyone, you have three choices: go out to a restaurant or bar by yourself, stay in your flat watching an incomprehensible foreign language TV channel, or work overtime to avoid going home to an empty house. But the more you work, the less of a life you have, so the more you work … suddenly you are trapped in a vicious circle.

Last month, Shell had 7,400 employees on international assignments, 400 of whom were in the 21-30 age bracket. The oil giant takes very seriously the challenges that their GenXpats face. "Younger expats commonly are not married and take the assignments as singles," a company spokesperson says. "In some locations this results in different challenges as many of the social networks tend to revolve around partners and children."

It seems that young expats who work for Shell in the Netherlands may well be luckier than most for, in addition to its briefings prior to departure and again in the host country, the company sponsors the 'Outpost' network which assists expatriates with day-to-day living.

But for Margaret Malewski even this strategy doesn't go far enough: "In an ideal world, employers should make an effort to recognise the challenges of expat life and continue to adapt their packages to reflect the changing profile of their expat populations." She does stress, though, that the onus is also on employees to find out about the destination before they get there, making the employer aware that they'd be happy to have a cheap studio flat in the city centre and use public transport but in return they want a monthly flight home.

What are some benefits and drawbacks of entering into an expatriate assignment alone?

What are some techniques for assimilating into the local culture?

The key to weathering the rollercoaster of emotions you will experience while abroad is accepting that culture shock is unavoidable, explains Caroline Pover who runs Being Abroad, an online and in-person support and information network for women living in Japan.

"It's important to stay open-minded and find support groups of people who have been there and done that," advises the former primary school teacher who left her home town of Plymouth for Tokyo eight years ago, aged 25.

Be patient with yourself and congratulate yourself often. It may not sound [like] much but when you first arrive even buying the right milk in the super-market is an achievement.

"I haven't had a 'I-hate-Japan' day for three years now. The trick is to work out what you want from being abroad and to realise that you don't have to adopt the country's entire culture. Nor should you hang on to your old culture. Pick and choose and create a new culture, one that is right for you."

From Presidency to Pop to Supermarkets, Andean Culture Blossoms in Peruvian Society

Rick Vecchio

When Dina Paucar takes to the stage, swathed in 40 pounds of petticoats and singing of love, hopes and her Andean hometown, she represents much more than just a pop craze.

The singer's popularity is emblematic of deep social change in race-conscious Peru, where the Indian and mixed-race majority are increasingly being recognized as a political, economic and consumer force.

The trend which has been building for some 20 years passed a landmark in 2001 when Alejandro Toledo became Peru's first freely elected president of Indian descent. Now it is being felt everywhere from college campuses to supermarket shelves to popular music.

At 36, Paucar, aka "the Beautiful Goddess of Love," is one of the nation's biggest stars. The one-time housemaid's fan base is the new generation of "serranos," from the word sierra, or highlands—Andean Indian and mixed-race mestizos raised in the shantytowns and slums that surround Lima and other cities.

Today, two-thirds of Lima's 8 million people live in those sprawling neighborhoods, where a burgeoning underground economy has produced an entrepreneurial class of its own.

"The people from these zones, who are basically Andean, are starting to have money to spend, and there is nothing more equalizing," said Rolando Arellano, president of the Arellano Marketing Investigation firm.

For them, "being called serrano is no longer an insult," Arellano said. "That's a very important social change and the case of Dina Paucar is clear. It is a vindication of the sierra tradition."

"RACISM IS STARTING TO DIMINISH"

That would seem inevitable, after four years under a president of mixed but mainly Indian extraction. But it is also being felt elsewhere in the Andean zone—in Ecuador, where Indians have repeatedly flexed their political muscle, and in Bolivia, which has just elected leftist Evo Morales, a full-blooded Indian, as president.

In Peru, the 80 percent Indian and mestizo majority has always occupied the lower rungs of society under a European-descended upper crust. But change is subtly felt on many fronts.

The Wong supermarket chain, which offers fancy pastas, cheeses and imported wines to the lighter-skinned elite, recently began selling guinea pig, cleaned and individually wrapped, at the fresh meat counter. To the upper class it's tailless rat, but in the Andes it's a delicacy.

For years, human rights attorney Wilfredo Ardito, who is mestizo, pressured TV network Frecuencia Latina to cancel "Paisana Jacinta," a slapstick comedy series featuring an overtly racist caricature of a stupid, toothless Andean migrant woman. Last year the network finally halted production of "Paisana Jacinta" and is cleansing the reruns of material that might be judged racist. It also ran a weeklong miniseries based on Dina Paucar's life and music, garnering record ratings and rave reviews.

Indian newcomers to the cities, many of them Quechua-speakers with poor Spanish, still face intense discrimination, Ardito, cautions. But he acknowledges that "There have been advances."

"For example, there are more people with Andean features in the private universities. Increasingly, there are Quechua last names in those places. Before, all doctors were white, but not anymore."

Dr. Alejandro Barrantes, a gastrointestinal physician, said integration in Peru's medical profession started in the 1980s but has become more marked in recent years.

A mestizo, he grew up in Huancayo, in the central Andes. He dreamed of studying medicine, but Huancayo had no medical school so he enrolled in Lima in 1987.

Now he sees more people with Andean roots entering all the professions. "Perhaps there are fewer barriers, or perhaps there is more dedication among the people themselves"

From Spanish colonial times, there was passive acceptance in Peru that prestige, wealth and power lay with the European-descended elite, later augmented by Asian-descended Peruvians such as the Wong family, originally Chinese, who founded and operate Peru's largest supermarket chain, and former President Alberto Fujimori, who is of Japanese ancestry.

Indians and mestizos might be descended from the mighty Inca empire, but in modern Peru they were ridiculed for their Quechua language and customs and relegated to work as maids, laborers or street merchants.

The outside world long ago fell in love with Andean music, popularized by the breathy flutes in Paul Simon's interpretation of Peruvian composer Daniel Alomias' tune "El Condor Pasa." But in Peru, the imperative for many Andean migrants was to assimilate into the mainstream, where salsa and Spanish rock predominated.

Paucar, who left home in the Andes when she was 11 to work as a street vendor and live-in maid in the capital, sings of her roots in "I Will Return," one of

How does history play a role in shaping and creating modern cultural values?

her biggest hits. "Now, I am far away, missing the village where I was born," she sings. "Oh, my children, I know I will return. Do not judge me. I did not abandon you. I just wish to build the things of which I always dreamed. I will return."

Her style of music is called huayno (pronounced WHY-no), a fusion of Andean and European instruments and rhythms, and she sees it as her mission to raise it "to a higher level so that no one is ashamed to dance to it."

"Dina is one of us," says Jorge Luis Gutierrez, a 28-year-old clothing salesman who left the Andes when he was 13.

"She is an example for all people who come from the provinces," he said at a recent Paucar concert. "Most everyone loves her."

What happens over time when two distinct cultures converge in the same geographic area?

ISSUE SUMMARY

Culture is a complex phenomenon, and it contains many subtle features that tend to vary within countries and across national borders. Language is undoubtedly one of the most important ingredients to culture, yet learning the language alone in a foreign country, while helpful, doesn't guarantee a smooth transition as an expatriate. Other factors such as mannerisms, local customs, workplace traditions, perception of time, and context also play a role in the formation of cultural values. Depending on the difference in values between two countries, often referred to as cultural distance, it may take months or years to develop a level of comfort in the foreign society.

Many managers and firms have been making significant efforts to adapt to local cultures. Language and cultural training seminars are becoming more common for managers who agree to take a foreign assignment. Many firms also adapt the language, style, or taste of their products and services abroad. Hasbro, Inc. changed the name of G.I. Joe to Action Man in France. Disney offers tours in two Chinese languages at its Hong Kong theme park. And Band-Aid has changed the color of its adhesive bandages to match local skin color in many Caribbean nations.

What are the sources of cultural values around the world today? Historical influences play a major role in the shaping of a country's cultural values. The effects of colonization can still be felt in many nations. In Latin America, for example, Spanish is the predominant language as a result of colonization by Spain, which ended in the early nineteenth century for most countries. The impact of colonization by the French, British, and Dutch, among others, played an instrumental role in the development of legal systems, governmental structures, and secondary languages in Africa. In many nations with strong indigenous populations, a value set has emerged that is the integration of traditional, imported, and modern values.

People around the world are being exposed to foreigners as an increasing rate, thanks to advances in technology, such as the Internet, cable television, and modern air transportation. Moreover, lower tariffs and the ease with which firms can transport goods across borders has led to an increased number of firms that have engaged in international trade. These newly global firms tend to bring their values, attitudes, and traditions to the global economy and to satellite operations abroad. In the future, it will become increasingly difficult for cultures to maintain their traditional values and worldviews as more and more outside influences enter their environments.

ISSUE HIGHLIGHTS

- Obtaining an understanding of the local language is an essential factor for cultural adaptation.

- Traditions and rituals in the workplace tend to vary by culture.
- Many firms adapt their products or services to the local market, such as Walt Disney's use of two Chinese dialects in its Hong Kong theme park.
- The context of a situation tends to receive more emphasis in Eastern cultures when compared to Western cultures.
- Culture shock tends to be more animated when an individual is traveling alone.
- A number of strategies are possible for adapting to the local culture, such as finding support groups and doing research prior to the trip abroad or expatriate assignment.
- Historical traditions can play a major role in shaping modern cultures.
- In many societies, two cultures collide, resulting in a more diverse and complex modern culture. Hong Kong (British and Chinese) and Peru (Inca and Spanish) are examples of modern integrated cultures.

CRITICAL THINKING

1. Language is a complex yet important part of culture. Yet languages tend to vary within countries, across borders, and in dialects. It is important for managers to recognize both the official and unofficial languages of a target nation. Expatriates preparing for foreign assignments should also make a reasonable attempt to learn the local language even if their native tongue happens to be the lingua franca in the assigned country. This will enhance credibility and respect, while opening up more windows into the local culture.

2. A number of researchers have examined how the importance of the context of a situation varies across cultures. In many Asian nations, for example, people place a significantly higher emphasis on the context of a situation than their Western counterparts. Western societies tend to emphasize the content of a situation more so than the context; as a result, communication in Western societies tends to be more explicit and precise.

3. Many cultures today are the result of the integration of various cultures over time. A number of factors influence the dominant set of cultural values at a specified point in time. Immigration patterns, colonial history, form of government, local indigenous groups, and prevalent subcultures all play a major role in the shaping of a nation's culture. Moreover, as more people around the world are exposed to different values, primarily through communications, their beliefs and attitudes are likely to be influenced, and even shaped to some extent, by foreign cultures.

ADDITIONAL READING RESOURCES

Suzanne Bourret, "Celebrating Cultural Differences," *The Hamilton Spectator* (August 19, 2005), p. G04.

Ed Frauenheim, "Crossing Cultures: Culture of Understanding," *Workforce Management* (November 21, 2005), p. 1.

Geert Hofstede, *Cultures and Organizations: Software of the Mind* (McGraw-Hill, 1997).

Geert Hofstede and Michael Bond, "The Confucius Connection: From Cultural Roots to Economic Growth," *Organizational Dynamics* (vol. 16, no. 4, 1988), pp. 5–21.

Gretchen Lang, "How Much Difference Does It Really Make; Cross-Cultural Training," *International Herald Tribune* (January 24, 2004), p. 13.

Janet Moore, "Minnesota Pair Live the Expat Life in Shanghai," *Star Tribune* (November 17, 2005), p. 19A.

J. Rokeach, *The Nature of Human Values* (Free Press, 1973).

Fons Trompenaars, *Riding the Waves of Culture* (Irwin, 1994).

W. Wines and N. Napier, "Toward an Understanding of Cross-Cultural Ethics: A Tentative Model," *Journal of Business Ethics* (vol. 11, 1992), pp. 831–841.

Trompenaars, Hampden, Turner: Culture for Business, http://www.thtconsulting.com.

Geert Hofstede's Web site: http:// www.geert-hofstede.com.

What Are Some Key Approaches Related to Competing in Foreign Markets?

he level of competition tends to vary enormously from nation to nation. Many firms have realized that a successful strategy in one region of the world may lead to failure elsewhere. Managers of multinational firms have recognized that a "one size fits all" approach to the global economy may be appropriate only in certain industries. As a result, many firms have elected to test unique and revolutionary strategies when entering new foreign markets. Moreover, it has become extremely common for firms to conduct a significant amount of market research not only before entering a market but also prior to determining how to compete in a given nation. The combination of technological advances and falling global trade barriers has led to an enhanced level of competition in most nations, and understanding the local dynamics prior to launching a new product or service can only increase the chances of sustainable success.

Varying strategic directions from market to market is not a new phenomenon. Firms such as Hasbro, Ford, and Nestlé have consistently either altered their products or created new products to fit local demand. Other firms, such as Levi's and Starbucks, have elected to maintain a more global strategy with only minor adjustments made between nations. The decision whether or not to alter a firm's strategy or product portfolio is generally the result of a number of factors, including local demand, purchasing power, and level of competition.

Many firms have decided to adjust their product offerings based on changing demographics and varying cost structures both at home and abroad. For example, the German firm that makes the hit toy series Playmobil, Geobra Brandstatter, switched from larger toys, such as the hula hoop, to the new smaller toy figures when material costs soared in the 1970s. This factor, combined with the sagging consumer purchases at home in Germany, led the firm to launch a global campaign in which figurines are created for global demand. Mark Landler assesses the Playmobil strategy and lagging German consumerism in his article, "German Industries Thrive, But Germans Won't Spend." Although some firms may have an excellent product line for certain markets, the actual mode of entry may be a key determinant of success. China has become a notoriously difficult market to penetrate, and a number of multinational firms have elected to either partner with a local firm or actually acquire a Chinese company in the same industry. Such is the case with Best Buy with its purchase of a majority stake in Chinese appliance and electronics retail giant Jiansu Five Star. In the article, "More Than a Face in the Crowd?" K.C. Swanson examines the recent venture by Best Buy into the Chinese market.

Another key issue related to strategy in international business is which markets to enter and when. Many firms typically enter foreign markets because of two key reasons: slumping sales growth at home or promising opportunities abroad. Depending on the industry and experience of the firm, the decision-making process related to internationalization may be either swift or prolonged. The recent move by Continental Airlines to offer extended service to the Irish market is indicative of a firm that endeavors to continuously assess route opportunities. By opening up additional flight paths to Ireland, Continental will solidify a trade link with the hottest economy in Europe. Constantin Gurdgiev's probing questions of Continental president Jeff Smisek are highlighted in the article "Wings across the Atlantic," published in *Business & Finance* magazine.

Achieving sustainable international growth over time generally requires a certain level of adaptability. A number of organizations have either created new products or updated existing products to incorporate changes that are necessary for global success. In John Schmid's article about the software developer Rockwell from Milwaukee, Wisconsin, he highlights a number of the adaptations and transformations that the firm has gone through over the years. Originally a control developer for firms in various industries, Rockwell has transitioned into an Information Age firm as a rapidly growing software developer. By tapping into research universities in far-away places such as India, Poland, and China, Rockwell has created a competitive advantage through the inclusion of myriad perspectives related to business solutions.

Economic development has led to profitable new opportunities in nations that were previously primarily looked to for labor and materials sourcing. A number of global firms now look to emerging giants India and China as potential destinations for their products and services. Consumer trends in the Indian market have developed to the point where companies such as Benetton, Tommy Hilfiger, and Louis Vuitton have entered India with burgeoning success. According to Yasmeen Mishra, marketing manager for Arvind Brands in India, the Indian market offers a customer who is "brand-conscious and wants to live the lifestyle of his/her international peers." Nonetheless, challenges exist for marketers in India such as limited income levels, distribution problems, and inconsistent service levels. Ajita Shashidhar reviews many of the benefits and drawbacks of doing business in India in an article titled, "The New Destination."

ISSUE ARTICLES

Mark Landler, "German Industries Thrive, But Germans Won't Spend," *The New York Times* (February 23, 2006).

K.C. Swanson, "More Than a Face in the Crowd?" *Daily Deal/The Deal, www.The Deal.com* (July 25, 2006).

Business & Finance Magazine, "Wings Across the Atlantic," *www.bfmag. com* (June 15, 2006).

John Schmid, "Wisconomy: Our Evolving State Economy," *Milwaukee Journal Sentinel* (September 10, 2006).

Ajita Shashidhar, "The New Destination," *Financial Times, Global News Wire—Asia Africa Intelligence Wire* (December 16, 2004).

ARTICLE 9.1

German Industries Thrive, But Germans Won't Spend

Mark Landler

The sturdy little pirates, policemen and farmers of the Playmobil toy series owe their existence to the oil crisis of the 1970's, which drove up the cost of plastic, forcing their German creator to switch from hula hoops to smaller, more economical toys.

Now Playmobil is drawing on its resilience to weather another, potentially more lasting, crisis: Germans are not spending money on toys, let alone more expensive items like cars, refrigerators, or television sets. That has left the German economy in a stubborn four-year-long slump.

"It would be difficult if we had to learn that this is a market where we can't grow any longer," said Andrea Schauer, the chief executive of Playmobil's manufacturer, Geobra Brandstatter. "But we would find strategies to overcome that, to live with that fact."

Last year, Playmobil was saved by buoyant sales outside Germany, particularly in France, Italy and Canada. Despite its deep roots in the centuries-old toy trade of nearby Nuremburg, Brandstatter is one of hundreds of German companies that no longer depend on their home country.

That helps explain a curious dichotomy here. German corporate executives are more confident than at any time in the last five years, according to recent surveys. Booming exports have lifted their profits and turned the German stock market into one of the world's star performers.

Yet German consumers remain in a funk. The unemployment rate is 12 percent, near a post-World War II record, and people are worried about losing their jobs. On the same day that Volkswagen reported higher profits recently, it announced it would eliminate up to 20,000 jobs.

The big question is when—and whether—this German industrial revival will spill over into the rest of the economy. Until it does, Germany will be fallow ground for a company like Playmobil, which sells elaborately detailed planes, pirate ships, and fairy-tale castles, along with its figures.

Playmobil has an additional problem, Ms. Schauer said in an interview at the company's headquarters in this northern Bavarian town. German couples, she said, are not having enough children.

What are some of the factors that have led to sluggish consumer spending in Germany?

"It's either one person working, and they want one to three kids, maximum. Or it's two people working, with no kids or one kid only," said Ms. Schauer, 46, who is married and has a 15-year-old son.

The good news is that Playmobil already reaps close to 60 percent of its 377 million euros ($448 million) in sales outside Germany. That percentage is likely to go up as Ms. Schauer seeks to expand the company's presence in the United States, Latin America and Asia.

The same tilt toward exports is being repeated throughout German industry, from automobiles and machine tools to athletic shoes. Demand for German goods in the United States, Asia and other European countries has allowed BMW, Siemens and Adidas to thrive, despite the weakness here.

In 2005, German exports grew 7.5 percent, and the country racked up a record trade surplus of $190 billion, making it the world's largest merchandise exporter. The overall economy, however, grew just 1 percent, putting Germany at the bottom of European league tables.

"You don't need a strong home base for sales anymore," said Dirk Schumacher, an economist at Goldman Sachs in Frankfurt. "You just need Germany to be a good base for manufacturing."

Germany's high labor costs are a problem for mass-market manufacturers like Volkswagen. But small specialized companies like Playmobil have found ways to keep their production in Germany.

The family-owned company still does the bulk of its manufacturing at a factory a few miles from here. The company's owner, Horst Brandstatter, even invested $76 million in the operations last year, buying 80 injection-molding machines to churn out more plastic figures.

Seventy percent of the world's toys are manufactured in China, according to Ms. Schauer, which raises the question of why Playmobil has not moved production there. Labor costs in Chinese toy factories average $1 an hour, she said, compared with $25 an hour at the factory in Germany.

Ms. Schauer said, however, that Playmobil could not manufacture toys of the same quality in China as in Germany, without eroding most of the cost advantages of the Chinese market. "You can get any level of quality in China," she said. "The question is, At what cost?"

One trademark of a classic Playmobil figure, she said, is that they are durable enough to be passed down through generations, rather than discarded after a few playing sessions.

Playmobil, she said, also wants to keep its production lines closer to its major markets in Europe, so it can quickly adjust production to fluctuating levels of demand. Shipping toys from China, she said, would give the company less flexibility in ramping up its production of, say, a World Cup soccer player, if the demand for that toy suddenly spurted.

This does not mean that Playmobil steers clear of lower-cost countries. It has a large plant on the island of Malta, where it produces 73 million figures a

Describe some key contributing factors related to the evolution of Playmobil's international strategy?

year. It also has a factory in the Czech Republic, which turns out components that are assembled into completed toys in Germany.

This manually intensive work used to be done by German housewives, working at their kitchen tables, Ms. Schauer said. But Playmobil outgrew this local cottage industry years ago. With an average hourly labor cost of $4.70, the Czech Republic is Playmobil's nod to the global economy.

Ms. Schauer said she was not ready to rule out producing in China at some point in the future. But "for the next five years," she said, "we feel that it's better to make the investment here."

Now if only Playmobil can figure out how to revive its home market. If Germany is no longer so critical for the company in sales, it remains vitally important as the place Playmobil tests its newest toys.

This spring, to coincide with the World Cup soccer tournament in Germany, it is introducing a series of soccer players, outfitted in their national colors. As a concession to the demands of the game, the figures will have a movable leg for kicking a soccer ball—a first for Playmobil.

The soccer players will appeal to the company's core market: boys, aged 3 to 9. But Ms. Schauer also wants to broaden Playmobil's appeal to older boys and more girls. It is also introducing a set of figures for three fairy tales: Cinderella, Hansel and Gretel, and Snow White.

Still, Ms. Schauer, who remembers being one of the first girls in her class to own a Barbie doll, is very careful about not messing with Playmobil's image. This is a company that makes firefighters, construction workers and Roman gladiators—not flaxen-haired fairy-tale nymphs.

"We don't want to pretend to be something we're not," she said, in a dig at the impossibly proportioned Barbie.

Ms. Schauer is confident that Playmobil will ride out these tough times. The bigger question is whether Germany will ever again supply legions of young children to play with Playmobil's toys. That, Ms. Schauer conceded, would require significant changes in society.

As one of the few women to rise to chief executive of a German company, she said she was excited to see Angela Merkel elected as Germany's first female chancellor last November.

But Ms. Schauer could not help noting that Ms. Merkel—who is married to a university professor and has no children—hardly sets an example to Germans to have big families. "I hope she understands that if the entire society functions like that, it's going to be tough," she said.

More Than a Face in the Crowd?

K.C. Swanson

Is it ever too late to get into China? Best Buy Co.'s experience may soon provide an answer, as it enters the Chinese market at a time when home-grown rivals have become formidable competitors.

The leading U.S. consumer electronics retailer with sales last year of $31 billion, Best Buy announced on April 1 that it would open its first branded store in China, a four-story emporium in the premier shopping district of Shanghai. On May 12, it followed up with the $180 million purchase of a majority stake in Jiangsu Five Star, the fourth-biggest Chinese appliance and electronics retailer. The exact size of the holding wasn't disclosed, but the deal gives Best Buy an indirect retail presence in 136 Jiangsu Five Star stores throughout eight provinces in China.

The move into China supports Best Buy's international expansion, a key piece of its long-term strategy, according to Robert Willett, CEO of Best Buy International. With 940 retail stores in the U.S. and Canada, the company has already nearly reached the 1,000 total stores it reckons North America can support.

At the company's annual meeting in June, Willett sketched out plans for a cautious ramp-up in China, at least in the beginning. "We're going to learn carefully, then scale fast. The road to international expansion is littered with failures," he said, referring to Wal-Mart Stores Inc.'s withdrawal from Germany and French supermarket group Carrefour SA's exit from other overseas locations. Best Buy plans to study their failures while also applying its own four years of experience operating in Canada. "We're in no rush. We want to learn from other people," said Willett, adding that the company's agenda is to be there "for the millennium."

This marks the first time an outside retailer has tried to enter China's appliance and consumer electronics industry. In the U.S., analysts have generally lauded Best Buy's moves as a natural expansion into a strategically key market—particularly as the North America market approaches the saturation point. Consumer electronics sales in China are expected to see double-digit growth over the next decade, up from an estimated $85 billion in 2006, according to Best Buy.

But while a push into China may look like a sensible strategy from afar, the Minn.-based company faces considerable challenges as it tries to win Chinese consumers. In just the past few years, the local retail landscape has

How has Best Buy hedged risk in its entrance into the Chinese electronics industry?

been transformed by a handful of hungry regional players, with at least one—Gome Electrical Appliances Holding Ltd.—now able to claim a nationwide footprint. Plus, the customer service-centric business model that has served Best Buy well in North America isn't necessarily suited to China, where consumers shop on price.

China's consumer appliance and electronics retail industry has grown with startling speed: Just three to five years ago, most Chinese still bought their appliances by bargaining with individual stall owners in big electronics bazaars. But over time, a handful of the more successful retailers started acquiring competitors and consolidating their purchasing power with suppliers, who are now undergoing a parallel consolidation trend.

Last year, China's top five consumer appliance and electronics retailers combined still owned only 24% of the home appliance market, according to the Ministry of Commerce. Still, they've developed brand recognition and staked out prime real estate in the biggest, richest metropolitan areas and have now begun expanding into second- and third-tier cities. Most importantly, they have developed tight supplier relationships that allow them to pass on ultra-cheap prices to their consumers.

"The basic business model is to grow as fast as they can to get sales volume, so they can get bigger discounts," says Graham Matthews, Shanghai-based partner in transaction services for PricewaterhouseCoopers.

Gome, the top-ranked player, opened its first retail appliance outlet in 1987. Though it didn't start expanding beyond Beijing until 2003, the company has recently seen explosive growth. Founder and chairman Huang Guangyu—whom Euromoney tagged as the richest man in China in 2004—presides over more than 420 stores. The company's listed arm, which trades in Hong Kong and last year included about two-thirds of its retail network, posted 2005 sales of $2.2 billion. Huang has said he plans next to transplant his business model of rock-bottom prices into Southeast Asia.

Industry watchers voice serious doubts about whether an American company steeped in a quality service culture can compete with such hungry rivals. "It's late," says Paul French, a Shanghai-based retail and consumer analyst at market research firm AccessAsia. "We're not exactly sure what Best Buy is going to do or why they're bothering." Best Buy must quickly scale a steep learning curve—with the possible rewards being relentless price wars and scant profits. Last year, Gome's listed arm eked out a profit of only 4.5% of revenues, partly due to its aggressive store expansion, compared with gross margins of 25% at Best Buy.

The newly purchased stake in Five Star should help its effort, shaving a decade off the time Best Buy would have needed to develop a comparably sized business through organic growth, says Citigroup Inc. analyst Bill Sims. The investment should also help Best Buy figure out what Chinese customers want and boost its foreign-sourced, private-label initiatives for U.S. stores, he added.

Plus, there is an upside to Best Buy's late entry. It has allowed the company to gain a partner experienced in the consumer electronics business. "We believe we've acquired some really good management there," said Willett of Five Star, speaking at the annual meeting. Granted, Five Star is still considered a regional player, having morphed from a state-owned enterprise into a private firm in 1998. And some analysts say Best Buy ended up with fourth-ranked Five Star only because the top-three players in the industry weren't willing to sell. But business has grown rapidly since Five Star opened its first retail store in Nanjing in 2001: In 2005, revenues totaled nearly $700 million, up more than 50% from the prior year, according to Best Buy.

To put Best Buy's entry in perspective, consider pioneers Carrefour and Wal-Mart, both of which started operations in China about a decade ago. Since retail was then still in its infancy, they had time to learn the finer points of Chinese commerce without having to face well-entrenched local competitors at the outset. Indeed, the two are credited with creating China's hypermart sector—giant stores selling groceries, clothing and household items at discount prices. Carrefour and Wal-Mart now boast a respective 76 and 52 hypermarts on the mainland. Under the 2004 rule that allows foreign retailers to open stores without JV partners, both have been accelerating their expansion into second- and third-tier cities.

What are some of the advantages and disadvantages to Best Buy's late arrival to the Chinese market?

Carrefour and Wal-Mart have a tangential presence in appliances and electronics themselves and are often named as potential competitors to fast-growing Gome. Some local analysts say that threat is overstated, since Chinese consumers prefer to go to more specialized stores with a wide selection for major purchases.

Best Buy faces similar competitive pressure on the home front, where Wal-Mart and other big retailers offer such mass-market products as digital cameras and computer peripherals, crimping prices industrywide, and direct-to-consumer brands such as Dell Inc. have stepped up their discounting, says Richard Hastings, a New York-based senior retail analyst at Bernard Sands.

In North America, Best Buy has heavily emphasized service. Over the past three years, it has become a leading practitioner of the marketing approach known as "customer centricity," which involves understanding the needs of customers and targeting the most attractive segments. Among other things, the company has promoted high-end home entertainment fare and focused on small business customers. It has also debuted several new concept stores tailored to such demographic groups as soccer moms. In its fiscal 2006 annual report, Best Buy says customer centricity means "treating each customer as a unique individual," adding that it aims above all else to offer customers a "differentiated experience."

But where customer centricity might lead in China isn't clear. In the Middle Kingdom, discounts rule, assiduous comparison shopping is the norm, and overly friendly service is considered suspect. "[Western] analysts who know Best Buy say, 'The decoration and service are really good, and at Gome and Suning the stores are dirty and staff sit around smoking,' " French says. But that assessment "fundamentally doesn't get retailing in China," he adds. "Best

Buy's stores do look very nice. [But] all it does is make people think they're paying for something they needn't pay for: 'Why should I pay so you can have nice carpet and a flash sign?' "

"If the prices in Best Buy aren't lower than Gome and Suning, it has no chance," says China Merchant Securities analyst Hongke Hu. "Chinese people may buy products from an American store they don't know, but the precondition is that this American store has a lower price."

For now at least, retail segmentation doesn't really exist in the Chinese electronics market. To be sure, Gome recently announced plans to debut a higher-end store format with sleeker stores and better service. But so far it's only an experiment involving a handful of stores.

Above all else, consumers simply demand the cheapest gadgets possible. Margins have gotten so tight that some industry watchers expect to see further consolidation in electronics. In theory, at least, that wouldn't rule out Best Buy making another acquisition, though it's given no indications it would consider one.

Best Buy has been quiet about its China strategy, so it's not clear how it will adapt its North American model. The company has, however, acknowledged hiring lots of Chinese nationals to study the market through focus groups, exit interviews from stores and home visits. Willett says Best Buy will also draw on Five Star's "considerable customer insights and strong local networks."

Best Buy's direct-owned store will need to reshuffle its traditional product line-up for China. Last year in North America, Best Buy drew 43% of sales from consumer electronics, notably higher-end fare like flat-panel TVs and MP3 players, and only 6% of revenues from appliances (with the remainder coming from home office goods and entertainment software). At specialty retail stores in China, typically more than half of revenues come from lower-end white goods, a category that includes big appliances like refrigerators and washing machines, and black goods, such as televisions and audio components, says Sandy Chen, an equity analyst for Citigroup in Shanghai.

On the marketing side, Best Buy plans to pursue the dual-branding strategy in China that has served it well in Canada. Following its 2001 acquisition of Future Shop, Canada's leading consumer electronics retailer, Best Buy now runs 119 Future Shop stores under the Future Shop brand along with 44 of its own branded stores. "We've learned a great deal about running two brands" in Canada, Willett said at the annual meeting, adding that the company plans to apply those lessons in China.

Best Buy says the newly acquired Five Star stores will continue to operate under their own brand and current management will stay in place. Meanwhile, analysts speculate that Best Buy's Shanghai-based, 86,000-square-foot flagship (and only) store in China will probably primarily fill a marketing role, raising consumer awareness of the Best Buy brand.

Branding aside, the most important task for Best Buy may be to leverage its buying power with suppliers. The consumer electronics chains in China "in general don't make a lot, but the money they do make is the discount they can negotiate from suppliers," says PwC's Matthews. "The advantage foreigners have is they have the export relationships with the same suppliers. If you consolidate that with domestic China [purchasing] all in one, you'd have much bigger volume than a Chinese company."

Best Buy says it has "well-established" links with manufacturers that it says want to gain broader distribution in both China and North America. The company opened its first procurement office in China in 2003 and has since added offices in two other cities.

If it can make good on those supplier ties, Best Buy could put serious pressure on Chinese rivals. But it's starting from behind. And as long as industry margins hover near the floor, even success may not taste too sweet.

ARTICLE 9.3

Wings Across The Atlantic

Constantin Gurdgiev

Last month, world leader in international routes services US Continental Airlines increased fights between the Republic of Ireland and New York to three daily as a part of growth strategy for an airline that has been in the Irish market since 1988.

"We are very committed to the Irish market. We are here because the Irish market offers great opportunities, not because the US market is becoming more competitive," says Jeff Smisek, president of the airline. "That said, some of our competitors are coming to the Irish market today because their domestic [US] operations are in such bad shape that they are hoping to find a lifeline anywhere in the world."

In the next few years, Irish aviation will undergo crucial changes. These include potential privatisation of Aer Lingus, completion of airport facilities upgrades in Dublin, Cork and Shannon, and regulatory changes triggered by the EUUS Open Sky agreements. Can the Shannon stop-over be an economically justifiable proposition in the new age of high-efficiency, value-for-money operations?

"Well, at Continental we have run at 87% capacity utilisation over the past decade or so. This also applies to our flights to Ireland, so for us the Shannon stop-over has been a contributor to high-capacity utilisation.

It hasn't been a problem. Even assuming that the Open Skies agreement goes forward, we currently do not have any intention to eliminate Shannon landing. "Do airlines anticipate a revision of landing charges in Shannon or Dublin as the result of the Open Skies agreements or new building programmes?

"No air carrier likes to see increases in its operating cost, including the cost of landing charges. If there is such an increase beyond the market rates, every air carrier will make long-term provisions to shift services elsewhere. So if there were to occur new increases in charges, these will have an effect on optimal frequency of services. In general, airports do compete against each other and those that have higher landing fees suffer.

Obviously the Irish economy—and with it the demand for airline services—is growing. We understand that some improvement in the airport capacity is needed and we are not against a measured increase in fees but only if this will

Why did Continental delay its opening up of additional flight segments between the United States and Ireland? What are the implications related to this new service route?

From *Business & Finance,* June 15, 2006. Copyright © 2006 by Business & Finance Magazine, Dublin, Ireland. Reprinted by permission.

bring more efficient and better services." If Open Skies agreements deliver more competition on the routes dominated by the traditional airlines, what strategy will Continental adopt to respond to the new pressures?

"Continental has tremendous assets, such as being the only airline with a hub in the immediate proximity of New York. So, from a business traveller perspective, we have a tremendous advantage over our competitors. We have invested over a billion dollars in the Global Gateway terminal at Newark, which now has dedicated customs and immigration facilities, and convenient check-in systems.

We can fly to 120 destinations non-stop and 230 destinations in total from New York. We are not concerned with increasing competition. What bothers us in the context of the European Union part of the Open Skies is that it effectively will continue to block our access to the most-demanded destinations in Europe. Heathrow will be one example, but also Paris and Frankfurt. This is why we are working with US Congress to prevent the US department of transportation from signing a damaging, one-sided opening of the travel routes."

In Europe, most growth today comes from the low-cost airlines. Can traditional full-service airlines survive in this world?

"Not only can they survive, they can thrive. Our service is transatlantic and we see the majority of business travellers today demanding first- and business-class seats, so they can be ready to go into work the minute they land. I am not concerned that there will be degradation of the service quality in exchange for lower fares. I think there always will be demand for higher standards."

Apart from increased competition, fuel costs present the largest problem in terms of rising business costs. Are there any secret hedging strategies that Continental employs?

"We have fuel costs reaching to around 70% of the operating non-capital costs. Up until recently, options were ahead of the oil-price curve. Instead of focusing on short-term strategies like price options, we focused on the long-term strategy of upgrading the fleet with new, more fuel-efficient planes. By the end of this year, we expect to fly aircraft burning 25% less fuel per passenger-mile than we did in 1998. We also manage our on-the-ground operations with minimised fuel-spend in mind. Sometimes, it is cheaper for us to fly fully fuelled than to refuel on return. We have technology and management strategies to generate savings and fuel efficiencies instead of fuel-price options."

Continental uses a modern, all-Boeing fleet—777-200ERs, 767-400ERs, 767200ERs and 757-200s—to operate its transatlantic services and, according to Smisek, has no interest in the Airbus A380 super jumbo.

"Our objective is to fly people non-stop from and to New York, rather than flying people from one hub to another hub and then to their final destination. We keep presence in the markets where there is demand for travel, where people actually want to travel to. This is a different strategy from flying A380. We believe that non-stop direct flights will be a much more successful strategy in the medium and long term. Under this strategy, it is really important that we select a right hub."

Continental's main hubs are New York, Houston and Cleveland—all mature US markets. Does this present a limit on Continental's growth?

"I see growth in passenger traffic from the US to Asia and Latin America. We are the second-largest carrier to Latin and South America. Ultimately we might be interested in eastern Europe or continental Europe, but right now we are facing aircraft availability constraints. We are taking in two new Boeing 777 aircraft and looking forward to purchasing more new generation, wide-body aircraft, but for now we are running at capacity. We do have interest in eastern Europe, but it will take us some time before we can get aircraft capacity available for that."

Continental just announced second year-in-a-row significant losses. Many industry analysts are increasingly doubtful that traditional airlines can achieve required returns on capital in today's markets.

Does Smisek think that an industry that has difficulty coping with the market changes in good times can really absorb any downturn in the economic environment?

How has Continental invested in its long-term global strategy?

"When you look at it from the relative points of view, United Airlines went bankrupt, US Airways went bust twice, Delta filed for bankruptcy protection, Northwest airlines have been there before. When you look at financial analysts' forecasts for an airline that is most likely to turn profit in the next few years, Continental is at the top of their charts. I am not particularly proud of this year's results, but given that we've been hit by a series of adverse events ever since the 9/11 terrorist attacks, Continental is doing much better than most of our competitors.

"Three to four years ago, Continental decided to invest heavily in new planes.

At the time, after 9/11, demand for aircraft was low and prices were low, as was the price of fuel. Many airlines claimed that our strategy will be the end of us, yet, now look around—the price of fuel went up and we are enjoying significant savings from efficiency. At the same time, the price of planes also went up, so those airlines who did not upgrade their fleet are now going out of business."

It's time to ask a question relating to our national airline—Aer Lingus—which is about to go into at least partial privatisation. Would Continental be interested in taking a stake in it?

"We have use for all our capital growing our own airline internally and have no desire to take any part in Aer Lingus. We are not interested in any potential mergers or acquisitions in Europe, as we very much believe that we have a great strategy for growth. We publicly announced that our growth target is 5% to 7% per annum, and this year we will be growing at around 8.7% on consolidated basis. We are growing at 4.7% domestically within the US, and at 12.5% internationally, in Latin America and on transatlantic routes. This means our growth in the US is significant relative to our competitors and certainly significant in the international markets as well," he says.

"This is not to say we are not watching industry trends, so if, for example, there is a consolidation wave, we may need to look into acquisitions to maximise the value for our shareholders and to make sure that our customers continue to have access to the services they demand. Barring that, we are not interested in investing in any other airline."

INSIDE THE HANGAR

Continental Airlines, headquartered in Houston, Texas, is the world's sixth-largest airline and has more than 3,200 daily departures. Continental serves 151 US and 137 international destinations—more than any other airline in the world. It is the leading US carrier across the Atlantic in number of cities served, with US hubs at New York (Newark), Houston and Cleveland.

Continental Airlines operates a fleet of 350 jet aircraft, and Continental Express flies 261 regional jets. In 2005, the airline took delivery of seven Boeing aircraft and inducted six 757-300s, giving it one of the youngest and most-efficient fleets in the industry.

Continental operates a twice-daily, non-stop service between Dublin and Newark and a daily service between Shannon and Newark. Jeff Smisek is the airline's president and a member of the board of directors. He is responsible for corporate communications, federal affairs, global real estate and security, human resources, technology, sales and marketing. He joined the airline in March 1995 as senior vice-president and general counsel. He studied economics in Princeton University and attended Harvard Law School. Smisek resides in Houston with his wife and two children.

ARTICLE 9.4

Wisconomy: Our Evolving State Economy

John Schmid

FactoryTalk software is hot. Tens of thousands of business users in 70 nations rely on versions of it. Programmers in Silicon Valley, China, India and Germany update it continuously.

And the fast-growing outfit that makes it is headquartered—incongruously, perhaps—near the coal heaps, ports and railroads on the industrial south side of Milwaukee.

Rockwell Software Inc., with 700 employees and growing, started 12 years ago, springing from a Milwaukee-based parent, Rockwell Automation Inc., that traces its roots for over a century as a maker of factory controls in a factory town.

"We create matter-less products," said Kevin Roach, vice president of Rockwell Software.

The emergence of a software developer in a city better known for smokestacks illustrates how a flagship of Wisconsin industry has reinvented itself to keep pace in a turbulent global economy.

As Rockwell bears increasingly less resemblance to its predecessor businesses, it mirrors the globalization-driven changes that are reshaping a broad swath of the industrial heartland. For any company that lacks such a culture of change, "the question is, how far do they drop?" said James Duderstadt, an engineering professor at the University of Michigan who specializes in competitiveness issues that affect Great Lakes states.

Keith Nosbusch, chairman and chief executive of Rockwell Automation, routinely uses the word "transformation" when he describes the company to Wall Street analysts.

The headquarters beneath the signature 17-story clock tower once teemed with blue-collar assembly workers, often employing more than one generation in a family.

Today, while Rockwell continues to make most of its money producing hardware, it is increasingly populated with electrical and software engineers who customize automation systems for pharmaceutical companies, oil refineries and automakers.

Rockwell also has satellite offices across the globe, in university towns such as Dalian, China, and Katowice, Poland, where it recruits local engineers. In

March, it inaugurated a development center in Singapore and announced plans to double its sales across Asia by 2009.

Currently, two-fifths of the company's $5 billion in annual sales and earnings comes from outside the United States.

"Many go to India because it's cheap," Roach said. "We go to India because it's a fast-growing economy."

This summer, Rockwell took another step as it announced plans to sell its Dodge and Reliance Electric divisions that make electro-mechanical gears, motors and other hardware. The sale, when complete, will lower Rockwell's worldwide work force to 16,800 from 21,000 and elevate the share of "knowledge workers" within the company to 70%.

Rockwell's model allows it to placate Wall Street, keep its headquarters in Milwaukee and compete with other giants of industrial automation such as General Electric Co., Emerson Electric Co. of St. Louis, Swiss-Swedish ABB Ltd. and Siemens AG of Germany. Some analysts compare Rockwell's metamorphosis with that of International Business Machines Corp., which went from making bulky mainframes to laptops, only to sell its computer hardware operations and focus on information services and consulting.

'INVENTION ON DEMAND'

Roach, who joined Rockwell in 2004, represents the emerging digital Rockwell.

"It's essentially invention on demand," Roach said. "We can deliver instantaneously."

The 44-year-old Boston native, who founded two technology companies including a robotics software firm, holds several patents and most recently worked at GE's automation division. He keeps busy hiring software executives and tweaking FactoryTalk.

Politicians wishing to support the Wisconsin economy should emulate Rockwell's strategy and promote investment in the research institutions that supply engineers, business leaders and patents, said Duderstadt of the University of Michigan. The engineers and research generated by the universities, in turn, would create new opportunities for local employers like Rockwell.

"To innovate, you need to invest in skills. You need to have the capital to invest in the future, and the quality of life that can sustain that kind of activity," Duderstadt said.

In Michigan, which has been brutalized by globalization, there has been a reluctance by political and business leaders to "shatter the old conventions that hold back the region," he said.

"We're spending heavily on keeping the last car plants alive instead of creating an entrepreneurial culture," he said. "And that's not an investment in the future."

Rockwell's global strategy relies on research universities. Across China, Rockwell cultivates ties with 18 of the best-known tech schools and universities.

Rockwell attributes much of its success to adaptation to change. How would you describe some of the major adaptations that Rockwell has implemented?

Its software development center in China is near the Dalian University of Technology, which boasts a big School of Software Engineering. This year, Rockwell Software announced an expansion in Katowice, Poland, where it said it takes advantage of Polish engineering schools.

Rockwell Software owes its founding to a couple of university students at the Milwaukee School of Engineering. Joe Menter was writing computer code in his apartment near the MSOE campus in 1985 when he met two business partners. They hired another MSOE programmer, and the four founded ICOM Inc., which grew rapidly. Rockwell acquired ICOM nine years later, calling it "one of the strongest and most successful companies in the automation software industry." ICOM formed the heart of Rockwell Software.

Since then, Rockwell has acquired industrial-automation software firms at the rate of nearly one a year. Last November, it purchased Datasweep Inc. of San Jose, Calif., which automates companies such as Lucent, Qualcomm and Johnson & Johnson. In May, Rockwell acquired GEPA mbH, a German automation software firm with European customers.

MORE THAN NUMBERS

Gary Herrigel, a University of Chicago professor who specializes in industrial evolution, said Rockwell has avoided a pitfall that lamed other established industries.

"Many hire MBAs and all they know is numbers and reducing costs," Herrigel said. "Many companies have constant warfare between production and innovation types and the finance departments. Wall Street likes numbers, but that ruins products."

Rockwell, by contrast, has corporate leaders with engineering backgrounds. Both Nosbusch and his predecessor, Don Davis, have decades of ties to Milwaukee and to Rockwell's predecessor, the Allen-Bradley Co. Davis joined Allen-Bradley in 1963. Nosbusch, a graduate of state universities in Madison and Milwaukee, joined in 1974.

Wisconsin has retained a stable of globally active engineering firms like Rockwell. Many are in the metro Milwaukee area, such as GE Healthcare, a separate division of GE, and Johnson Controls Inc. Some, such as ABB Automation Products Inc. in New Berlin, which began as a division of Milwaukee's big Harnischfeger machinery works, expanded their international reach when foreign parent companies acquired them.

Each represents an indispensable asset for the Wisconsin economy, Duderstadt said, because they inject a pool of international engineers and managers into the state.

"The people that drive innovation are creative people with strong education and high energy," he said. "They like to congregate where there are other people like them and where there's a good quality of life."

The innovators in metro Milwaukee are awarded four patents for every one in the economy around Madison, home to one of the nation's leading research universities, according to the Milwaukee 7, a consortium of planners from the seven-county metro area. Milwaukee's patents come mainly from private sector employers like Rockwell and GE and not so much from its universities, the consortium's researchers say.

ADAPTING TO GLOBAL CHANGE

Few Wisconsin companies have adapted to global change as methodically as Rockwell.

Allen-Bradley was founded in 1903 when 25-year-old Lynde Bradley patented a crude speed control for electric motors and went into business with his partner, Stanton Allen, on $1,000 in seed money.

The company opened its first foreign production site in Britain in 1969 and launched an international division in 1973. By 1985, when the California-based defense and aerospace group Rockwell International acquired Allen-Bradley for $1.65 billion, the Milwaukee company boasted 27 manufacturing locations outside the U.S. and a presence in 60 countries.

In 1999, having jettisoned many of its military-oriented holdings, Rockwell moved its corporate headquarters to Milwaukee from California.

By then, Allen-Bradley's engineers had defined new markets for themselves, developing factory-floor controllers that maximized output for individual machinery.

What are some of the key challenges that Rockwell has faced in its evolution in the past two decades?

Automakers that once groused about costly assembly-line downtime for model changeovers suddenly had the choice of merely reprogramming their controllers.

That led Rockwell into the computer hardware business and eventually pushed it further into information technology. Today, its FactoryTalk system helps coordinate all sorts of factory operations, including monitoring wear-and-tear on equipment, predicting breakdowns and scheduling repairs. The result: increased productivity, a Holy Grail for economies around the world.

"We were always in the factory business," said Rockwell spokesman John Bernaden. "But today we're more like Microsoft than anything else."

12 Years ago that Rockwell Software Inc. was started by Milwaukee-based Rockwell Automation Inc.

Number of employees	Rockwell Automation's annual sales, earnings	Amount of sales and earnings originating from outside the U.S.
700 and growing	$5 billion	40%

ARTICLE 9.5

The New Destination

Ajita Shashidhar

India seems to have made it to the international fashion map, with super-premium apparel and accessory brands beginning to eye the Indian market. While the summer of 2004 saw the entry of the $ 2-billion lifestyle brand Tommy Hilfiger, Louis Vuitton recently set up its second store, in Mumbai at the Taj Mahal Hotel. Similarly, United Colors of Benetton is in for a complete makeover (after buying out the 50 per cent stake held by the DCM Group), while Madura Garments is planning to bring in Giorgio Armani into India.

No longer do upmarket fashion-conscious Indians need to scout abroad for an Armani or Tommy Hilfiger casuals. While Tommy Hilfiger has five stores in the country, Louis Vuitton has a store each in Delhi and Mumbai. Both the brands plan to expand their retail network considerably in the coming years.

IS THE TIMING RIGHT?

Benetton, one of the premium Western brands that has found a place in India

Do these premium brands actually have a market in India? The marketers of these brands as well as analysts feel the timing is absolutely right. They say that Indian consumerism is at an all-time high. The youth have a huge amount of disposable income and they want to feel good and enjoy life.

"The Indian economy is soaring. I think the Indian people love brands," said Tommy Hilfiger, Honorary Chairman and Principal Designer of Tommy Hilfiger Inc, in an earlier interview to Catalyst.

Adding to Hilfiger's statement, Yasmeen Mishra, Marketing Manager, Arvind Brands (which markets Tommy Hilfiger in India), says, "India (like China) is fast emerging as one of the fastest growing markets for luxury goods across categories. We are seeing an influx of many international brands such as Maybach, Porsche, Patek Philippe, Bvlgari and Louis Vuitton. The Indian customer is well-travelled, affluent, brand-conscious and wants to live the life-style of his /her international peers. Exposure to global trends has contributed a great deal to fuelling this global lifestyle over the years. International brands therefore consider this an opportune moment to reach out to this customer who has the attitude and the desire to spend on labels."

Says Jagdeep Kapoor, Managing Director, Samsika Marketing Consultants, "Indian consumers have become world-class customers who want world-class brands. Their purchasing power has gone up and so has their aspiration. Therefore, there is a large market for premium brands in India."

Hemchandra Javeri, President, Madura Garments, says premium brands have a nascent but rapidly growing market in India. "There are several crore-patis in India, and there is an increasing awareness of brands and their value."

As far as the international brands are concerned, Javeri says, "India is the last big market left to tap and the long-term opportunity is very attractive."

For the premium category of brands, India is just happening as a market, says Harish Bijoor, CEO, Harish Bijoor Consults. "In the markets of the West, there is saturation and certainly brand disdain as well. Consumers are asking why they must pay 300 per cent premiums for products they can get of equal quality at a third of the price tagged on. As consumers get brand-wary for premium offerings in the advanced consumer markets of the West, consumers in India are letting down their guard. They want to buy more brands, eat more brands and drink more brands! It is but a part of the evolution of markets for branded products and services."

Agreeing with Bijoor, Sanjeev Mohanty, Head (Sales and Marketing), United Colors of Benetton, says that there is a definite slowdown in the European and US markets, which has prompted a number of premium brands to look at developing markets such as China and India. He also says that India has more affluent younger consumers in the age group of 25-40 than anywhere else in the world. "But the entry into this segment has not even warmed up. One will see a flurry of activity in the Indian premium and super-premium segments only by 2006–07. However, the market for these premium brands would be limited only to the top metros where the disposable incomes are high, especially among the youth."

THE CHALLENGES

The Indian luxury market, says Saloni Nangia, Manager, KSA-Technopak, is a Rs 2,000-crore market and is steadily on the rise. But the major deterrent here, she says, is the lack of quality retail space. "The upcoming malls are equipped only to cater to the existing brands."

That is the reason, she says, most of these brands prefer to operate from five-star hotels. "These brands can't afford to compromise on the experience and ambience, as the segment they are targeting is made up of those who shop abroad regularly and have knowledge of luxury brands."

How would you assess the major cultural and economic success factors related to doing business in India?

Equally challenging, says Mohanty of Benetton, would be to run a profitable retail model. "One mistake can wipe out the bottomline," he says. He adds that the quality of manpower, recruiting, training, motivating as well as retaining it would be a great challenge. "The perception about shop-floor persons in our society is not that great, so most people see it as a short-term career prospect. Internationally, it is just the reverse. Benetton recognises this and we are in the process of changing that."

Apart from this, the key challenge which affects every niche premium brand in the country, according to Bijoor, is distribution. "This is a nightmare for the marketer of a niche premium brand. The issues are that of holding inventory at diverse locations, managing styles and fashions, phasing out stock, moving out stock and making it available for a population base that is as large as India. Add to that the issue of having to largely do all this themselves, as distribution intermediaries are rare in the country at the moment."

Agreeing with Bijoor, Javeri of Madura says that reaching consumers in a cost-effective way would definitely be a challenge for these premium brands as retail infrastructure is developing only now, and the market is scattered across the major cities.

"Also, Indian consumers are very discerning and demanding of value and service. What works for international brands in other markets may not work here and they will need to adapt their marketing mix to India's specific needs," says Javeri.

Bijoor feels that these brands need to invest in market research within the country and need to have their fingers on the pulse of the young folks who crave for these brands. "And with it all, there needs to be Indianisation," he says.

But does Indianisation mean that these brands would have to review their pricing or introduce products at lower price-points?

"Certainly not," says Mishra of Arvind. "Tommy Hilfiger is a premium life-style brand across the world and in India also it will operate in the same way. The Indian consumer is now aware, more than ever before, of international brands and quality and is willing to pay for what he/ she wants."

Similarly, Mohanty of Benetton says, "We are very comfortable with our pricing strategy. We definitely would like to have a super-premium range to cater to a more discerning consumer for our flagship stores and therefore take the average weighted prices up. But we have no intentions right now to fundamentally change our price mix."

Analysts also feel that down-pricing would not be in the interest of these brands. "If brands down-price their offerings, then the value of the brand in the minds of consumers is hurt," says Bijoor. "I therefore think a good strategy would be to hold high price-lines but market innovatively. Look at what Bacardi has achieved in this country with its innovative Bacardi Blast," he adds.

Kapoor of Samsika says that as these brands cater to the topmost end there should be no limit to the pricing because of snob appeal.

HOW TO GET IT RIGHT?

"What these premium brands actually need to do is choose the right segment, give world-class products and service and constantly monitor trends," says Kapoor.

On the other hand, Kabir Lumba, President (Buying and Merchandising), Lifestyle International, says these premium brands should be able to manage their expectations well and shouldn't aspire to do exceptionally well within a short period. "They should instead try to offer international experience as the Indian customers are well-travelled. They need to offer the same product and the pricing should be at par with the pricing in Dubai, Singapore or any other Asian country."

What has led to India's rise in its level of attractiveness as a market for global brands?

"Indianise, invest in brand-building, hold the price line and skim the top end of the market ... and never ever have factory sales or factory shops for your brands! The intelligent consumer in the market will buy only from these," says Bijoor.

ISSUE SUMMARY

———————————————————————————————●

Firms that elect to enter foreign markets generally face a higher level of uncertainty and complexity in their daily operations. The attainment of success abroad is a result of numerous factors and decisions. The selection of the best possible target market given numerous alternatives is clearly a crucial success factor. The timing of market entry is also important. National economies and consumer buying patterns tend to fluctuate over time, as do the number and quality of local competitors. It is not uncommon for firms to delay entry into foreign markets not only because of the high chance for failure but also because of the extensive initial costs involved with international expansion. Yet the potential for deep profits abroad and potentially massive market opportunities more often than not outweigh the initial setbacks.

The percentage of world trade that occurs strictly among industrialized nations has been declining in recent years, partly due to the entrance of India and China into the global business arena. Indeed, just a decade ago, multinational firms almost exclusively looked to India and China as locations for cheap labor or raw materials. The combination of an emerging middle class in these two nations with massive populations has led to a significant consumer base that has triggered the interest of many multinational firms. Best Buy's entrance into the Chinese market in 2006 suggests that the consumer electronics industry in China is alive and well. The penetration of high-end retailers such as Tommy Hilfiger and Benetton into India is also indicative of increased purchasing power among the middle and upper classes. The expatriate communities in many developing countries are also growing and can play a significant role in a firm's decision related to when and where to enter a potential market. Starbucks, for example, has entered seven different locations in China, either through company-operated stores or joint ventures.

As globalization continues to redefine the business environment in numerous nations, it is important for firms to continuously reevaluate their competitive strategies and core competencies. It is entirely plausible that a competitive advantage in one nation may quickly disappear in a different nation due to the nature and scope of local industry rivalry. Firms such as Rockwell, Continental and Playmobil have achieved success in foreign markets by being willing to adapt, reassess product offerings, and build new relationships. One of the keys to survival in international business is having the ability to recognize when a product's shelf life has expired and having the vision to generate new and exciting products, or services, that appeal to the local consumer needs. Although investment in research and development can be costly, it should be looked to as an insurance policy against shifting consumer trends in the future.

ISSUE HIGHLIGHTS

- Geobra Brandstatter, the German manufacturer of the Playmobil toy series, has pursued a strategy of aggressive international growth in recent years due to lagging consumer spending in Germany.
- Playmobil has limited any outsourcing of production to nations within a reasonable geographic distance from strategic target markets.
- In April 2006, Best Buy opened its first branded store in China as part of a larger international expansion strategy.
- To further pursue the thriving Chinese electronics industry, Best Buy purchased a majority stake in the Chinese electronics firm Jiangsu Five Star.
- Continental Airlines increased daily flights to Ireland from New York to take advantage of growing demand along the North Atlantic corridor.
- Continental uses a modified hub and spoke strategy with three domestic hubs in the United States: New York, Houston, and Cleveland.
- Rockwell International has evolved from a precision control manufacturer to a modern high-tech software designer.
- One major competitive advantage that strengthens Rockwell's position is its cultivation of relationships with research universities worldwide.
- India has become an attractive market for consumer goods due to globalization and rapid economic growth.
- Many high-end brands have initially entered the Indian market by selling their products through five-star hotels.

CRITICAL THINKING

1. Firms that are faced with little or no growth in revenues have a number of strategic options that may help accelerate long-term objectives. One alternative is to develop and market new products. If sales at home are flat, the firm can take mature and/or new products abroad to viable foreign markets. Depending on the firm's strategy, management may elect to adapt products to local demand or market products with a global identity. Best Buy, for example, may decide to offer certain products in China and not in the United States due to local consumer preferences.

2. After making a decision to enter a foreign market, a firm must assess the level and scope of local competition. Pursuing a low-cost strategy in one nation may not be a plausible alternative in a different nation due to crowding at that end of the market. Moreover, the number of players in a firm's given strategic group is likely to vary considerably across borders. Although Benetton has identified a solid consumer base for its products in India, minor adjustments to style and pricing may be necessary to maximize performance.

3. One of the keys to long-run success is the continuous reassessment of a firm's strategy and brand performance. A number of firms have gone through either evolutionary or revolutionary transformations as a result of globalization and now generate the majority of their revenues from products that were not part of their portfolios two decades ago. Rockwell International's shift toward software development and Playmobil's move into smaller play figures were both the result of identifying new market opportunities based on internal core competencies.

ADDITIONAL READING RESOURCES

D. Barboza and M. Barbero, "Wal-Mart is said to be acquiring a chain in China," *The New York Times*, October 17, 2006, Section A, Page 1–2.

A. DeRosa, "Sealed Air alters global strategies; Canada site to close," *Plastics News*, July 31 2006, Page 1–2.

J. Main, "How to go Global and Why," *Fortune*, August 28, 1989, pp. 70–76.

Michael E. Porter, *The Competitive Advantage of Nations*, New York: Free Press, 1990.

H. K. Steensma, L. Marino & K.M. Weaver, "Attitudes toward cooperative strategies: A cross-cultural analysis of entrepreneurs," *Journal of International Business Studies*, 4th Quarter, 2000, pp. 591–609.

www.playmobil.com, The Web site for Playmobil toys.

www.compete.com, The Council on Competitiveness, a nonprofit group that focuses on enhancing competitiveness domestically and abroad.

www.bestbuy.com, The Web site for Best Buy.

CONTRIBUTORS TO THIS VOLUME

EDITORS

CHRISTOPHER J. ROBERTSON, Ph.D., is an associate professor in the College of Business Administration at Northeastern University in Boston, Massachusetts. He received his B.S. (Accounting) from the University of Rhode Island, and his M.B.A. and Ph.D (Strategic Management) from Florida State University. Dr. Robertson is a two-time Fulbright Scholar (both times in Lima, Peru) and has also lived in both Ecuador and Spain. He has published numerous refereed journal articles on strategy, corruption, and international business in journals such as *Strategic Management Journal, Journal of Business Ethics, Journal of World Business, Management International Review, Journal of Business Research, Organizational Dynamics, Business Horizons,* and *Latin American Business Review*. Dr. Robertson's professional work experience includes work as an internal auditor for Hasbro, Inc., consulting for various small businesses, and many summers as a bartender in his hometown of Newport, Rhode Island.

STAFF

Larry Loeppke *Managing Editor*
Susan Brusch *Senior Developmental Editor*
Jill Peter *Senior Developmental Editor*
Beth Kundert *Senior Production Manager*
Jane Mohr *Project Manager*
Shirley Lanners *Permissions Coordinator*
Maggie Lytle *Cover*
Tara McDermott *Design Specialist*
Julie Keck *Senior Marketing Manager*
Mary Klein *Marketing Communications Specialist*
Alice Link *Marketing Coordinator*
Tracie Kammerude *Senior Marketing Assistant*

AUTHORS

SARA ANDERSON is a director of the Global Economy Project at the Institute for Policy Studies, a progressive think tank dedicated to a variety of issues.

DAVID ARMSTRONG is a staff writer for *The San Francisco Chronicle* where he focuses on a range of issues that included international trade matters and controversies surrounding the World Trade Organization.

FREDERIK BALFOUR is the Asia correspondent for *Business Week*.

RADLEY BALKO is a freelance writer living in Arlington, Virginia. Balko publishes his own blog, The Agitator, and writes occasionally for Tech Central Station and Foxnews.com, where he has a regular column.

OWEN BELL is a litigation partner for White & Case in New York where his focus is on litigation related to securities, commercial, bankruptcy, and international law cases. He has also managed internal investigations related to the Foreign Corrupt Practices Act.

EMMA BIRD is a freelance reporter who recently completed an assignment as an expatriate in Italy.

KEITH BRADSHER, the *New York Times* Hong Kong bureau chief, was a finalist for the Pulitzer Prize. His most recent book is *High and Mighty* (Public Affairs).

ALEX BRUMMER is the *Daily Mail* city editor in London. Mr. Brummer's work focuses on financial matters related to the British and global economies.

JOHN CAVANAGH has been director of the Institute for Policy Studies since 1998. He is the co-author of 11 books on the global economy, most recently *Alternatives to Economic Globalization: A Better World Is Possible*. He is a graduate of both Princeton University and Dartmouth College.

ALAN CLENDENNING is an Associated Press foreign correspondent stationed in Sao Paolo, Brazil.

HERMAN E. DALY is a professor in the School of Public Affairs at the University of Maryland and the author of a classic on the subject of environmental economics, *Steady-State Economics: The Economics of Biophysical Equilibrium and Moral Growth* (W.H. Freeman, 1977).

CHRISTOPHER DICKEY is the Paris bureau chief/Middle East regional editor for *Newsweek*.

DANIEL W. DREZNER is assistant professor of political science at the University of Chicago. Beginning in the 2006–7 academic year, he will be an associate professor of international politics at the Fletcher School of Law and Diplomacy at Tufts University. He retains a blog at www.danieldrezner.com.

R.G. EDMONSON is the bureau chief for the Washington bureau of the *Journal of Commerce*.

ALAN M. FIELD is the associate editor for international trade at the *Journal of Commerce*.

JAMES FLANIGAN is the senior economics editor for the *Los Angeles Times*.

PAUL L. E. GRIECO, a doctoral student at Northwestern University's department of economics, previously worked as a research assistant at the Institute for International Economics.

CONSTANTIN GURDGIEV is the editor of *Business&Finance,* Ireland's largest business publication, dean of finance with CBSM, and a research fellow with Trinity College, Dublin. He also is a founder and an academic director of the *Open Republic Institute* (www.openrepublic.org), Ireland's only independent economic and social policy think tank.

JORGE HEINE is the Chilean ambassador to India. He previously served as Chile's ambassador to South Africa. Dr. Heine, the author of eight books, graduated from the University of Chile Law School and York University in England. He also received his M.A. and Ph.D. from Stanford University.

GARY CLYDE HUFBAUER is the Reginald Jones Senior Fellow at the Institute for International Economics. He was formerly the Marcus Wallenberg Professor of International Finance Diplomacy at Georgetown University and deputy assistant secretary for international trade and investment policy at the U.S. Treasury Department. He has written extensively on international trade, investment, and tax issues. His most recent books include *NAFTA Revisited: Achievements and Challenges* (2005) and *Reforming the U.S. Corporate Tax* (2005).

AMY KAZMIN is a foreign correspondent for *The Financial Times* where she covers business and human rights issues in Southeast Asia.

ROY KHENG is an assistant editor with *China Knowledge Press*, a premier provider of trade and investment information on China.

REBECCA KNIGHT is a journalist and assistant analysis services editor of *The Financial Times of London*. She received her undergraduate degree from Wesleyan University.

MARK LANDLER, based in Frankfurt, Germany, is the European Economic Correspondent of *The New York Times*. Mr. Landler was previously *The New York Times* Hong Kong bureau chief and a reporter for *Business Week*.

PETER T. LEACH, a senior editor at the *Journal of Commerce*, is an expert in international logistics and supply chain management.

ROBERT MATTHEWS, an occasional contributor to *The Financial Times*, is a Visiting Reader in Science at Aston University, Birmingham, where he writes about science-related issues. His latest book is *25 Big Ideas: Science That Is Changing Our World* (Oneworld Press).

JAN NELSON is a staff writer for *Employee Benefits News*.

OECD (Organization for Economic Co-Operation and Development) is an international organization that fosters cooperation and collaboration among nations. The OECD is known for its research publications related to economic and social issues. The OECD has 30 member nations and works with more than 70 additional nations on a regular basis.

RALPH PETERS is a member of *USA TODAY*'s board of contributors and the author of the forthcoming book *New Glory: Expanding America's Global Supremacy*.

IAN PUTZGER writes about global air transportation–related issues for the *Journal of Commerce*.

RICHARD READ is senior writer for international affairs and special projects at the Portland, Oregon–based newspaper *The Oregonian*. Mr. Read is a Pulitzer Prize–winning writer.

ANDY REINHARDT is a writer for *Business Week* where he covers European management issues.

GAIL REINHART is a senior consultant in client services in the Calgary office of relocation firm TheMIGroup. She is also on the board of directors of the Canadian Employee Relocation Council.

ADRIENNE ROBERTS is a writer for the *Financial Times* where she covers issues related to corporate strategy and international logistics.

DAN ROBERTS is a writer for the *Financial Times* where he covers corporate governance and strategic management issues.

DEXTER ROBERTS writes about Asian economic issues for *Business Week* and is based out of Beijing, China.

KENNETH ROTH is the executive director of *Human Rights Watch*.

CHRIS ROWLANDS is a writer for *Works Management* where he focuses on issues related to globalization and manufacturing processes.

JOHN SCHMID is a business writer for the *Milwaukee Journal Sentinel*.

AJITA SHASHIDHAR is a business writer in India and has contributed to periodicals such as *The Hindu* and the *Financial Times, Global News Wire*.

JENNY STRASBURG is a staff writer for the *San Francisco Chronicle* where she focuses on social responsibility in the workplace.

K.C. SWANSON primarily focuses on the high-tech sector and is a staff reporter for *The Street.com*.

DAVID TEATHER has been a business writer for *The Guardian* (*London*) since 1999. Mr. Teather previously worked in New York for *The Guardian* as well as a writer for the London-based *Daily Express* and *Sunday Business*.

SUFIA TIPPU, a freelance writer based in Bangalore, India, is an occasional contributor to *The Edge Malaysia*.

RICK VECCHIO is a writer for the Associated Press based in Lima, Peru, where he covers political, social, and economic issues.

CARLTA VITZTHUM is a writer for *Business Week* and is interested in outsourcing–related issues from the European perspective.

ANDREW WARD is a writer for the *Financial Times* where he covers trade related issues.

MURRAY WEIDENBAUM is the chairman of the Weidenbaum Center at Washington University in St. Louis. He is also the author of *Business and Government in the Global Marketplace*, 6th ed. (Prentice Hall, 1999) and *Looking for Common Ground on U.S. Trade Policy* (Center for Strategic and International Studies, 2001).

LARRY WERNER is director of community publications at the Minneapolis-based *Star Tribune*. Mr. Werner was previously a business editor with the *Star Tribune* and a reporter with various newspapers, including the *Dallas Times-Herald* and the *Detroit Free Press*.

DEBORAH WILLOUGHBY is a reporter for the *Montgomery Advertiser* where she covers local economic and cultural issues.

DAVID ZUSSMAN is the Jarislowsky Chair of Public Sector Management at the University of Ottawa.

INDEX